THE COMPLETE BOOK OF DRAWING
MALE & FEMALE

THE COMPLETE BOOK OF DRAWING MALE & FEMALE

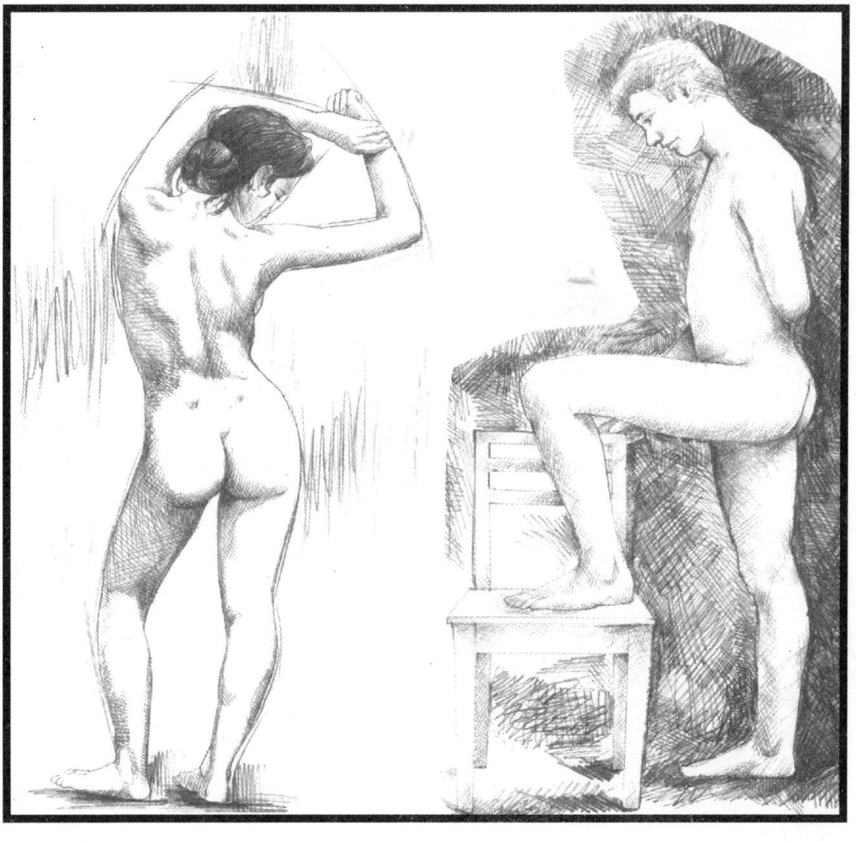

ADARSH BOOKS

THE COMPLETE BOOK OF DRAWING
MALE & FEMALE

Artist : Keshaw Kumar

ISBN : 81-87138-95-5

Published by :
Adarsh Books
New Delhi-2

Reprint - 2016

Distributed by :
ADARSH ENTERPRISES
4393/4 Tulsidas Street, Ansari Road,
Daryaganj, New Delhi-2
Phone : 23246131 - 32
Fax : 91-011-23246130
email : adarshbooks@vsnl.com
nirmal@ndb.vsnl.net.in

Designed by :
Jay Mata Graphics
1/3615, Ramnagar,
Shahdara, Delhi-110032

Printed at :
N.H.P. Offset Press
P. Ganj Ind. Area, Delhi-92
Phone : 9810002678

Visit us at : www.adarshbooks.com

INTRODUCTION

The figurative art applied to the study of human body, male and female, requires an artistic acumen. Those who decide to draw the human body, experience difficulties, or at least uncertainties, even though they themselves can often endanger their artistic awareness. Perhaps this happens because the artist sees only a model holding a pose, rather than the inner structure. This may be described as investigating the inside of the body in order to understand its outward appearance. I believe that discerning observation must, if not given priority over, at least be accompanied by a thorough knowledge of classically interpreted anatomy, essentially of the locomotor system and the outer form. Study of parts of the body (trunk, limbs); of details of the head (eyes, nose, etc.) and of the whole head; study of the whole figure, nude and clothed—this sequence goes from the particular to the general, following a progressive 'technical' mastery of drawing and is a method in harmony. I have put together some observations essential for understanding the complex structure of the adult human body, be it male or female, as well as ideas for experimenting with graphic techniques. I have presented a repertory of poses for male nude. This section is very important I believe, because in it I try to advise on how to transcend the purely objective study of the nude in order to add a different interpretation which while still figurative and anatomically correct, can be more spontaneous and emotional. I have presented a fairly wide selection of female nude model in poses useful for studies of the body and its movements. I have drawn poses of the female nude, some of which are in yoga positions and I have put the poses into groups (standing, sitting, lying drawn, foreshortened, etc.) Each illustration is made with an intention of giving only an indication and aimed at pointing a way to find and observe, through the body of the model, an understanding of the inner anatomy of the outer form. I have taken all the drawings from life almost, except for those which show the model in slightly off balance or firing poses, or those that cannot be held for more than a few moments.

CONTENTS

Anatomical Proportions

Proportion of the human body in the total height of a man corresponds to about seven and a half times the length of his head. Memorise the corresponding points at each level, from both front and back side.

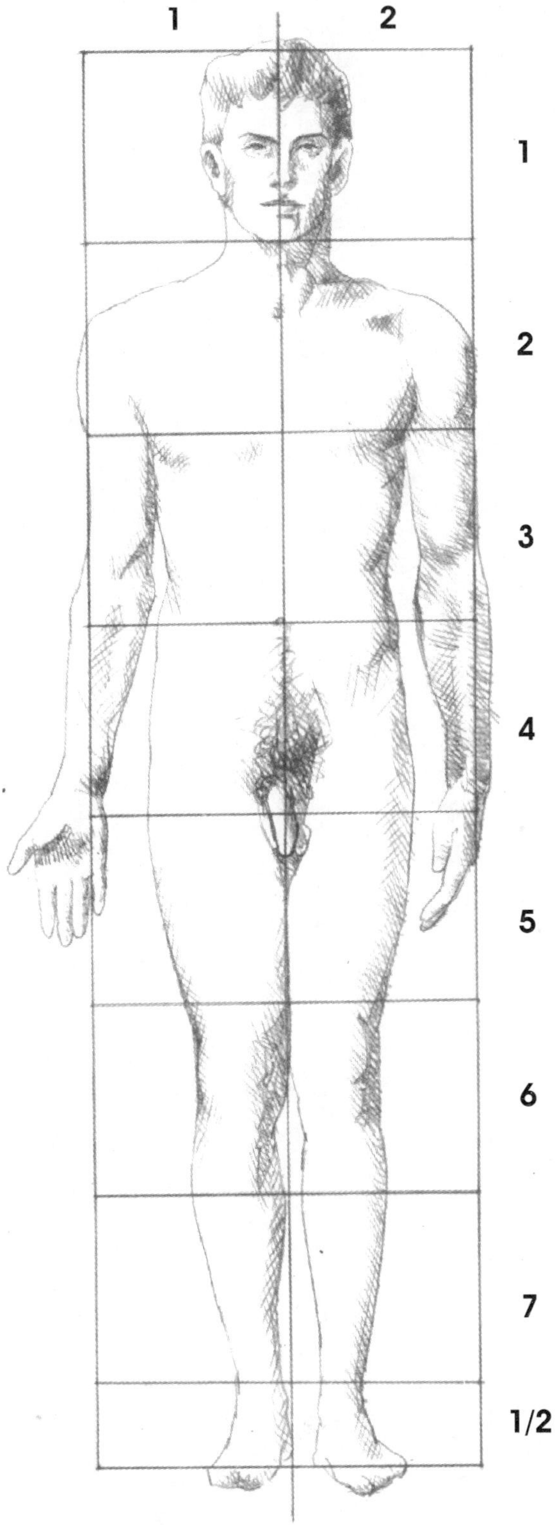

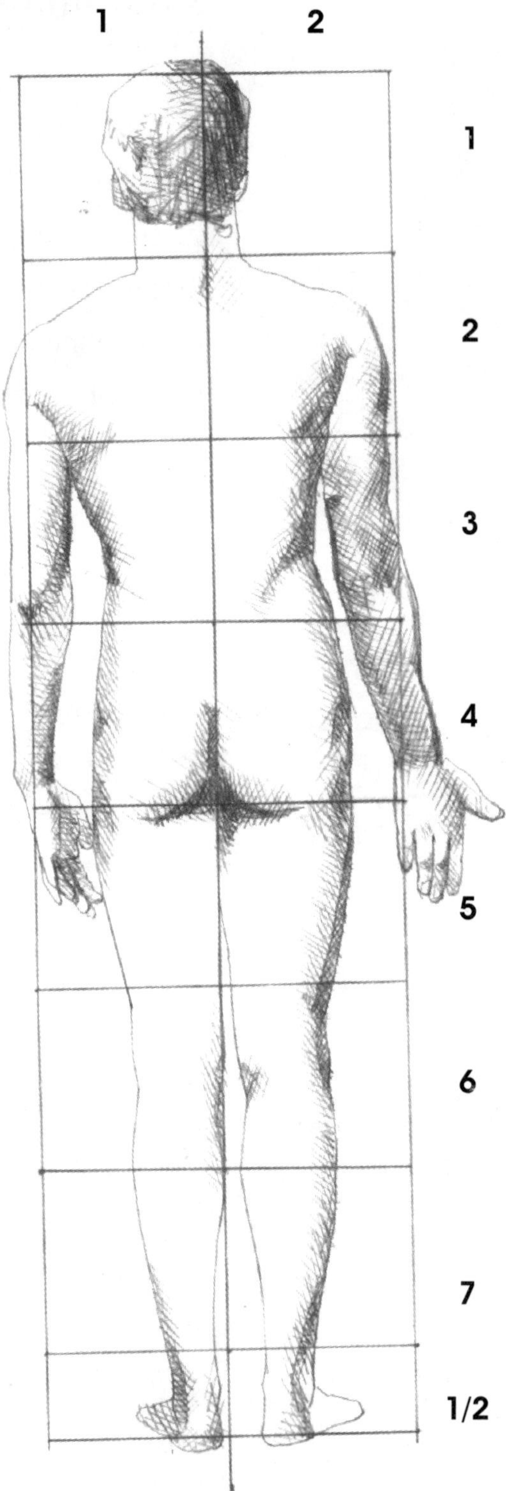
1
2
1
2
3
4
5
6
7
1/2

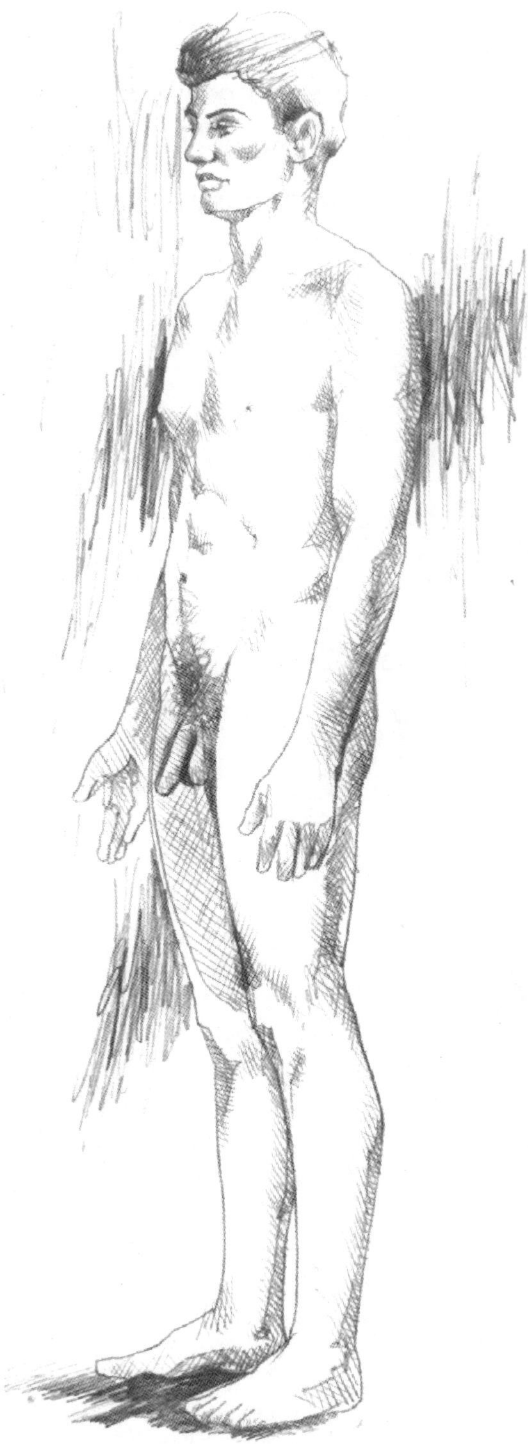

Observe how the preceding diagrammatic projections are integrated into three-quarter view of the male nude. You must be careful to reproduce the volume and balance of the figure.

Study attentively the transverse sections of front view of the male and female nude and compare and comprehend the different morphological differences and characteristics.

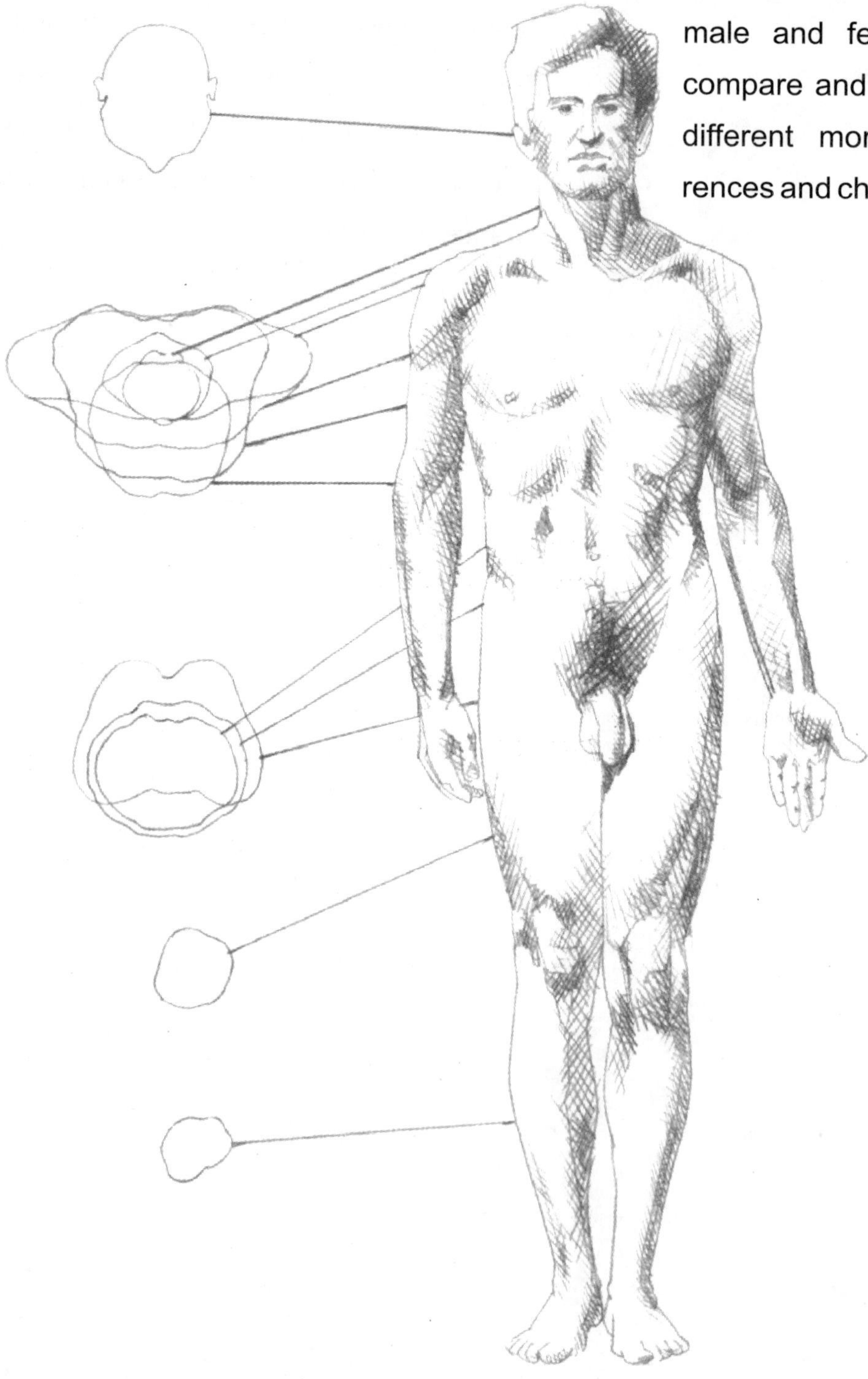

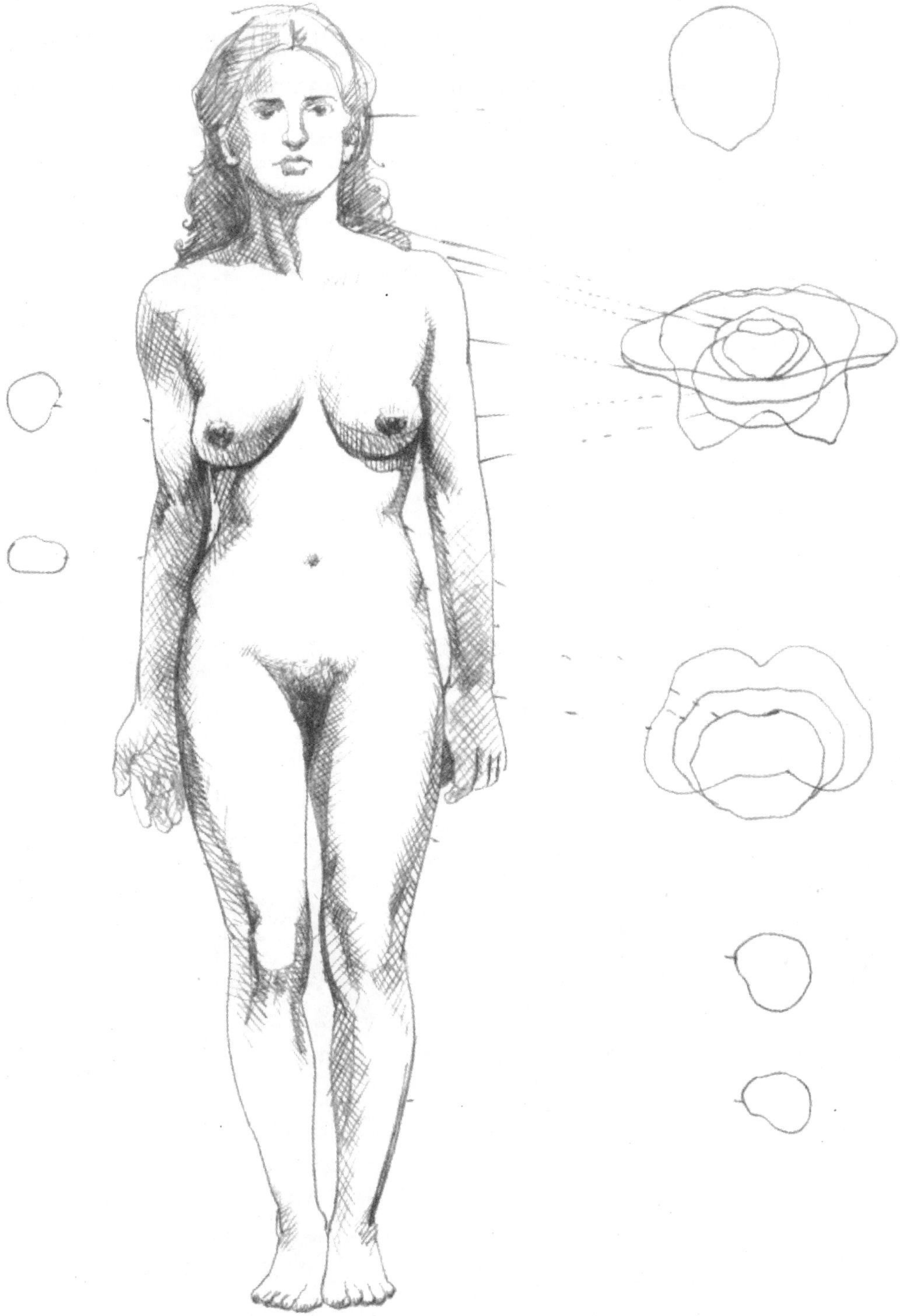

Plans

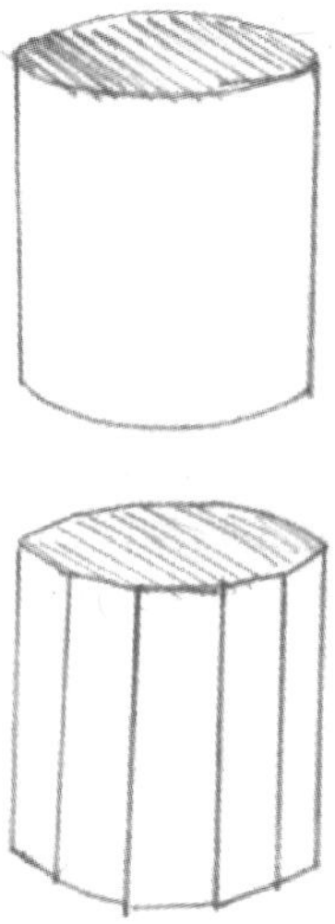

Simplification of the surface and articulations of the body in planes using a lay figure have been demonstrated below.

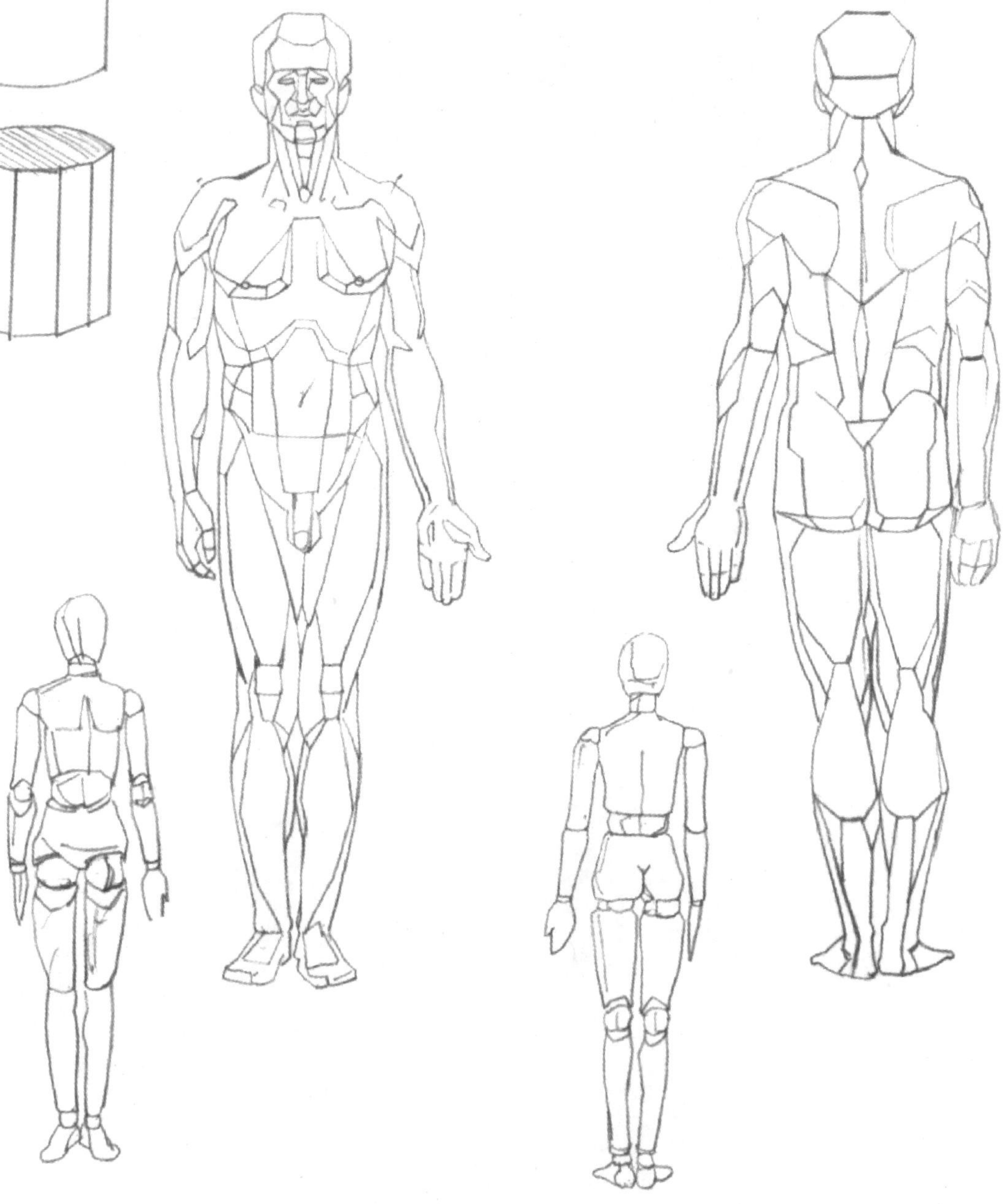

Note the different physical aspects of male and female bodies. The male form fits more easily into rectangles and angles, while the female corresponds to a more delicate rounding.

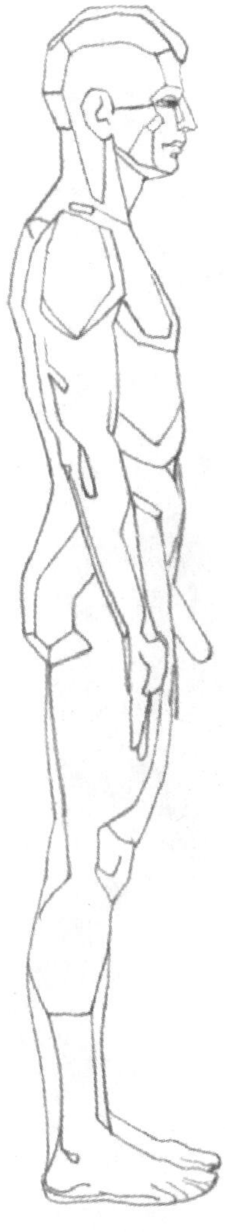

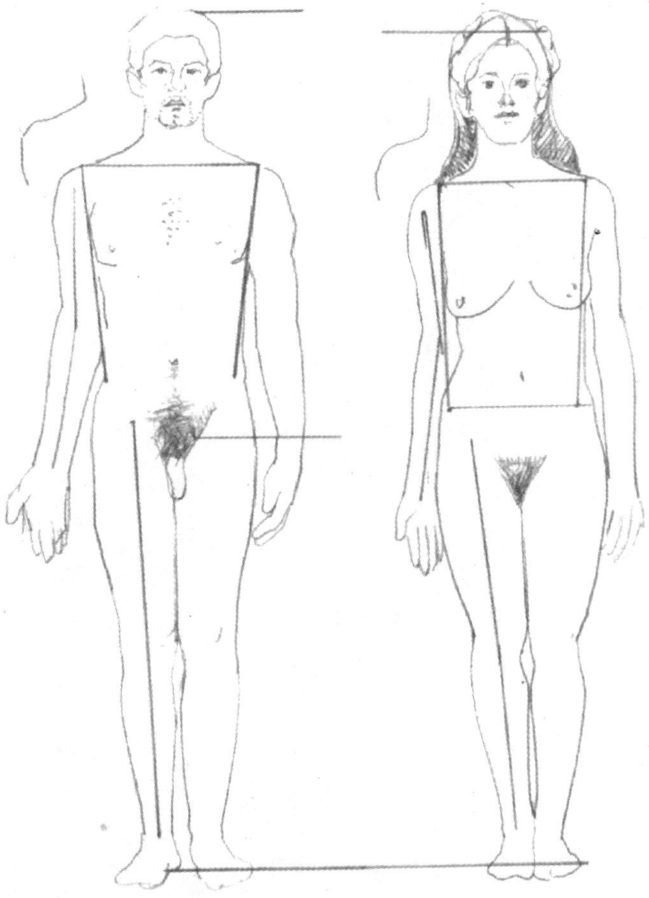

The Figures in the Upright Position

Observe the opposite direction to the axis of the pelvis shoulder (as shown in the diagram) and the distribution of the weight on one leg and by the resulting lateral flexion of the vertebral column. The right leg is slightly flexed which widens the fold of the buttock and makes it less sharply defined.

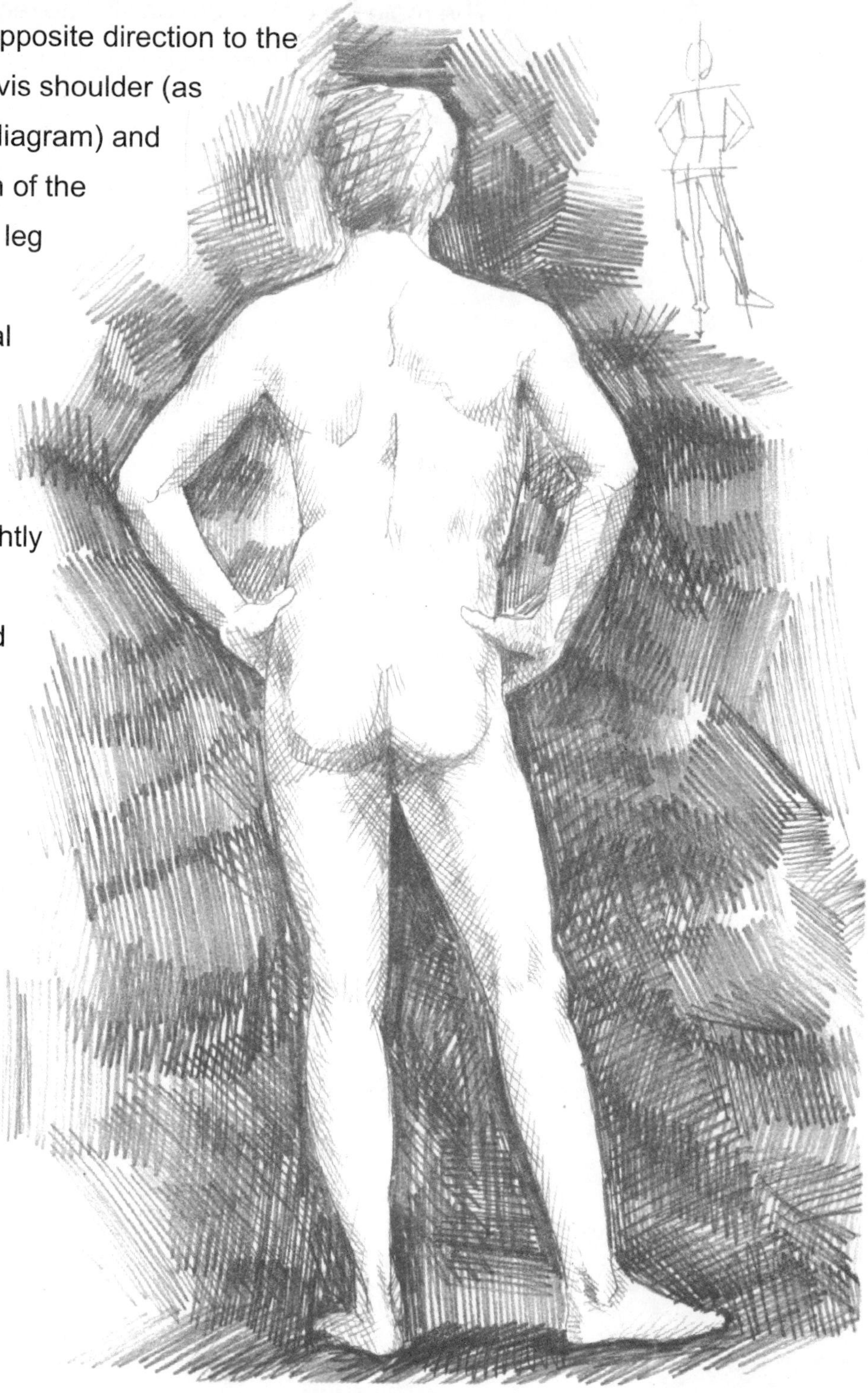

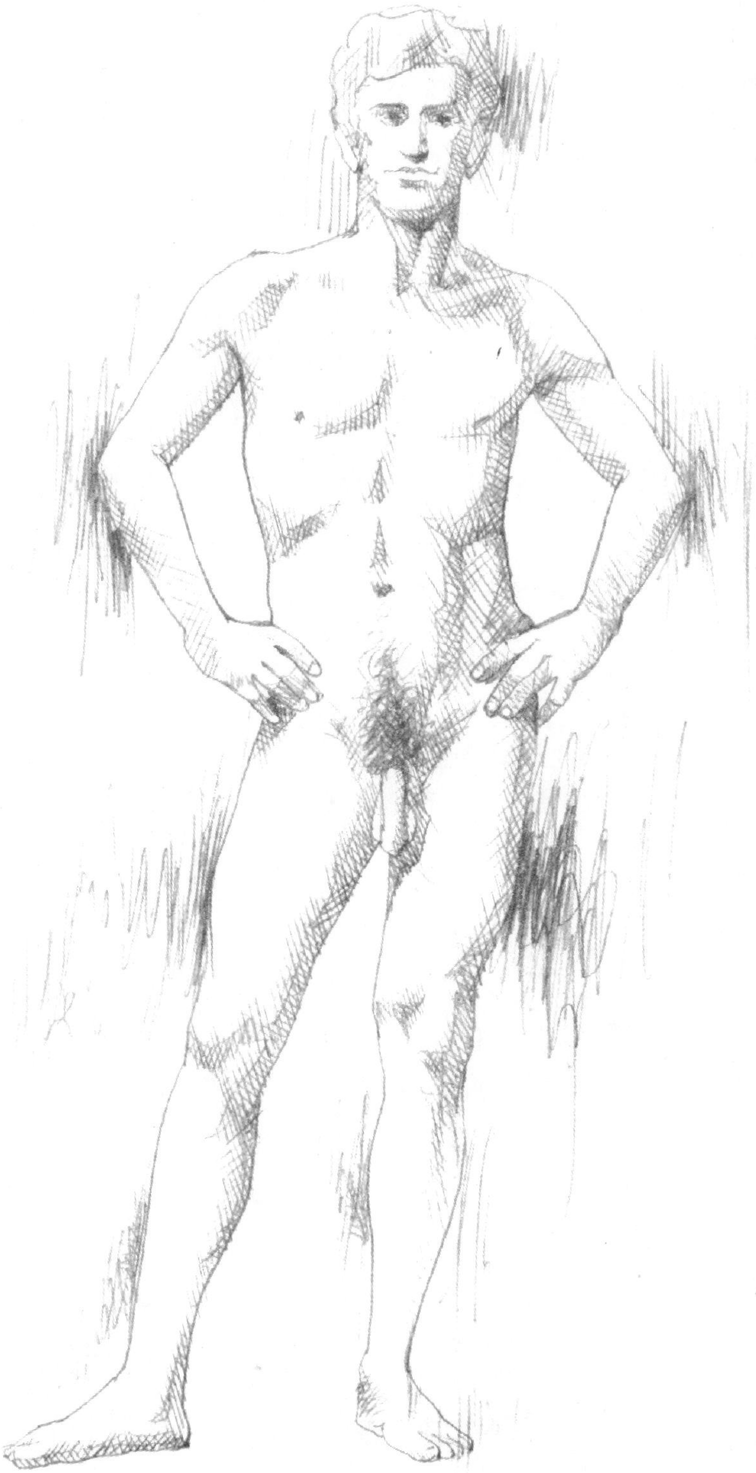

The same pose is seen from the front, the tilt of the pelvis is clearly seen and corresponds to the lowering and flexing of the right leg. Observe the different levels of the knees.

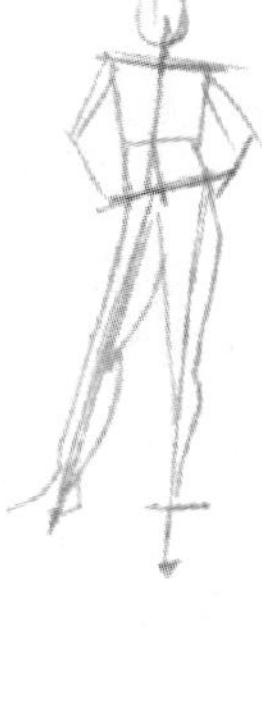

Back view of the male nude.

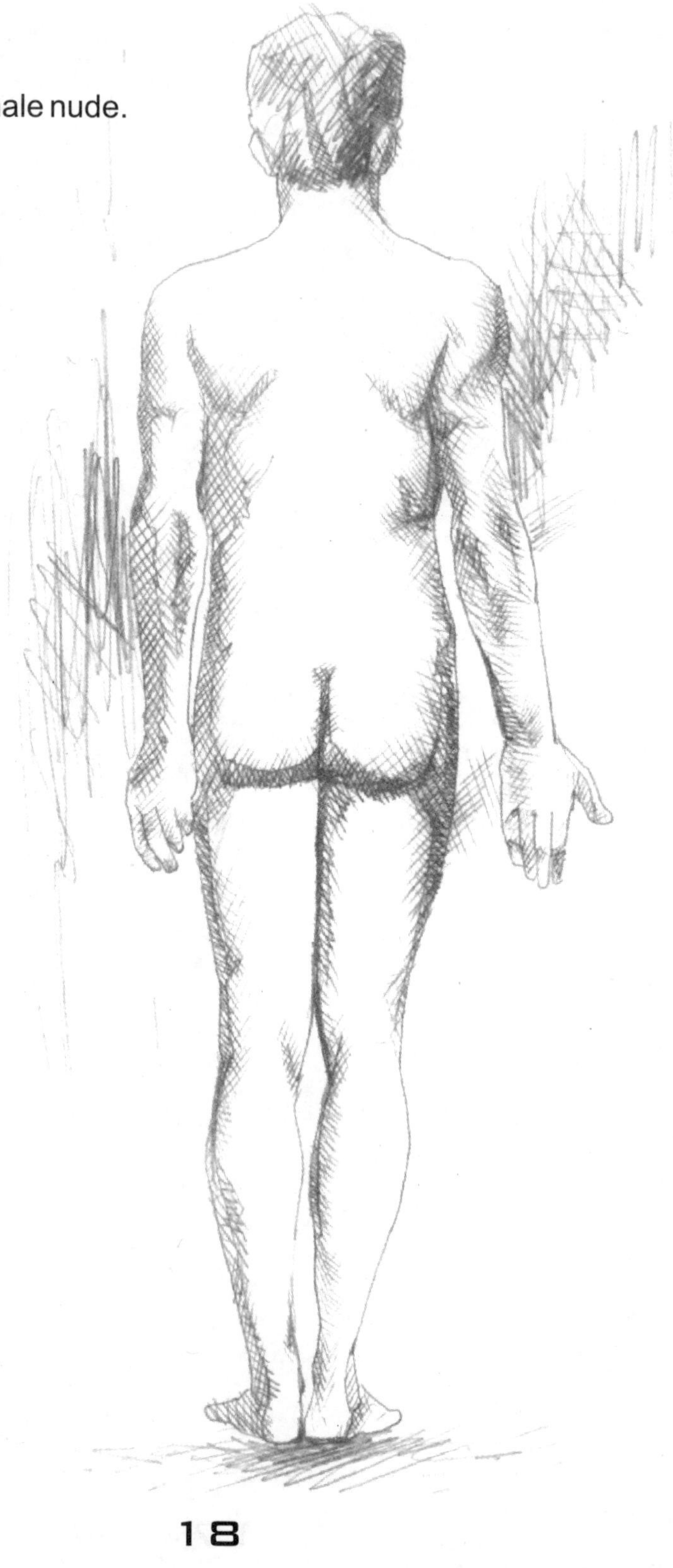

Tone drawing of different styles of male nude.

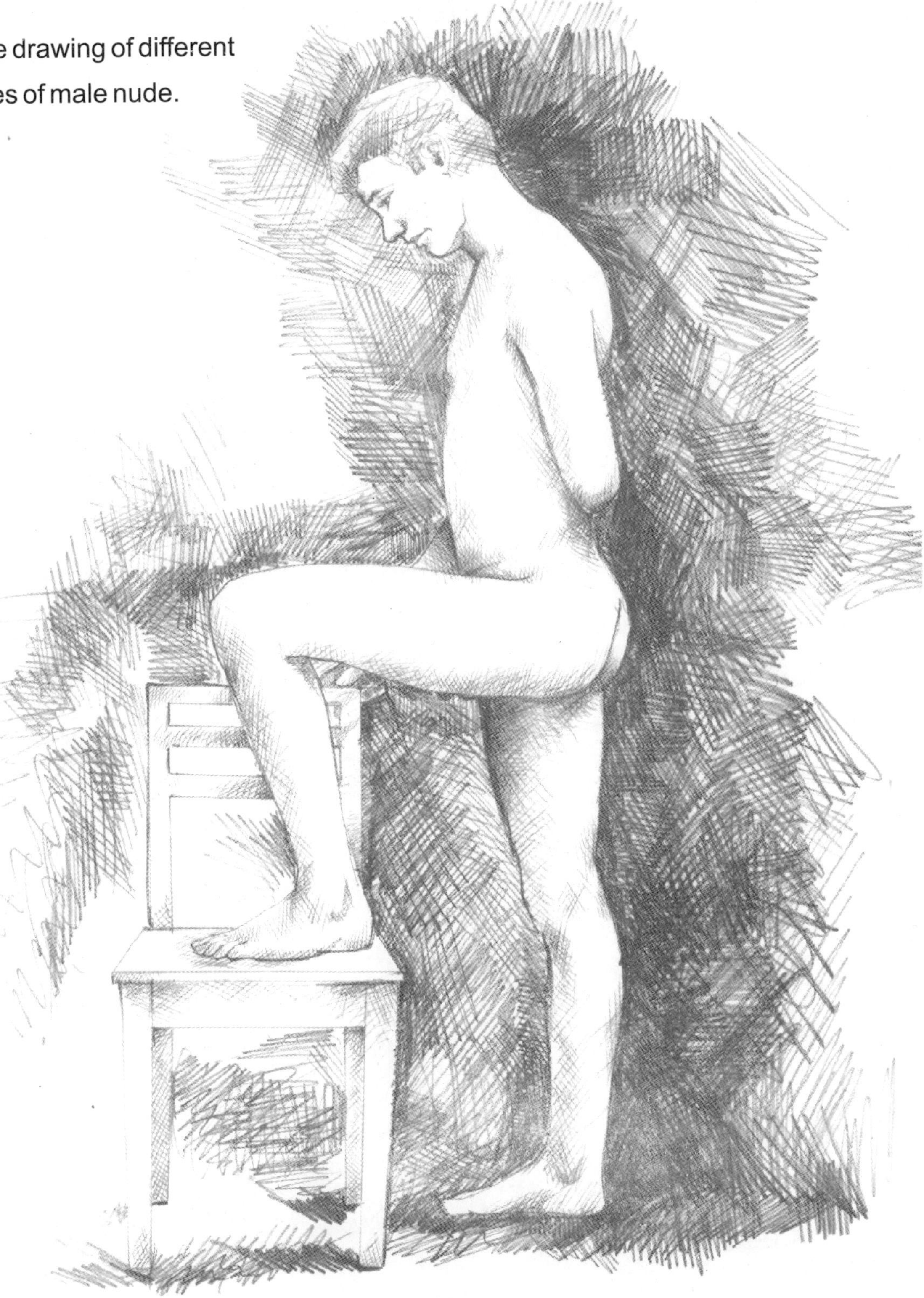

The Seated Figure

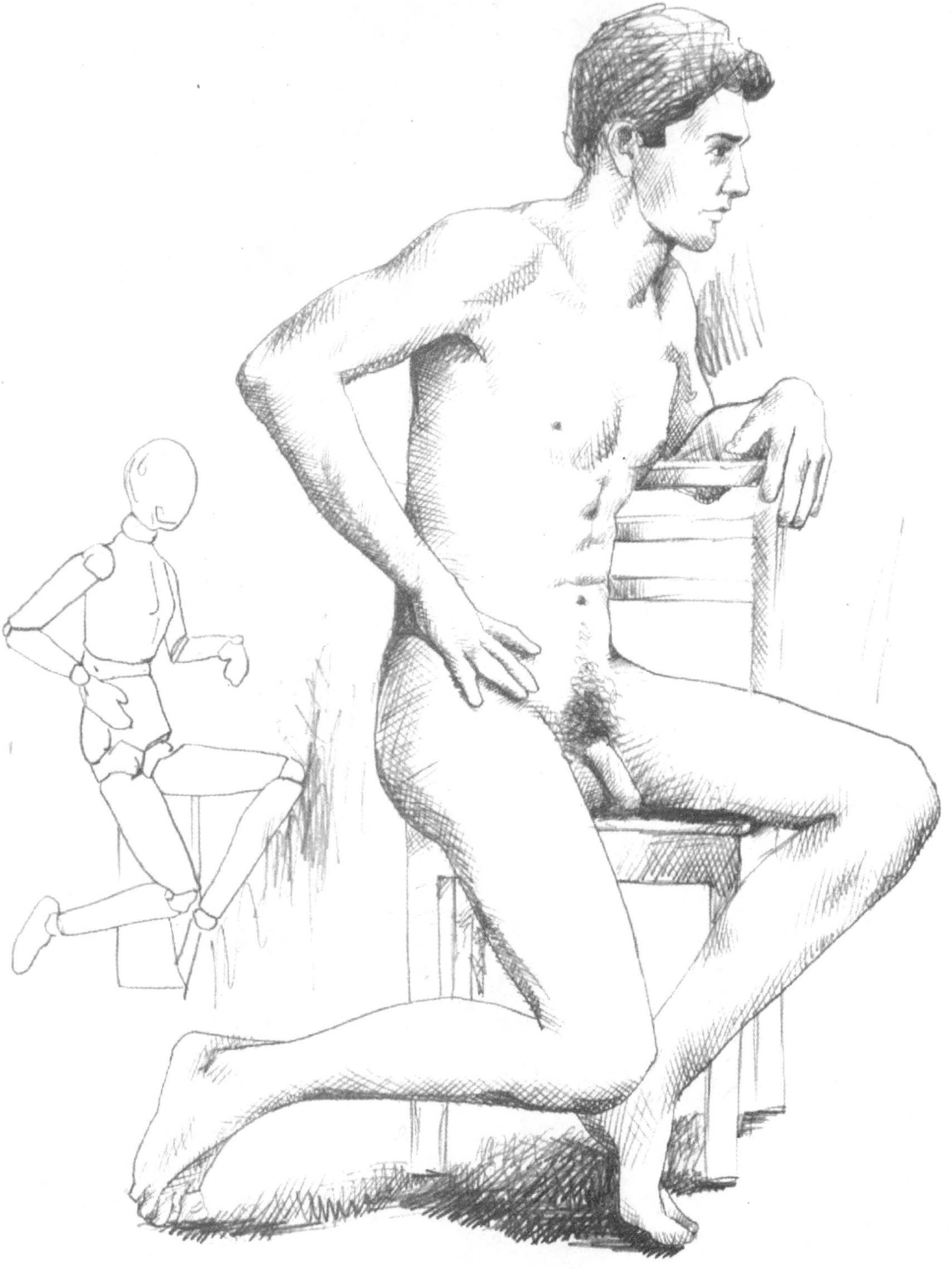

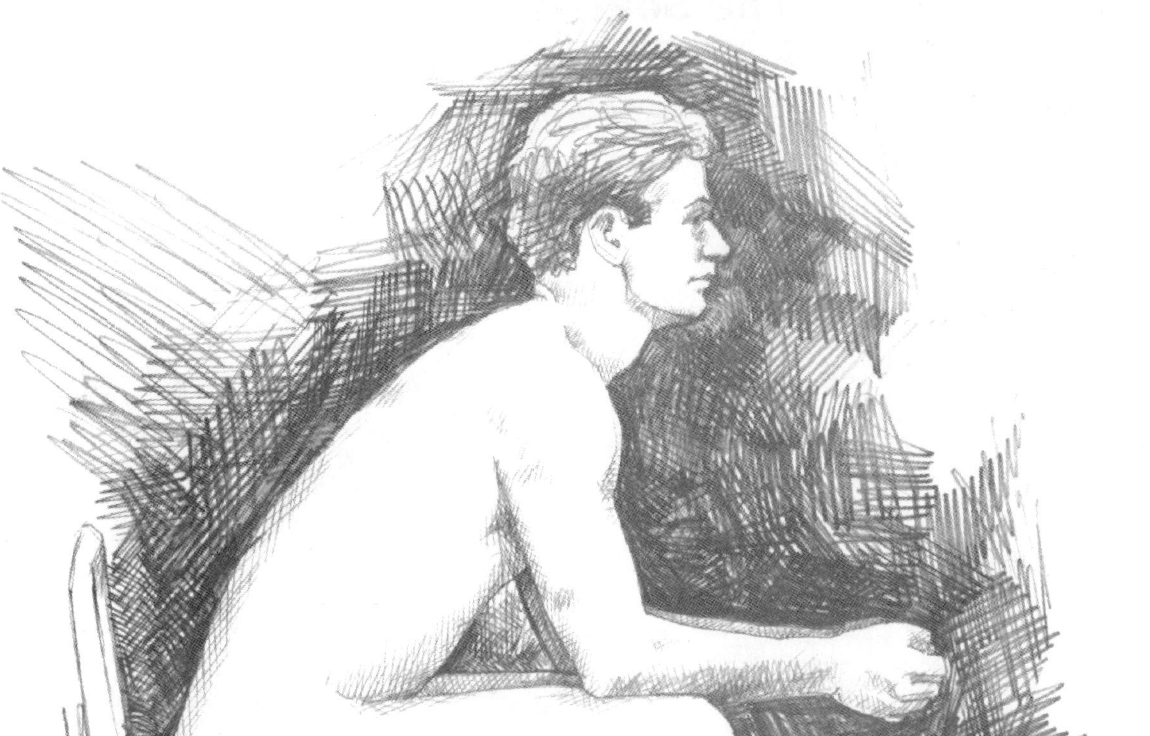

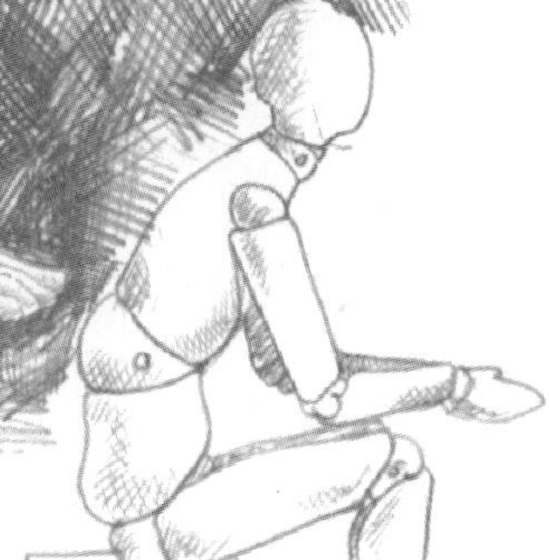

The seated male nude figure presents some difficulties because of the foreshortening of the limbs. So, at first observe the side to avoid these problems. The lay figure will help you capture the orientation of the body's axis.

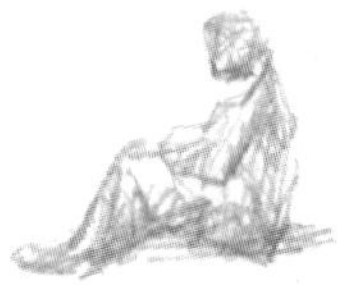

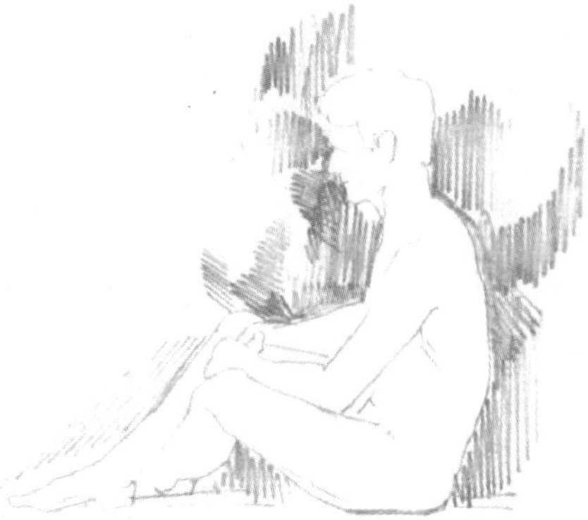

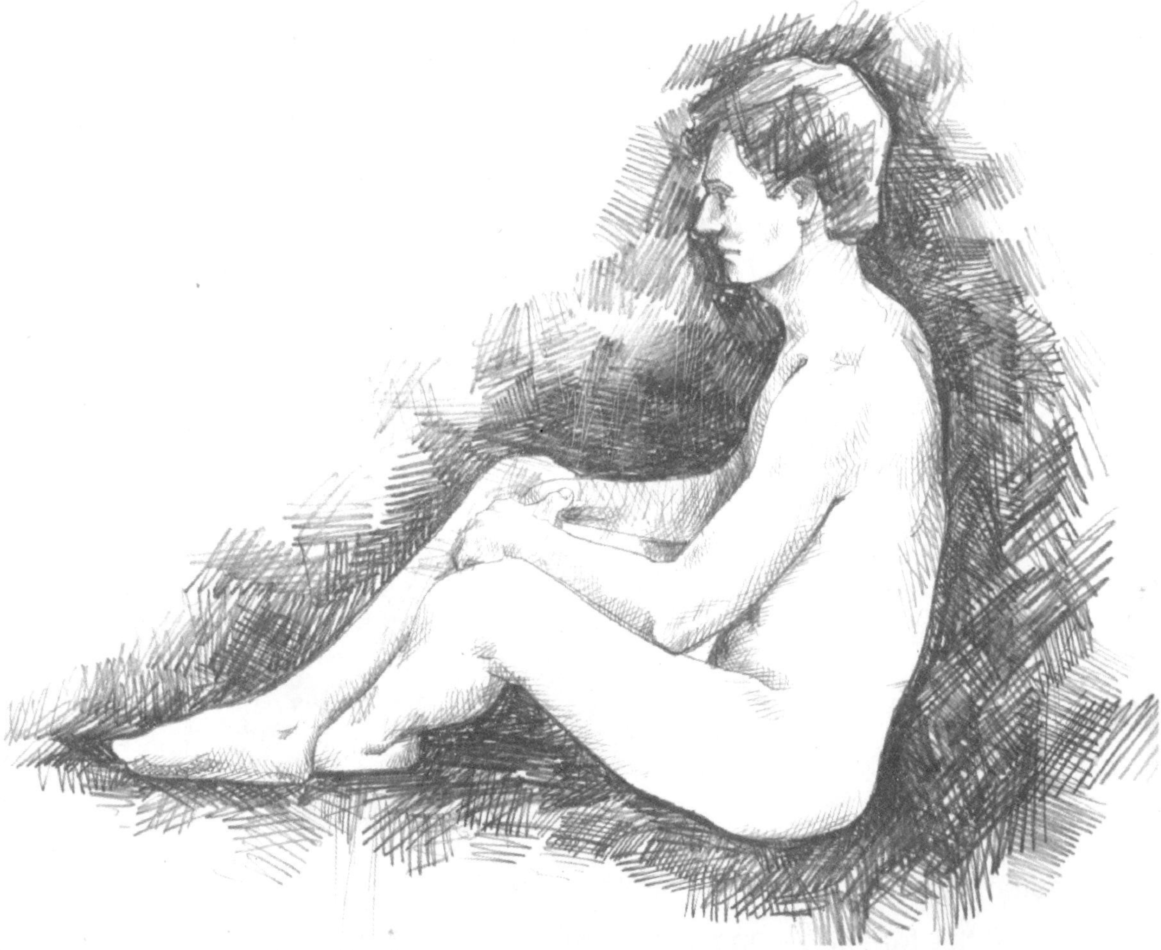

The model is seated on the floor in the easy and natural pose. The trunk and pelvis transfers the weight to the ground. The two small diagrams above show the rectangular triangle structure of the composition and suggest the basic outlines.

The model is drawn, seated on the floor, from two different viewpoints. The front view of the model shows the interesting arrangement of the left arm and the legs. The foreshortening of the right foot is difficult to draw. The head and shoulder are thrust slightly forward to keep the balance.

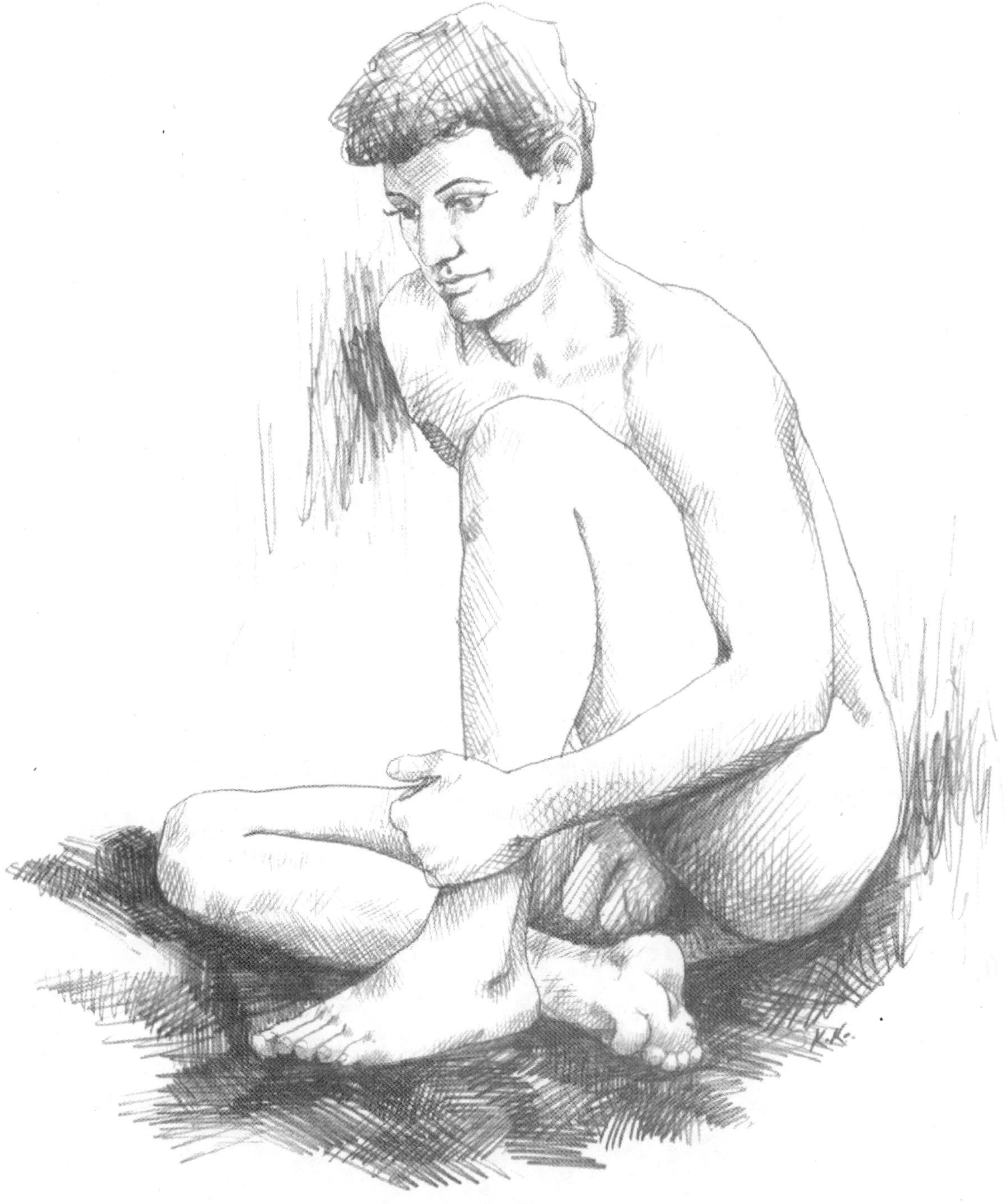

The back view of same model, you can see how the lateral curve of the vertebral column and the slope of the shoulders are tilted in the opposite direction to the pelvis. This is caused by the flexion of the left thigh and the stiffened right arm which is supporting the trunk and shares the weight of the body.

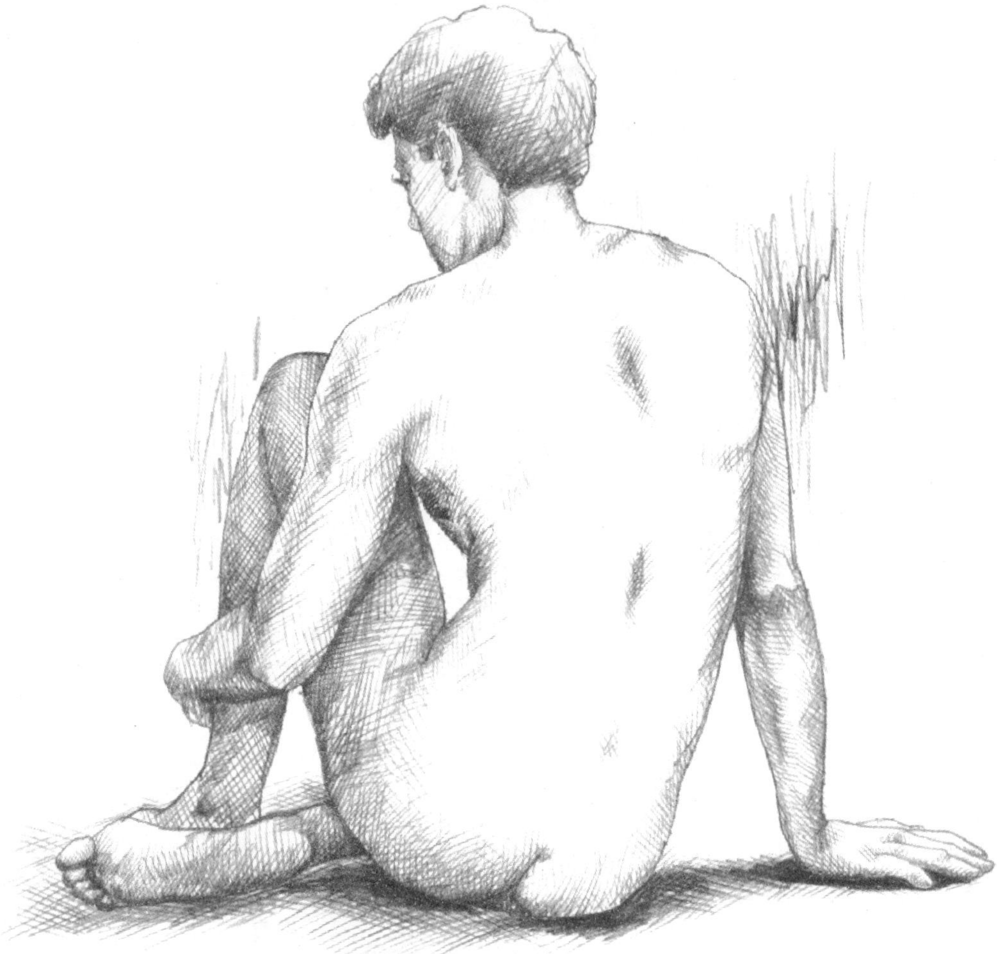

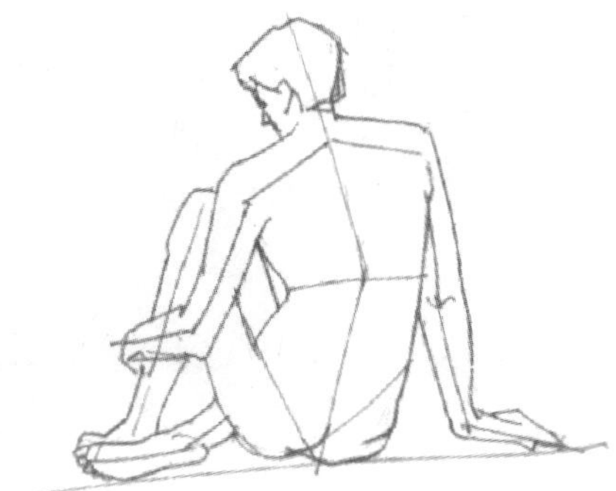

In the drawing the right leg is outstretched, but a slight flexing is evident in biceps femoris. Before putting the model into a reclining position, make use of the lay figure to facilitate the outlining of a constructive diagram for your composition.

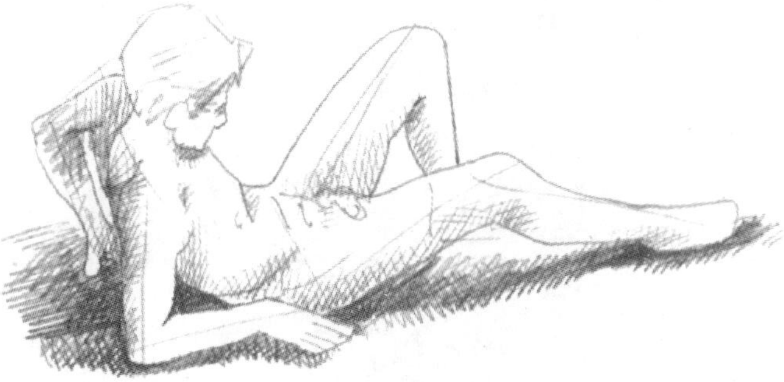

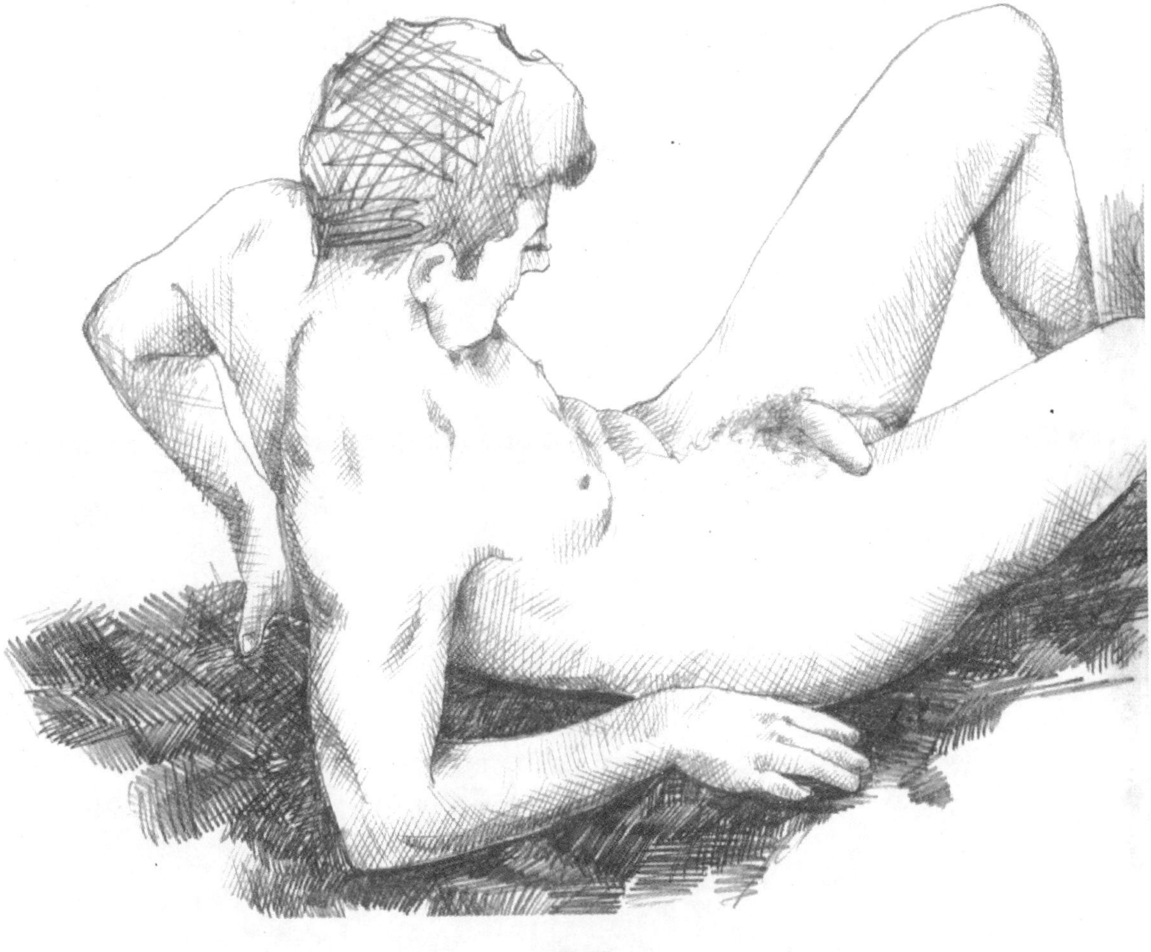

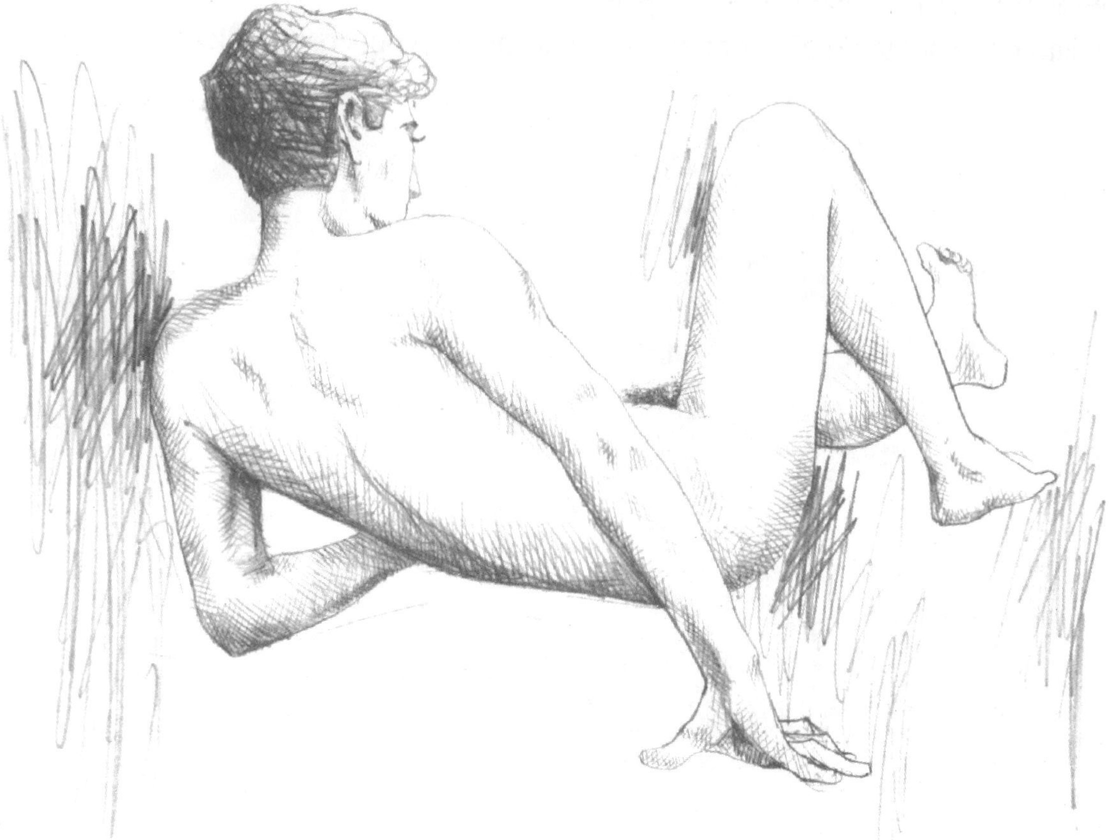

The pose of the model has to contract the abdominal muscles and those of the thigh.

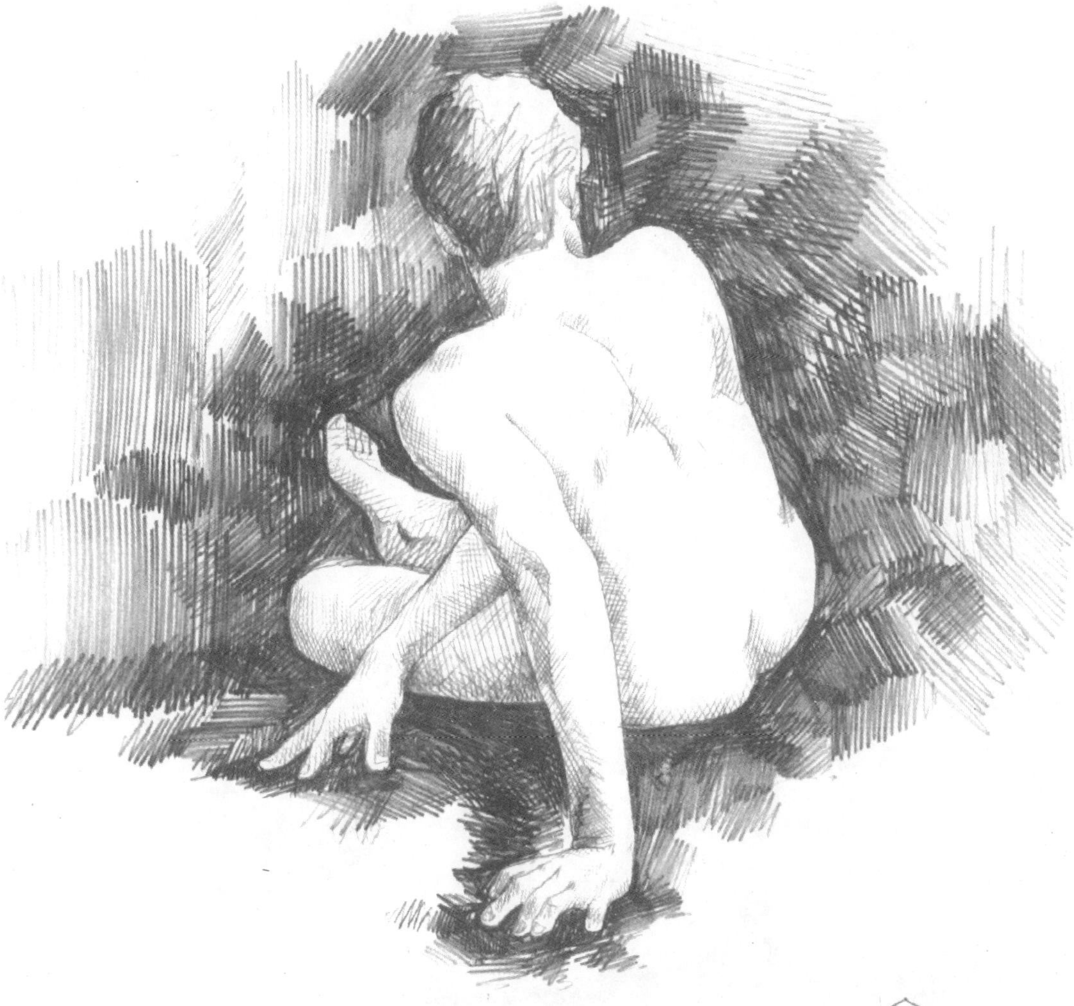

In this figure the weight of the body is supported on one arm. The supporting action is mainly skeletal and the muscles of the region are not called upon but it is the entire arm that props up the body.

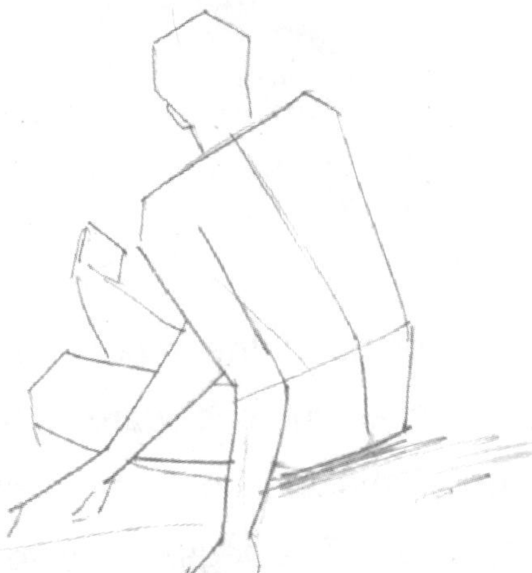

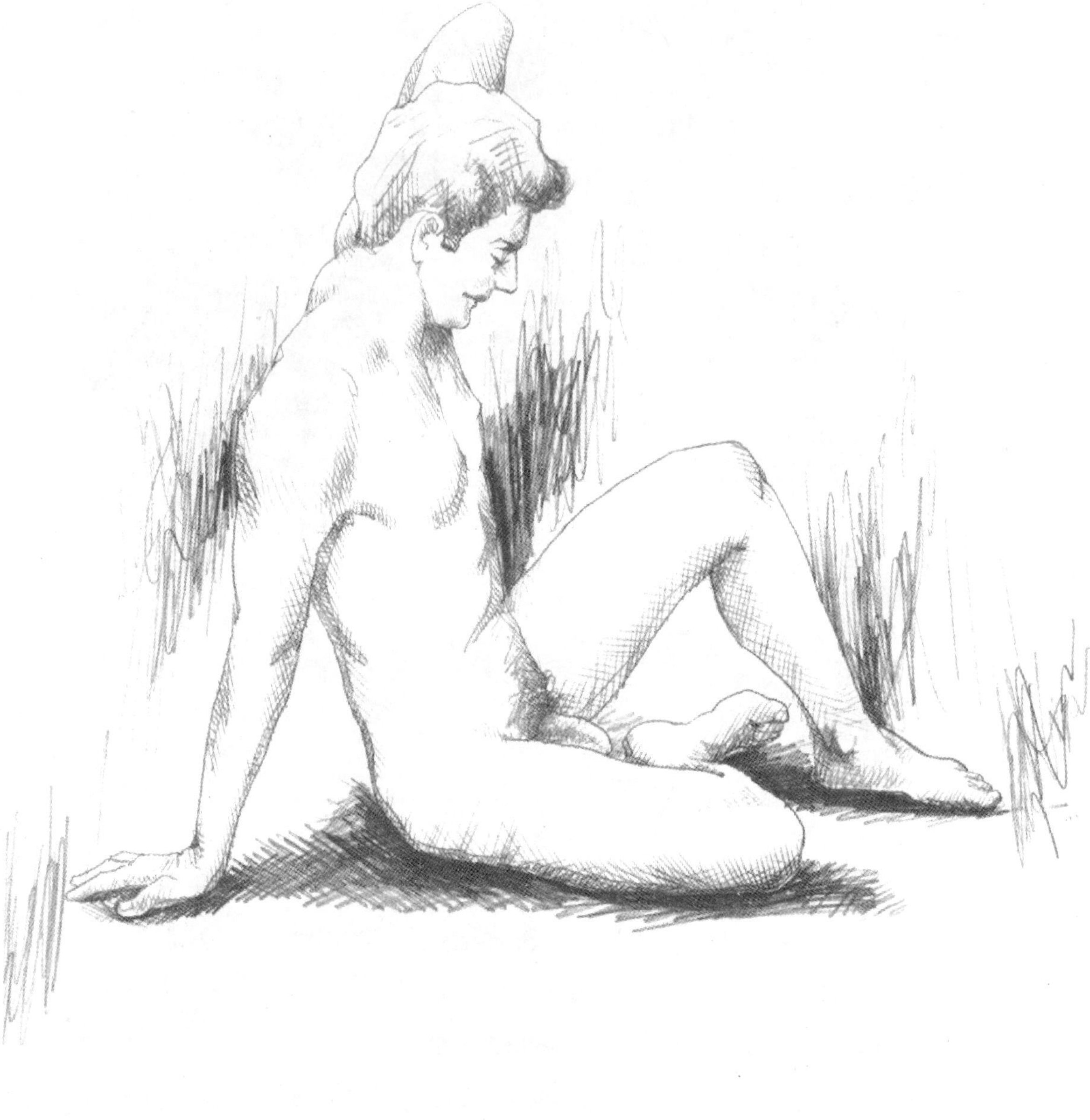

The pose of the model indicates backward slope of the trunk which makes necessary the backward shift of the right hand and the forward extension of the left foot. Note the contraction of the triceps, the deltoid and the rectus abdominis muscles. The legs, however, are not displaying any movement and, so, look relaxed.

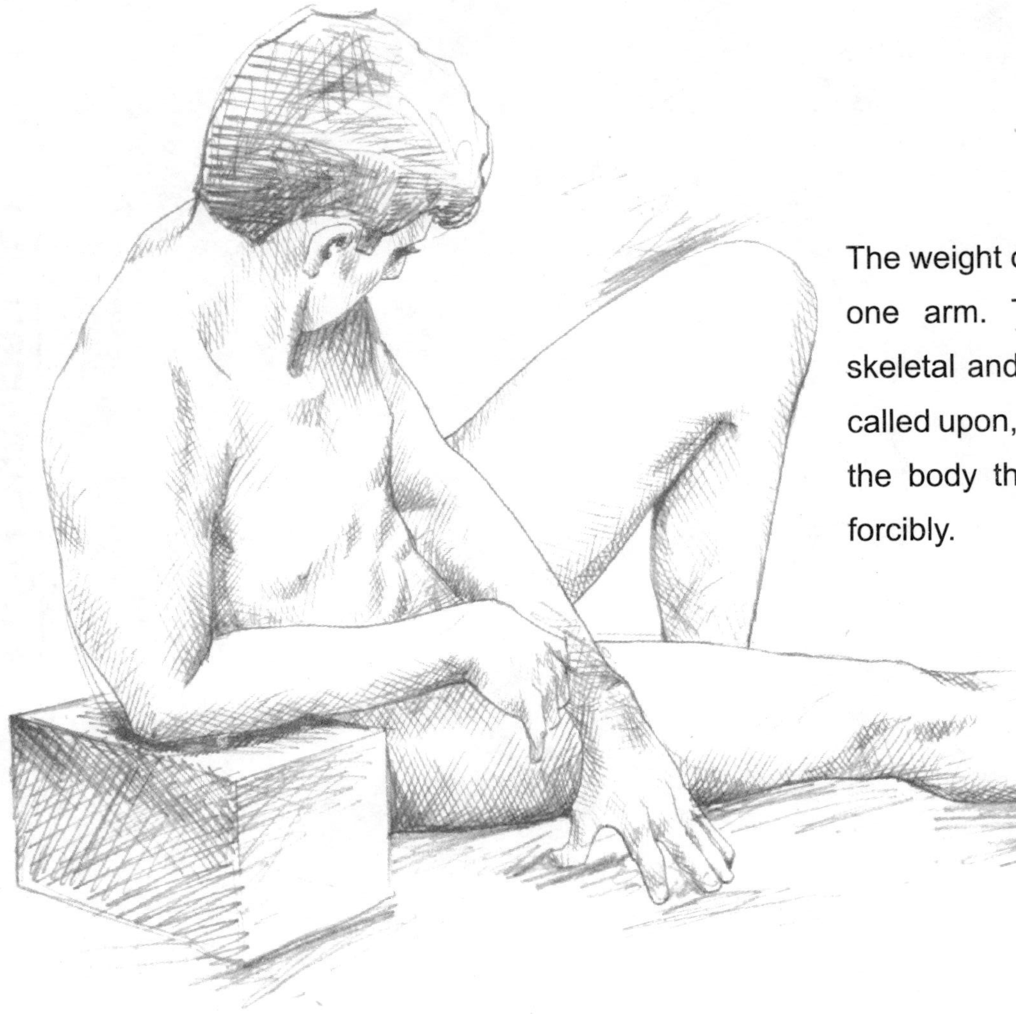

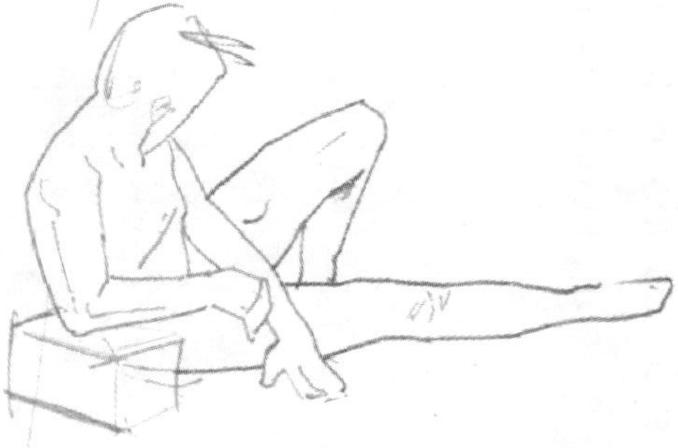

The weight of the model's body is supported on one arm. The supporting action is mainly skeletal and the muscles of the region are not called upon, but it is the entire arm that props up the body that makes some muscles contract forcibly.

The Reclining Figure

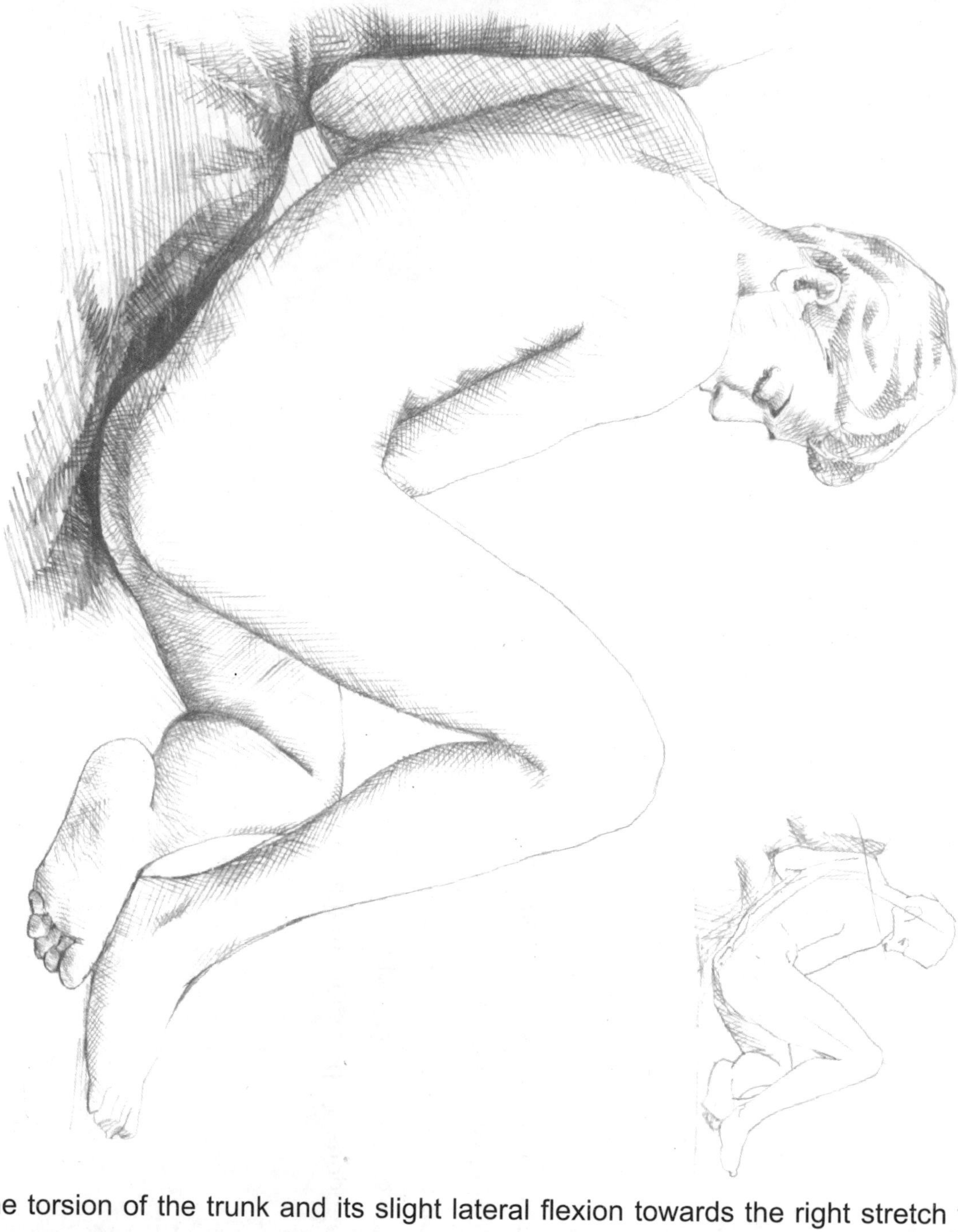

The torsion of the trunk and its slight lateral flexion towards the right stretch the vertebral column in a continuous curve and cause the transverse axes of the shoulders and pelvis to converge.

The Foreshortening Figure

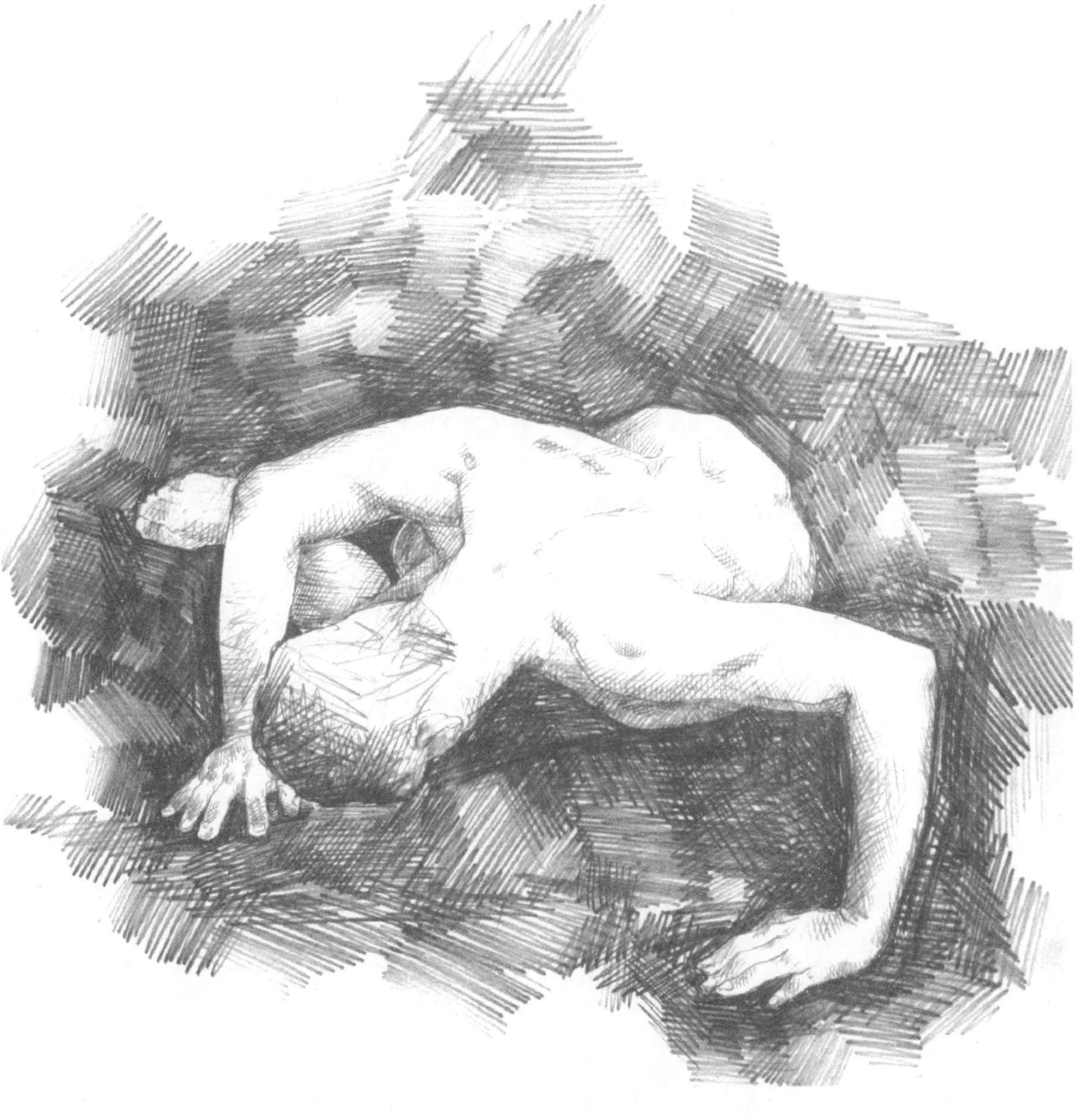

Carefully observe this foreshortening figure because it is an important verification of perspective, composition and especially, anatomy: the flexion of the head and neck, the pushing forwards of the scapulae, the parallelism of the arms and forearms and their function. The weight is sustained mainly by the left limb, the muscles of which are contracted more strongly than those of the right arm.

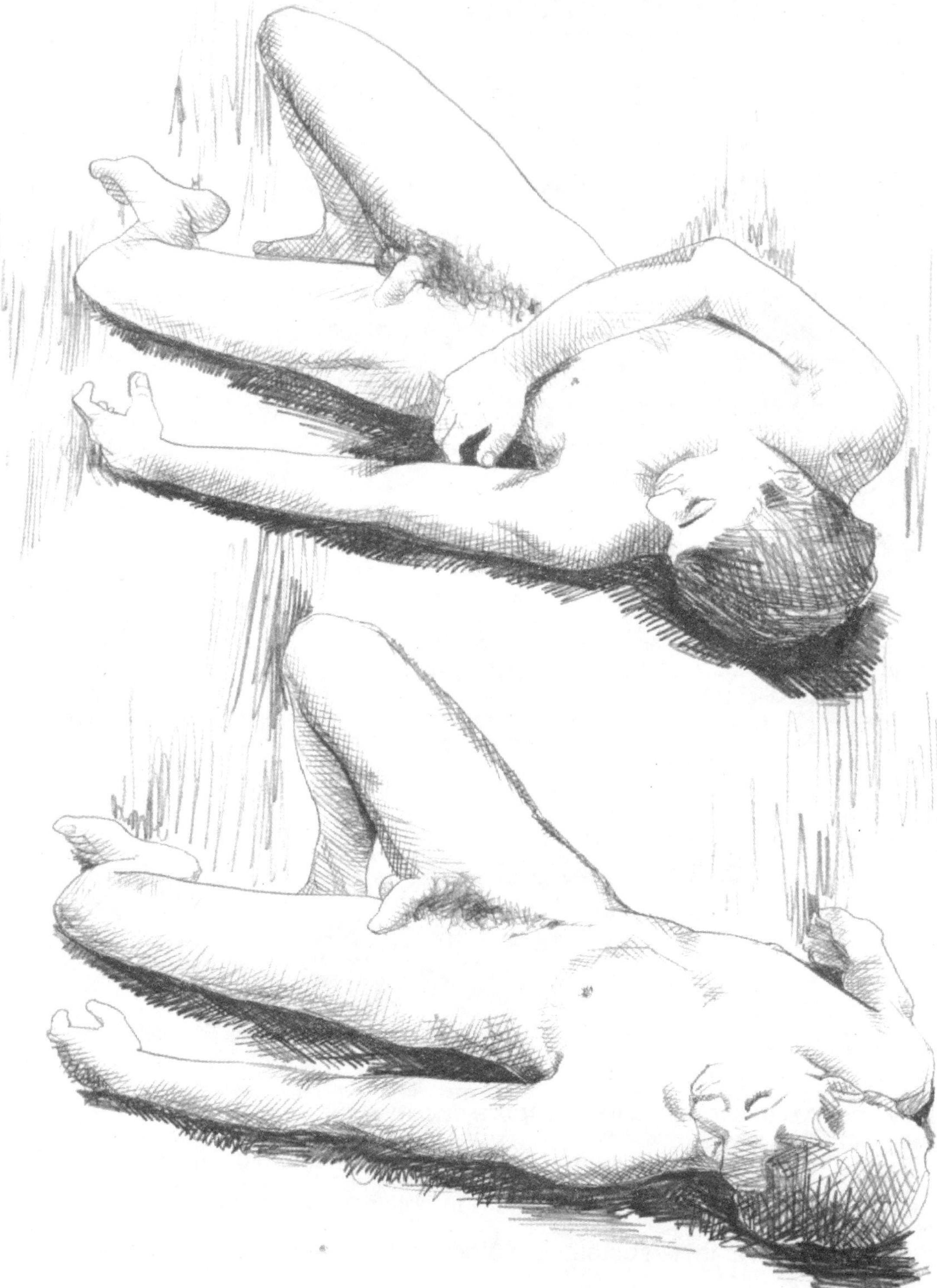

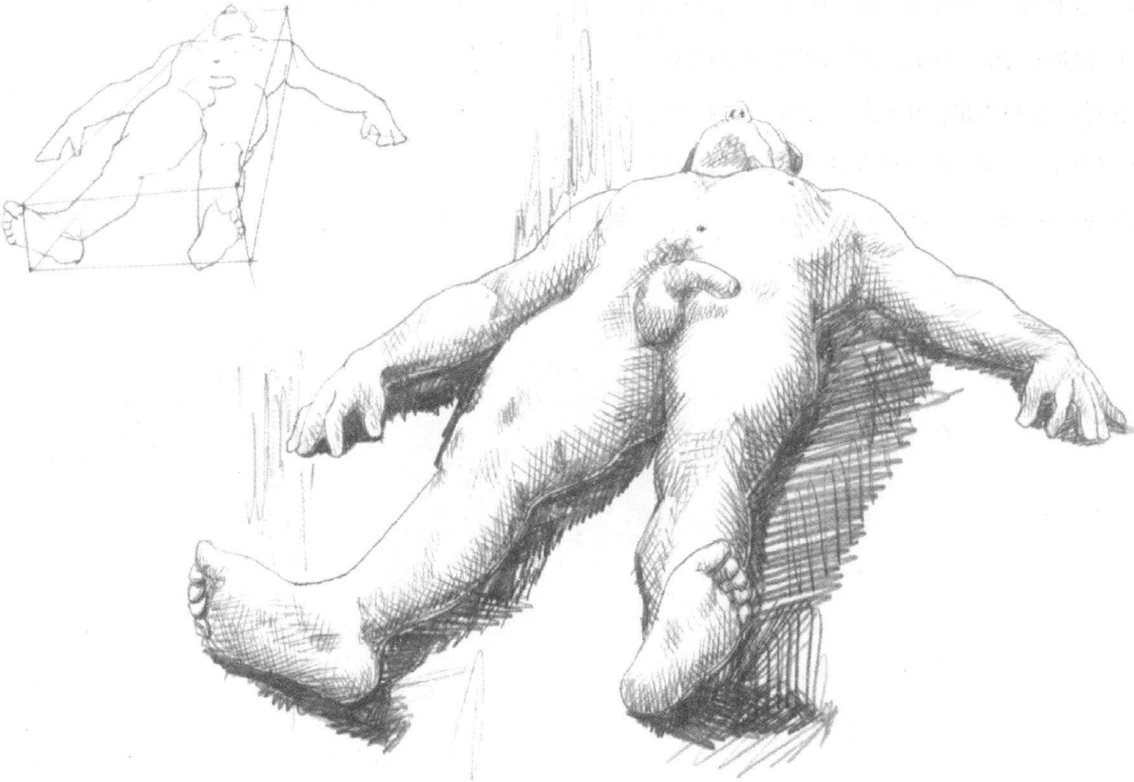

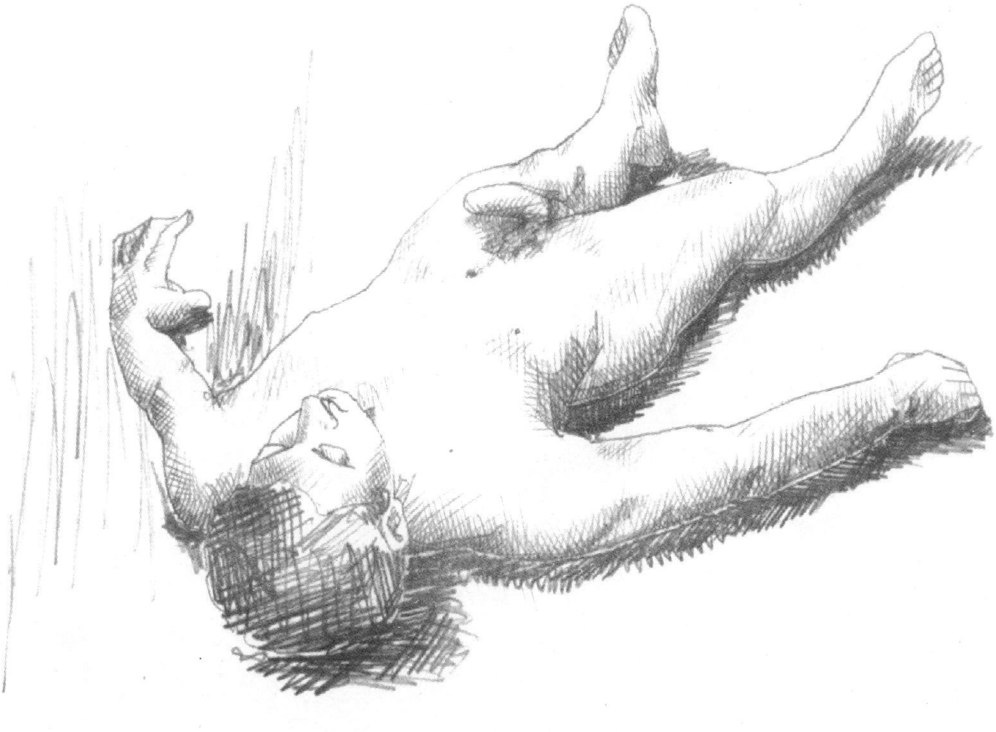

In these positions the model's muscles are relaxed and inactive; study carefully such pose and the force of gravity which flattens and spreads them sideways.

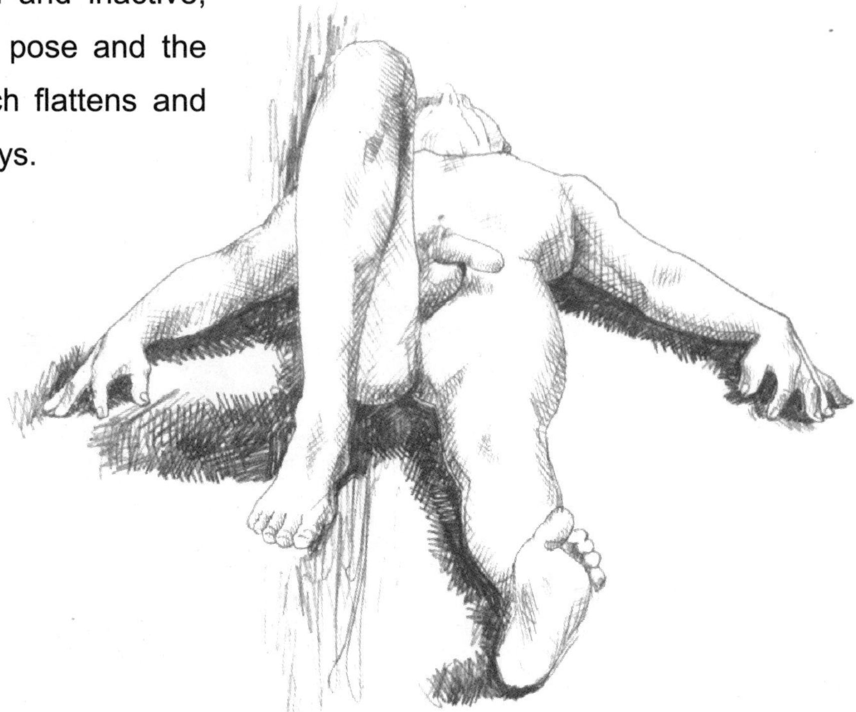

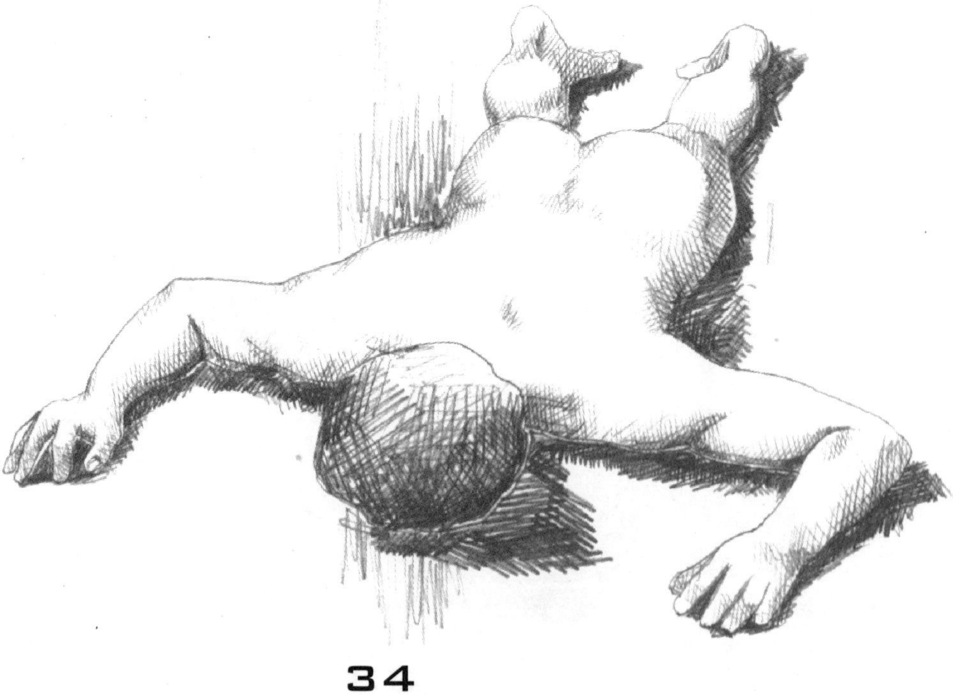

Observe the contraction of triceps, deltoid, trapeziums and latisimus dorsi, the protrusion of the right greater trochanter and the proximity of the scapulae to the median line. The ,muscles of the left shoulder are providing most of the support.

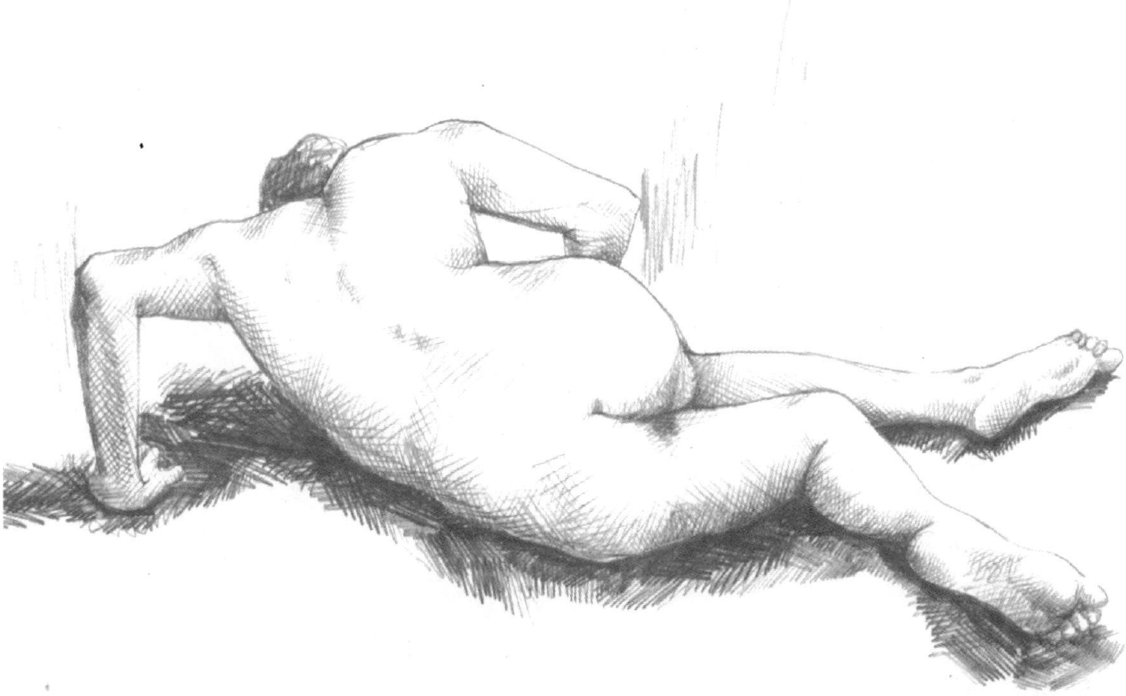

The Kneeling Figures

The drawing of the model in this pose looks for the bony reference points to get the correct proportions. Observe the length of the trunk in relation to the thigh and make a note of the point at which the right heel touches the buttock.

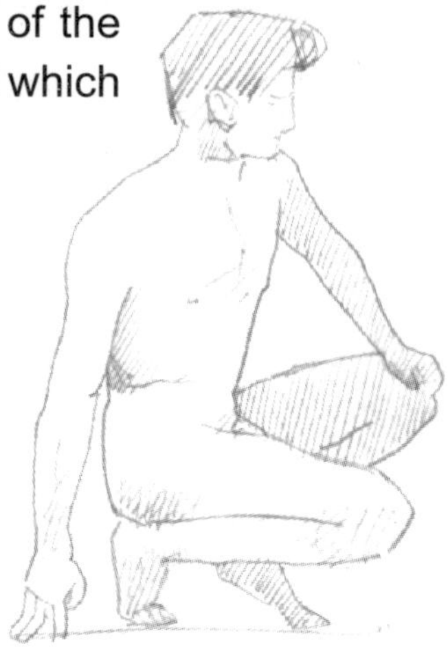

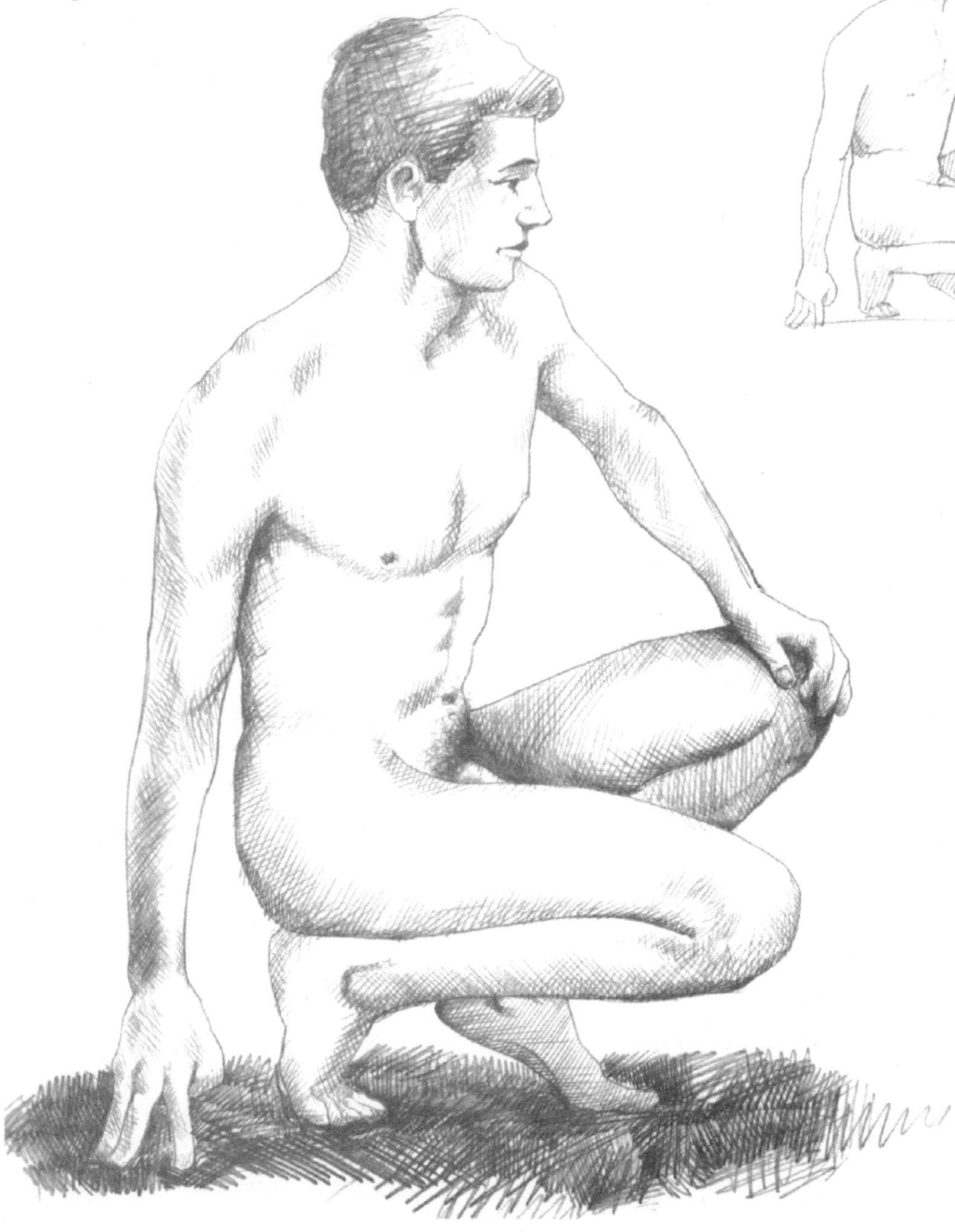

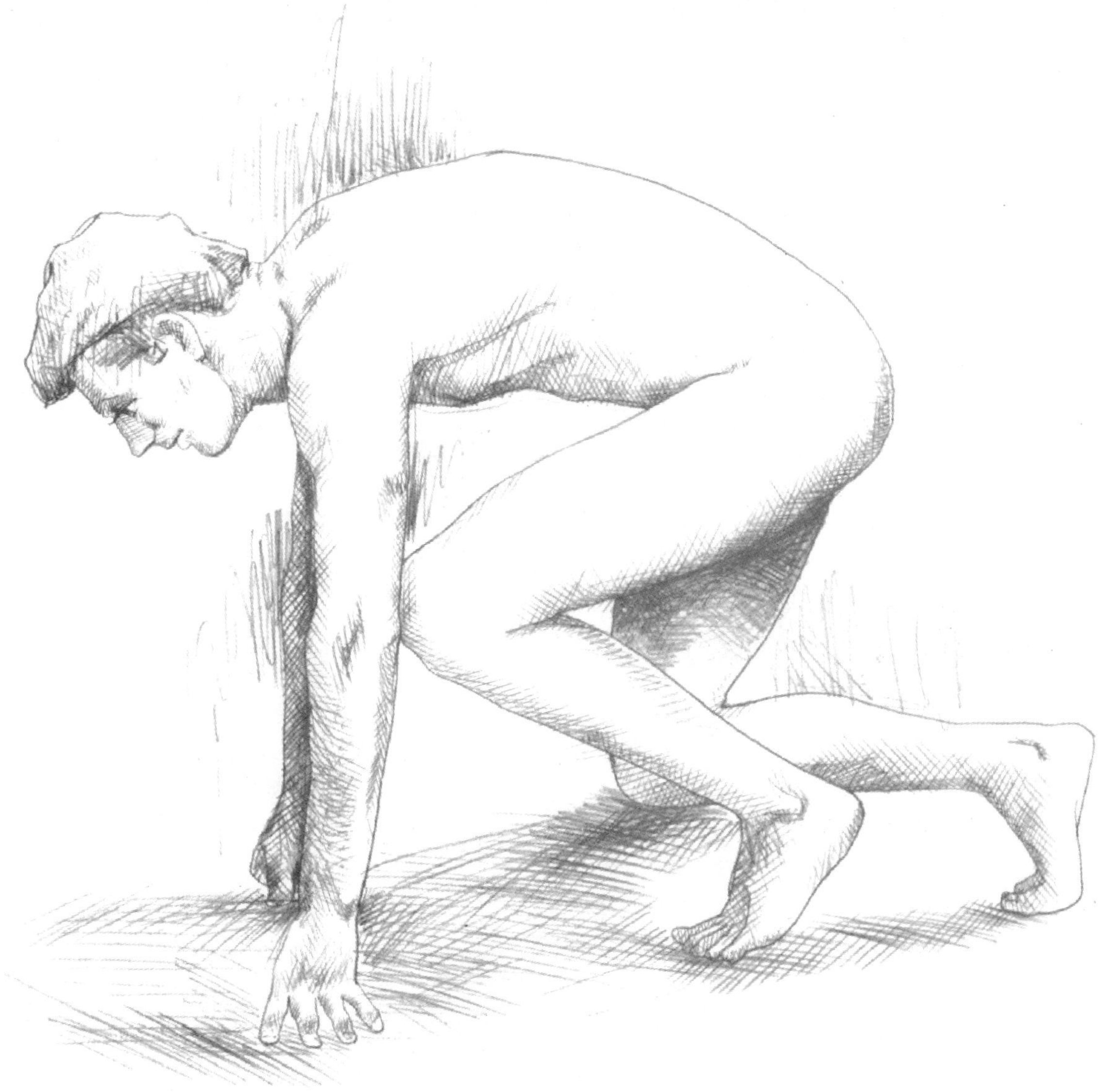

This sporting position of the model is of great interest because it shows off the musculature of the athlete ready to launch into the race: for example, latisimus dorsi, triceps, serratus anterior, tensor fascia latae and the tendons of biceps femoris are all much in evidence. Such poses can be held only briefly, so it is generally better to study them from photographs.

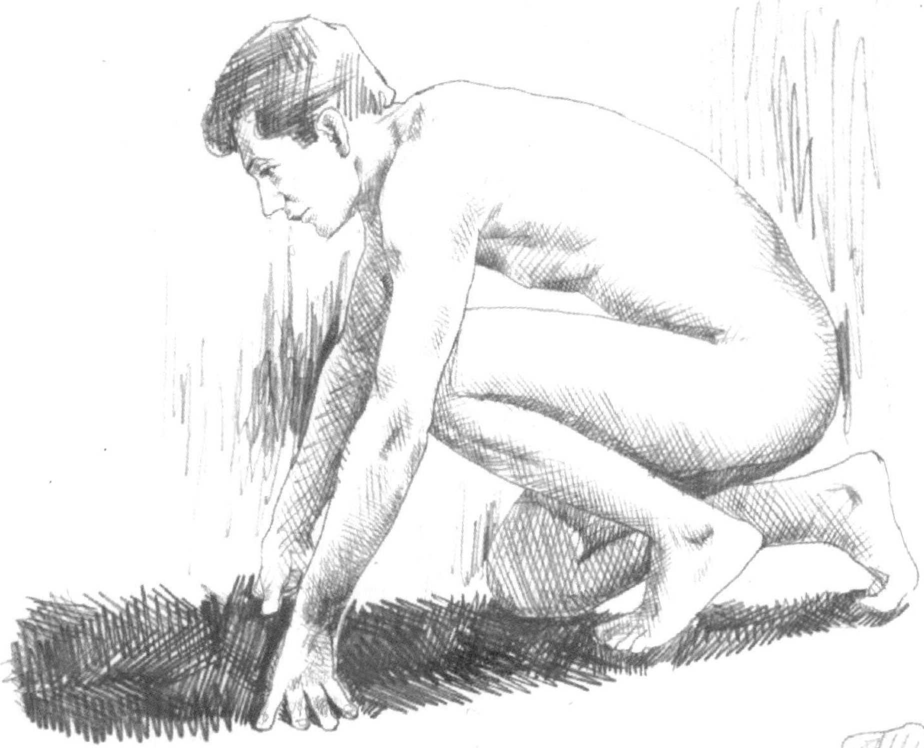

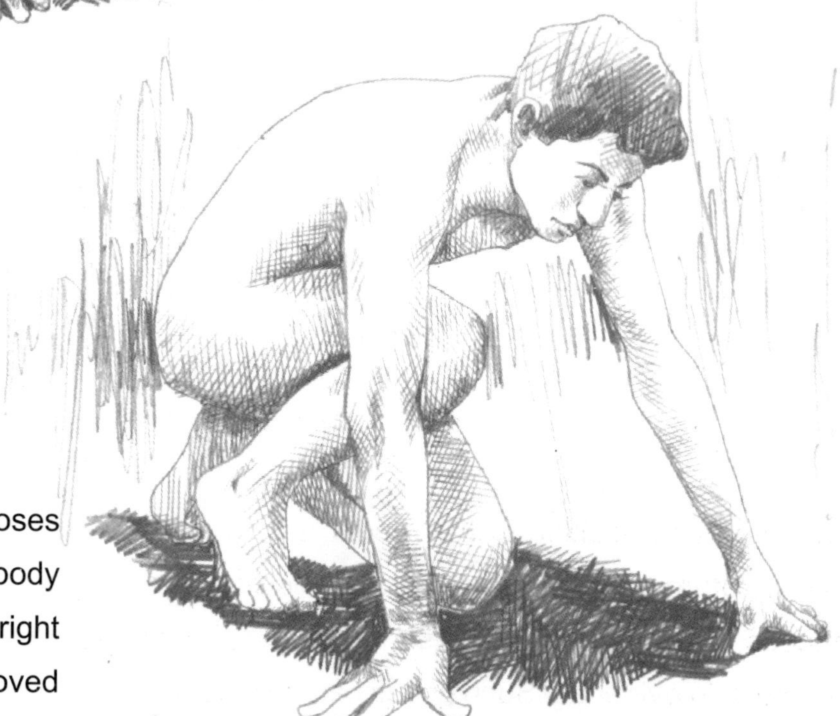

The drawings of two poses show the athlete's body weight falling on the right knee, the weight is moved forward on to the out-stretched fingers and toes.

In these types of positions the model must keep his balance by slightly contracting the muscles of the back and abdomen and the front muscles of the thigh.

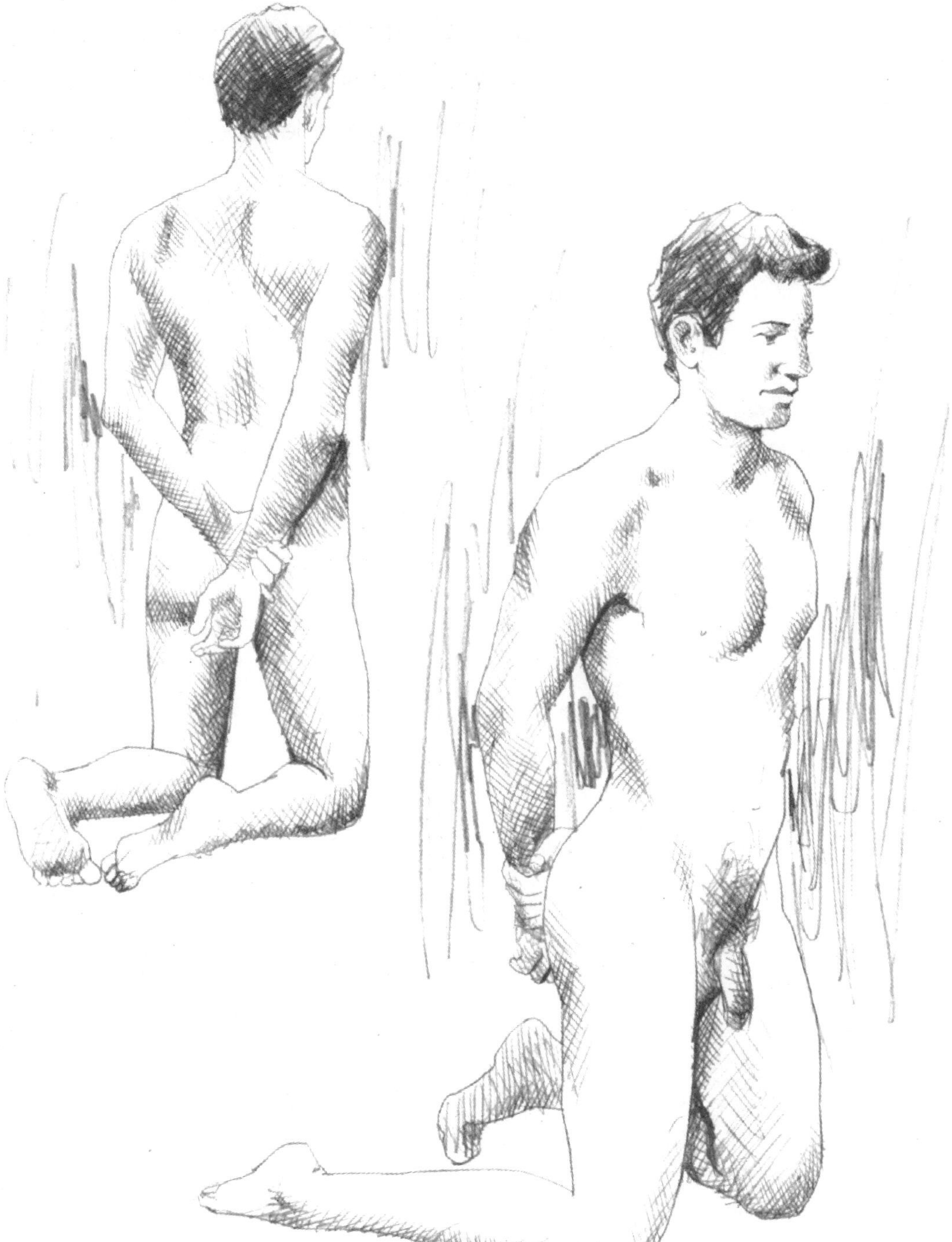

This model's weight of the body is sustained only by the right leg, resting on the ground. The forward thrust of the trunk, arms and head indicates an interrupted action, hardly balanced by the left foot, which is slightly touching the ground.

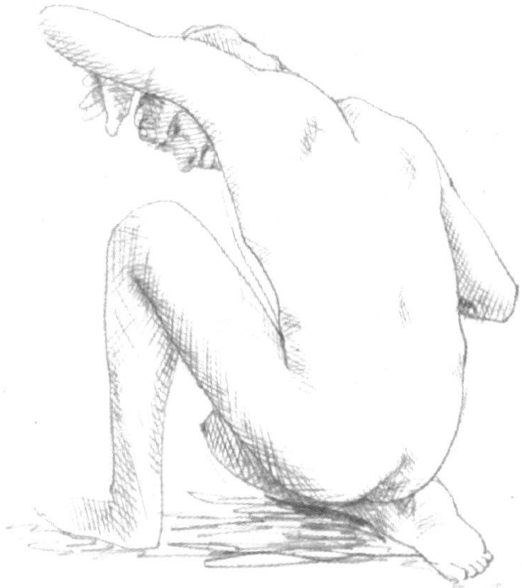

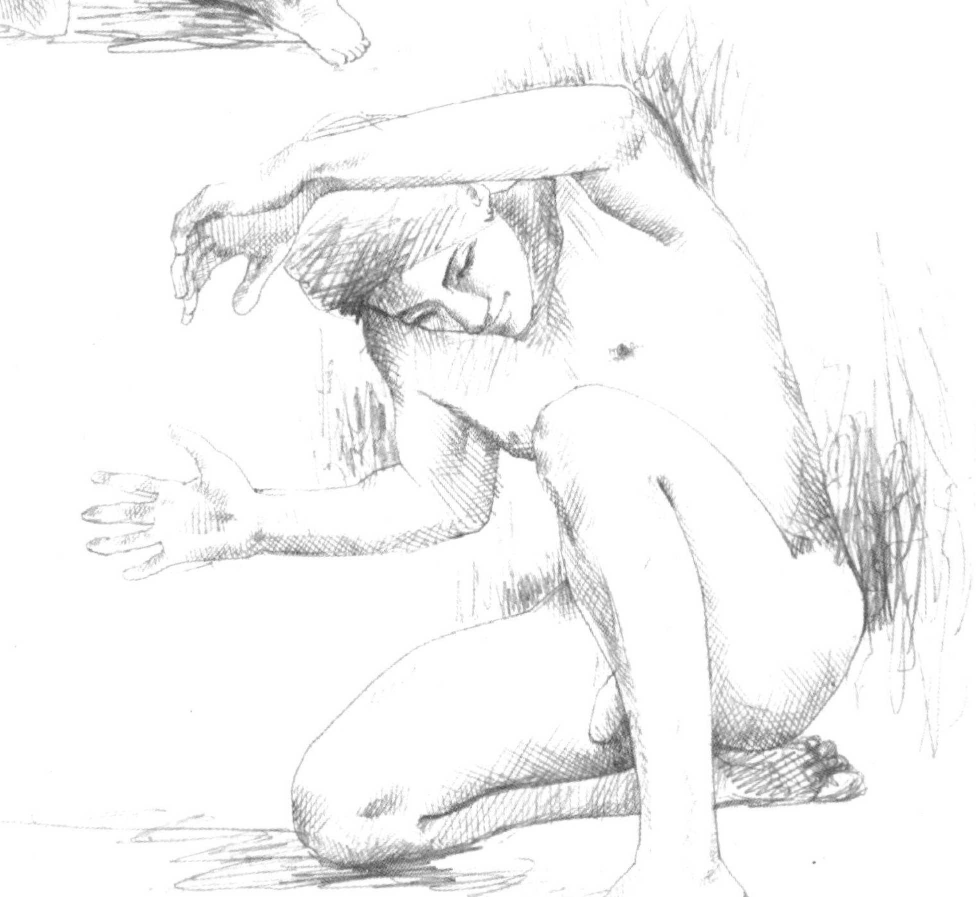

In this figure, the weight of the body is over the left knee and foot, while the balance is quite securely assured by the right foot and outstretched figure of the right hand.

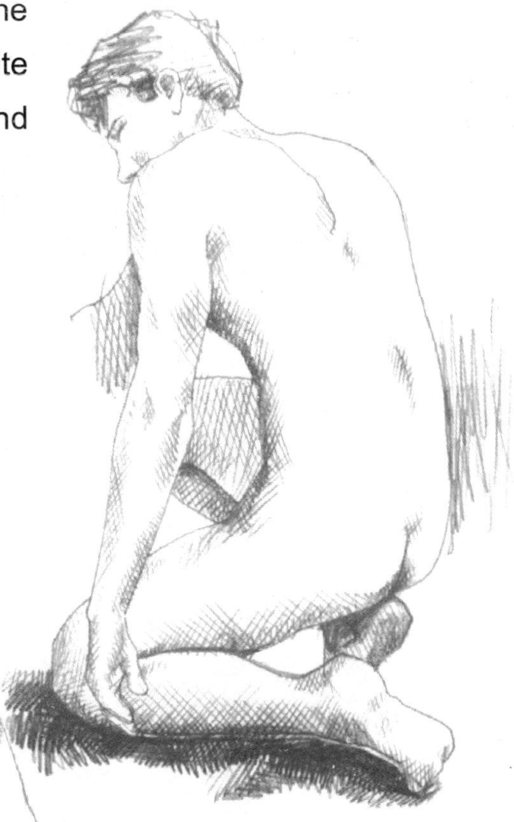

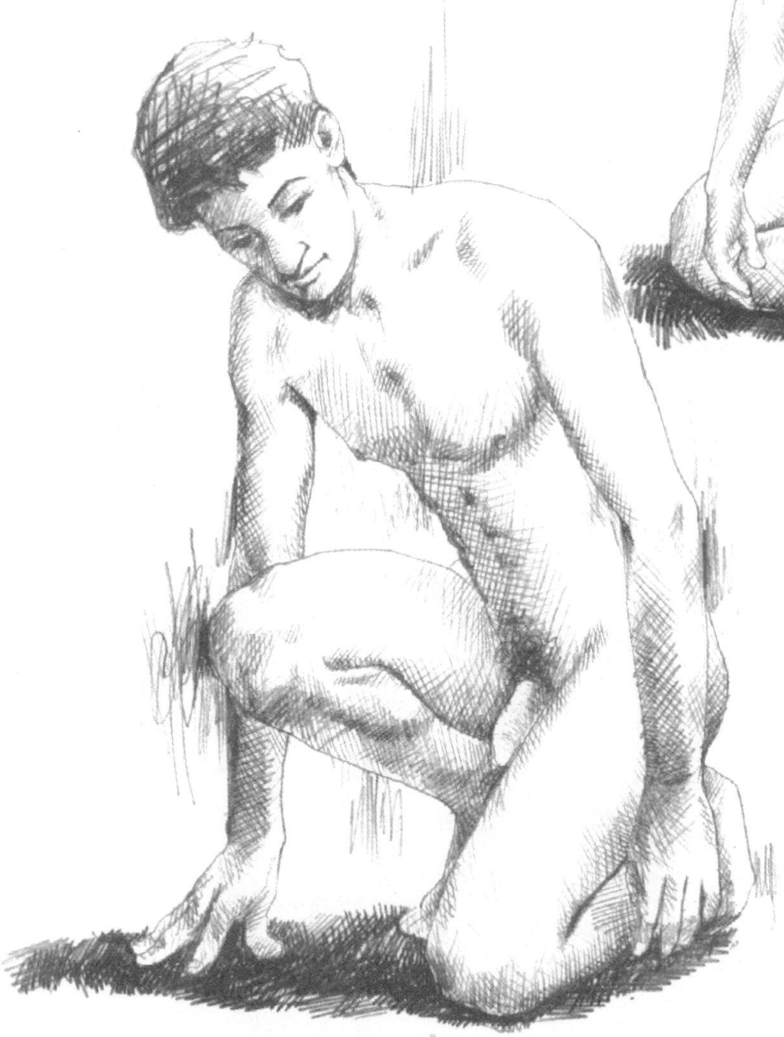

Look for the bony reference points to get the correct proportions. Note the length of the trunk in relation to the thigh and make a note of the point at which the right heel touches the buttock.

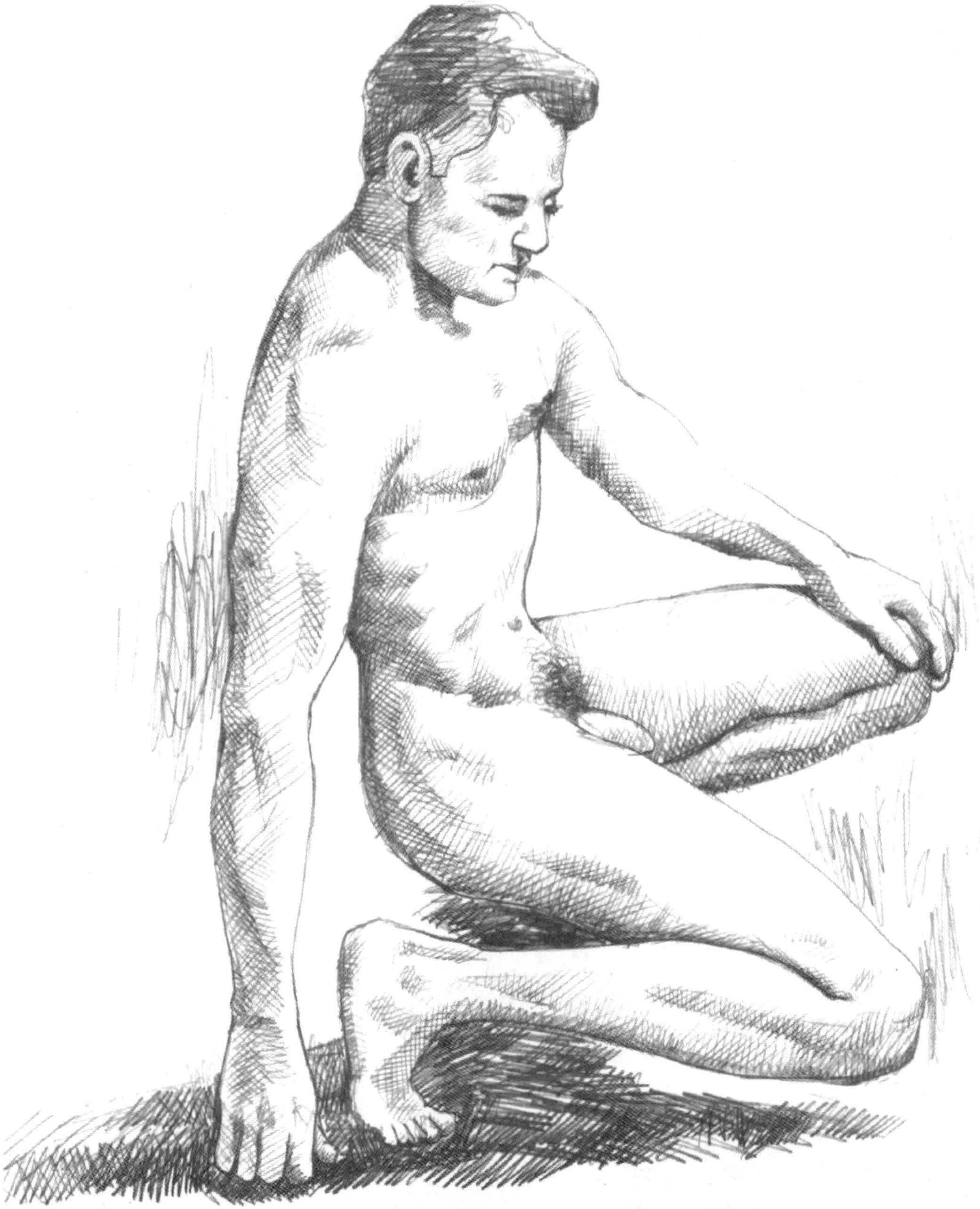

Standing Figures

Observe carefully the positions of these models; the different characteristics of the bodily structure and muscular development of the model in various poses.

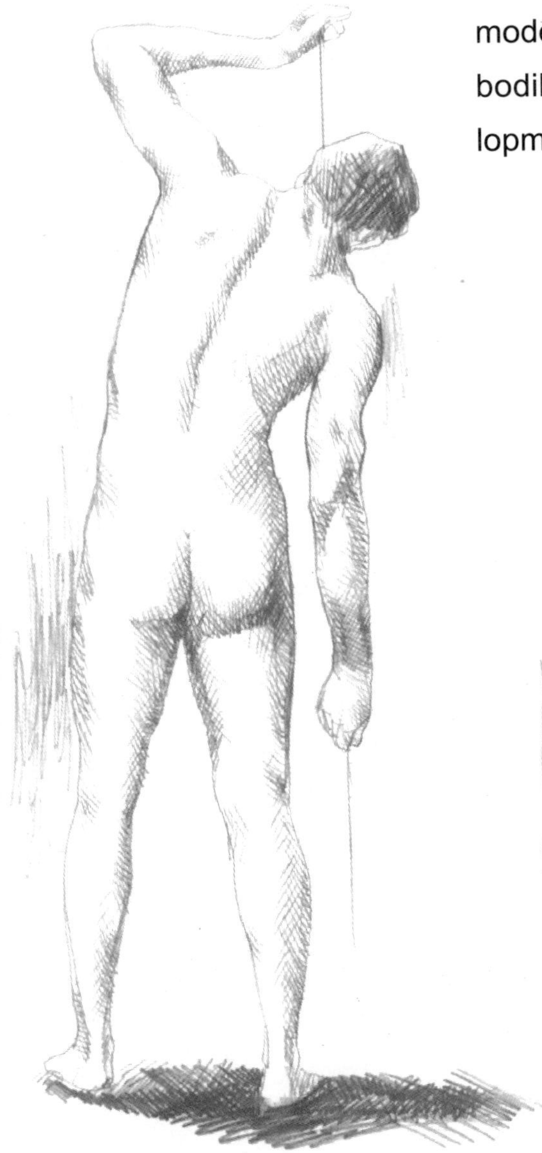

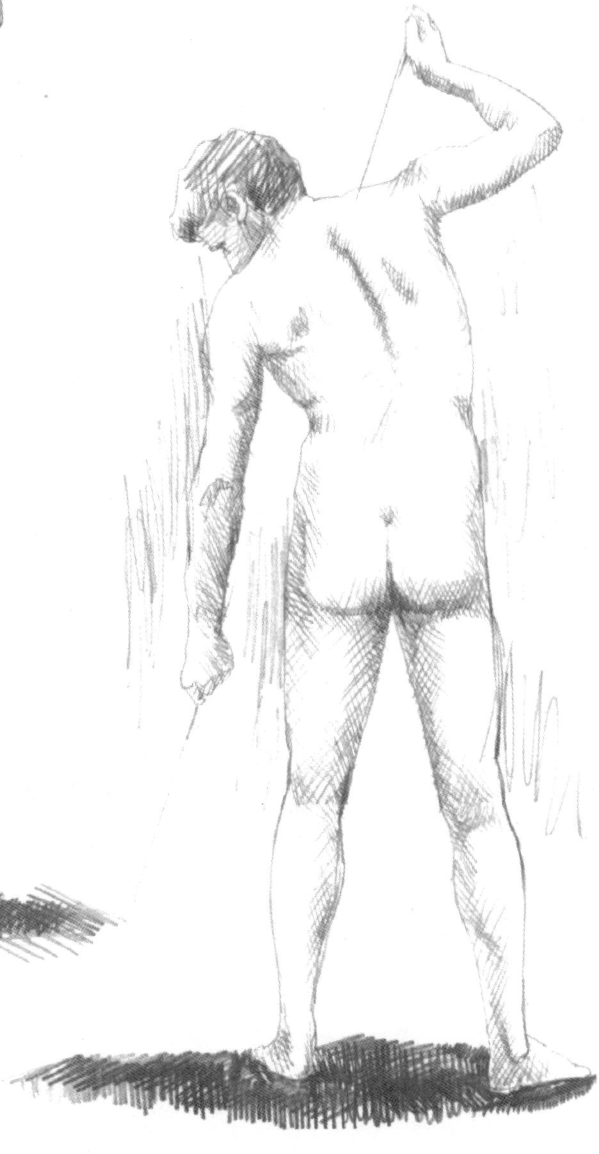

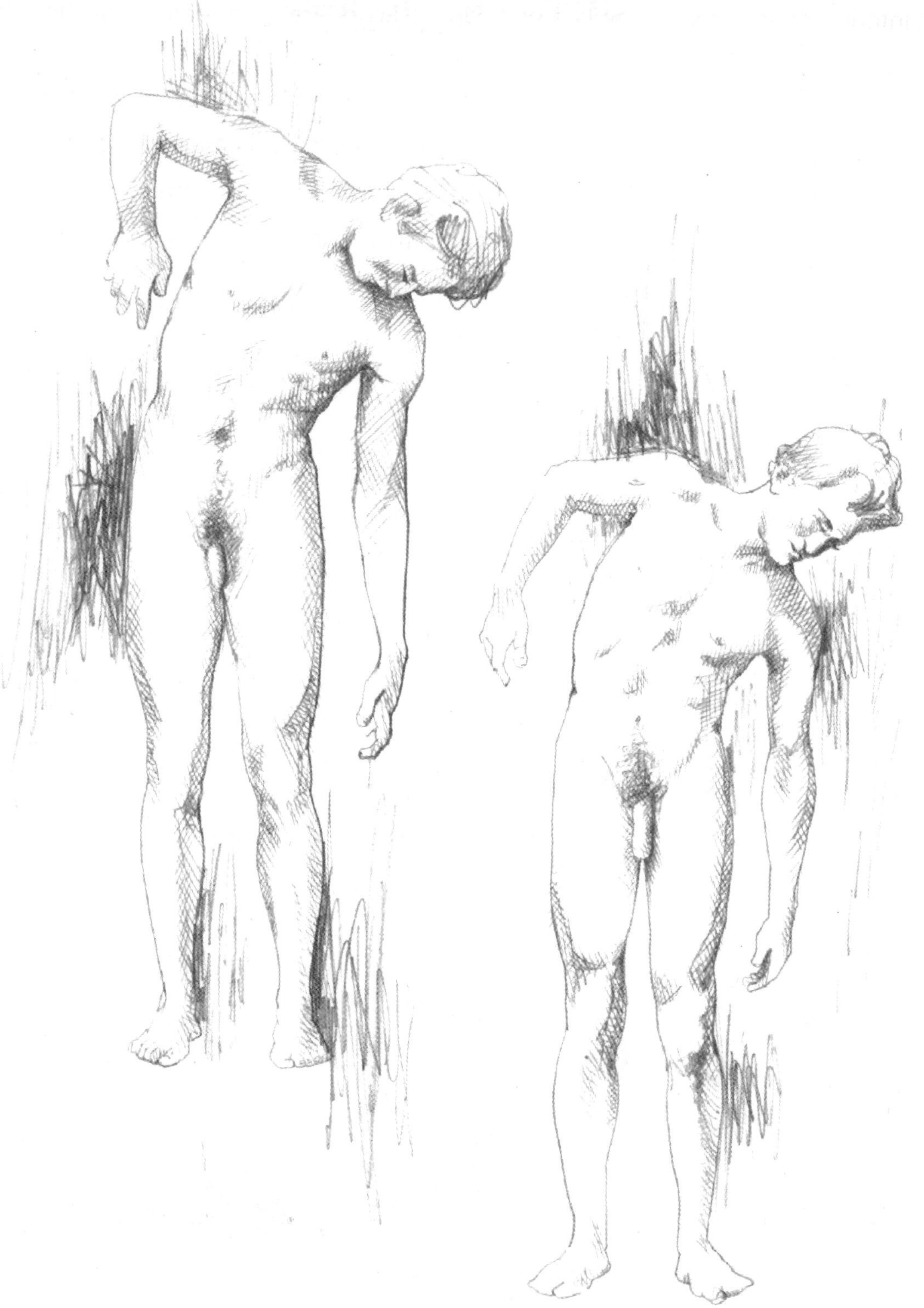

It is interesting to draw a complicated action. It is generally better to study them from photographs, the changes in the axis of equilibrium but, most of all, try to 'sense' the feeling of control in the position of the model when he is most effectively demonstrating it.

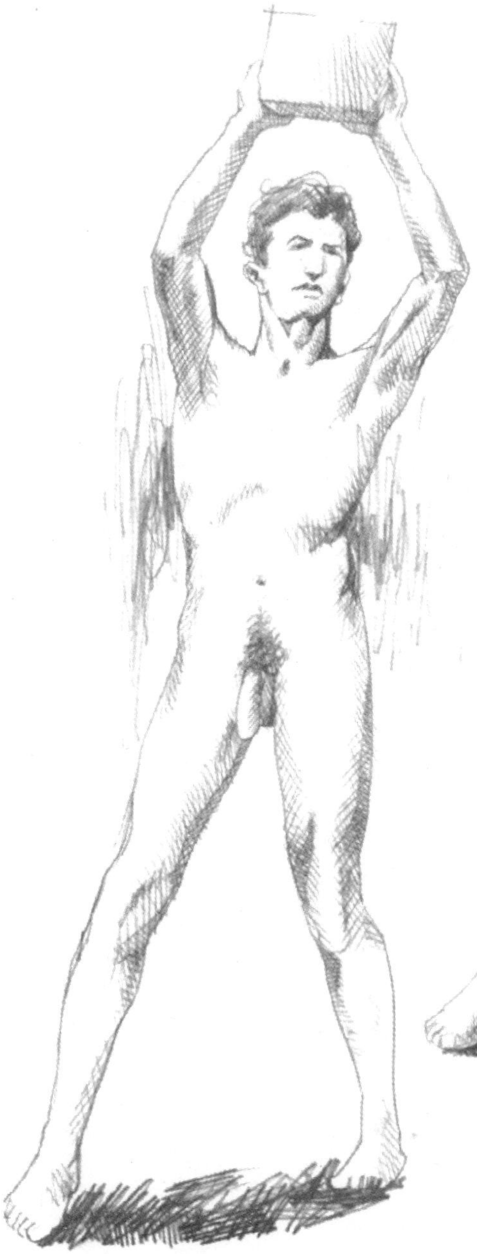

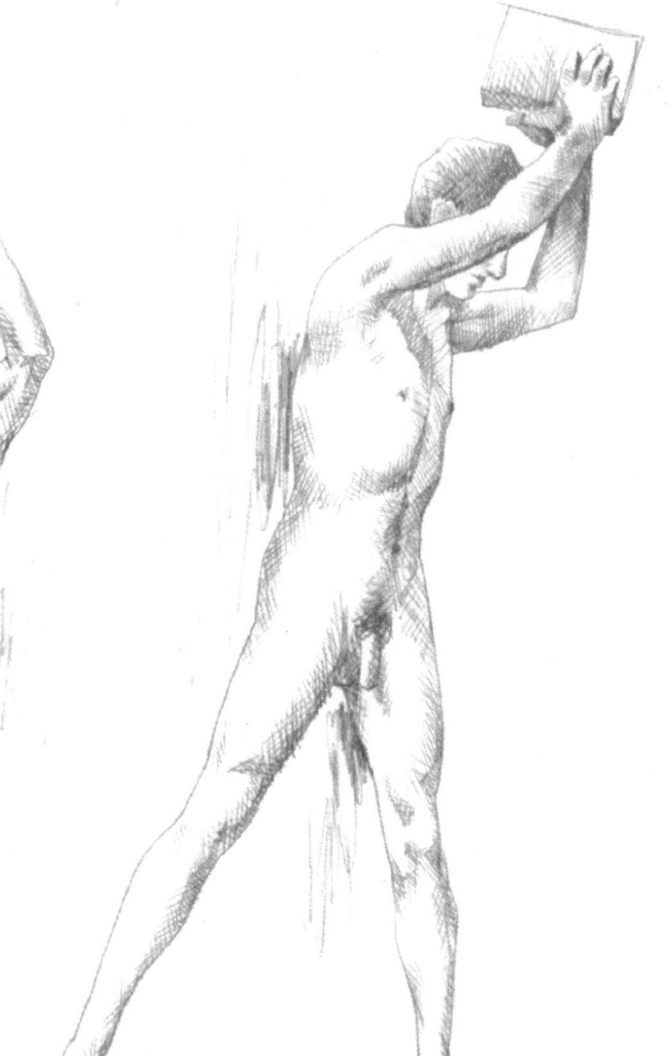

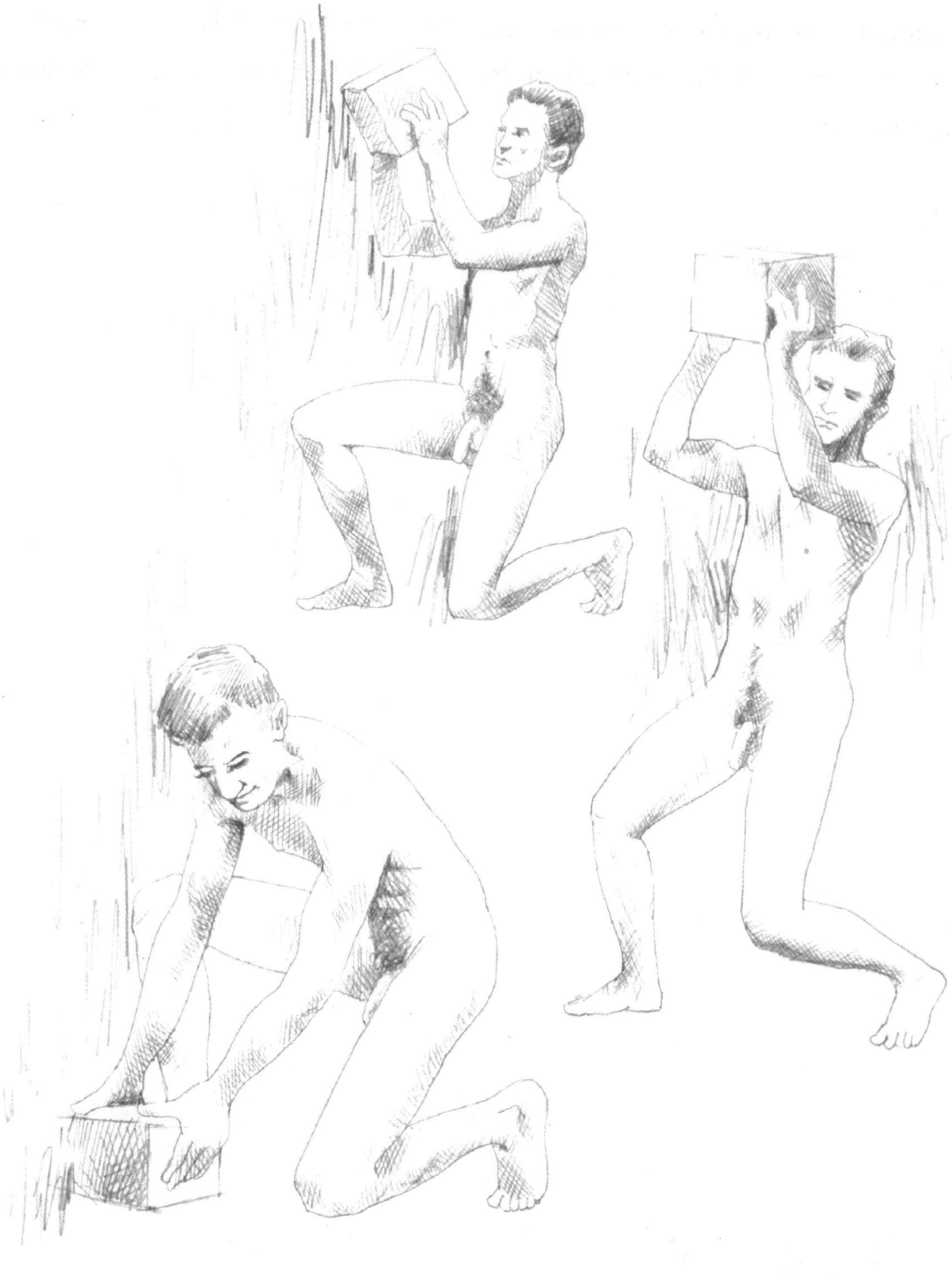

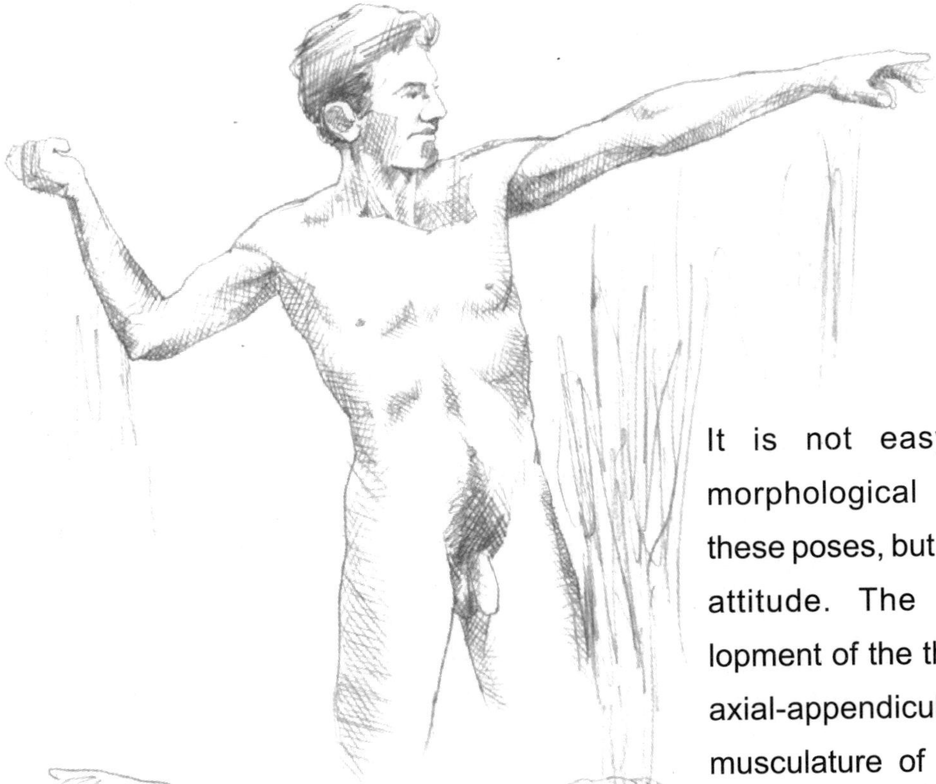

It is not easy to see the morphological differences in these poses, but also the model's attitude. The greater development of the thorax due to the axial-appendicular and dorsal musculature of the model is in strong contrast to that of the other.

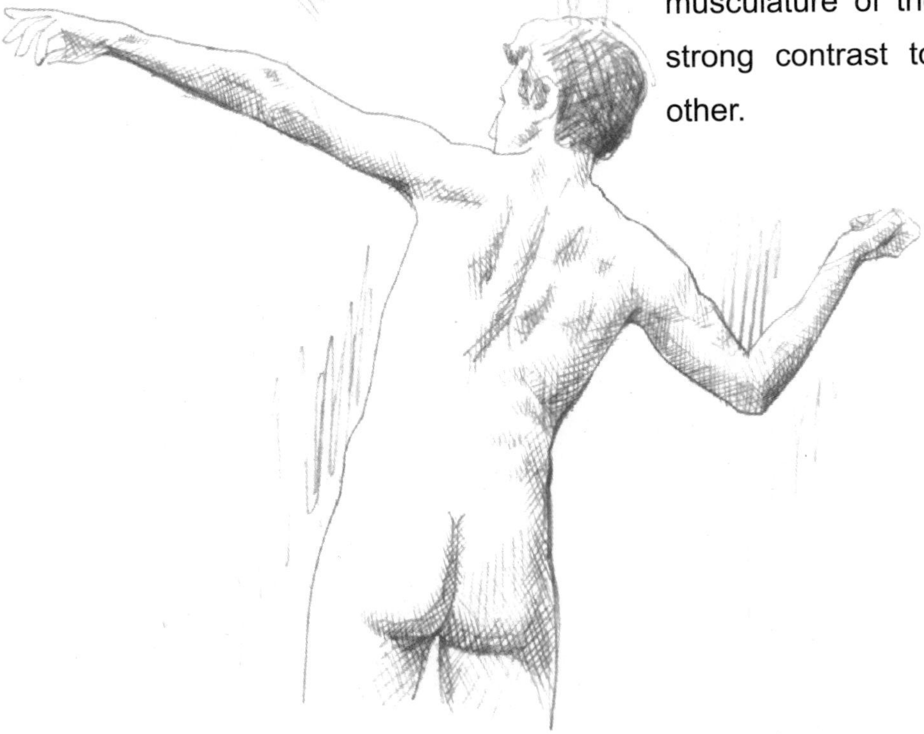

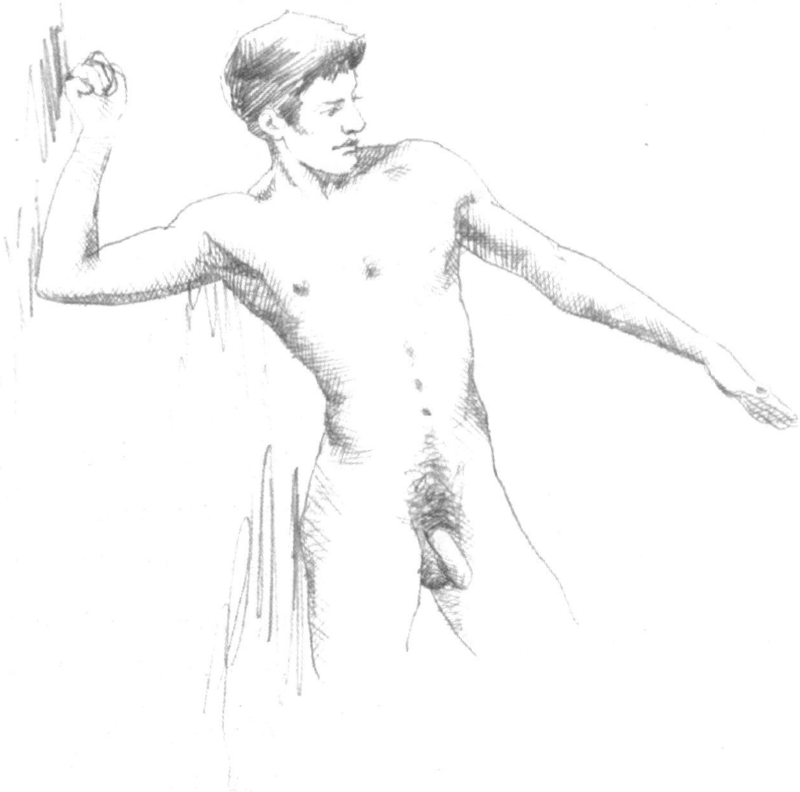

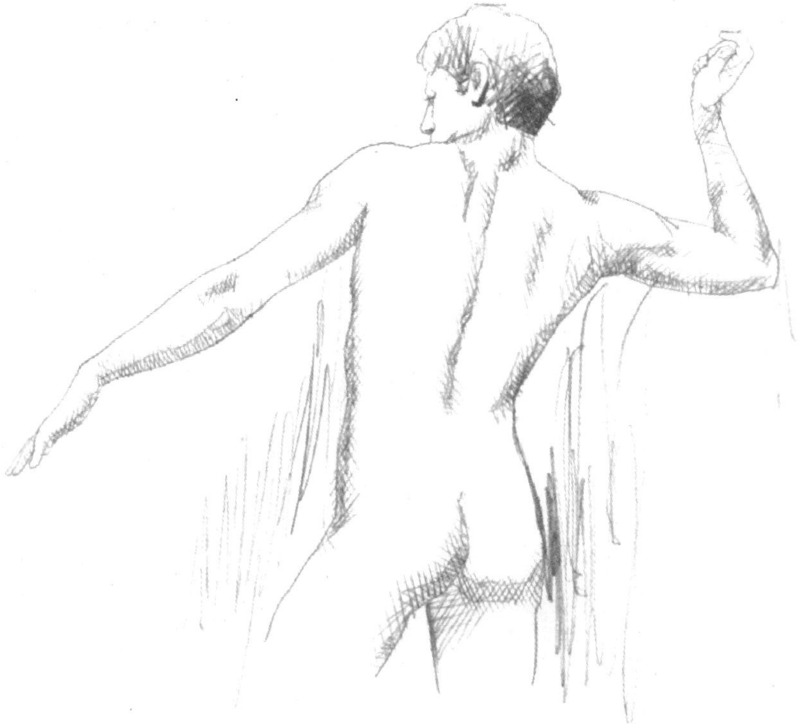

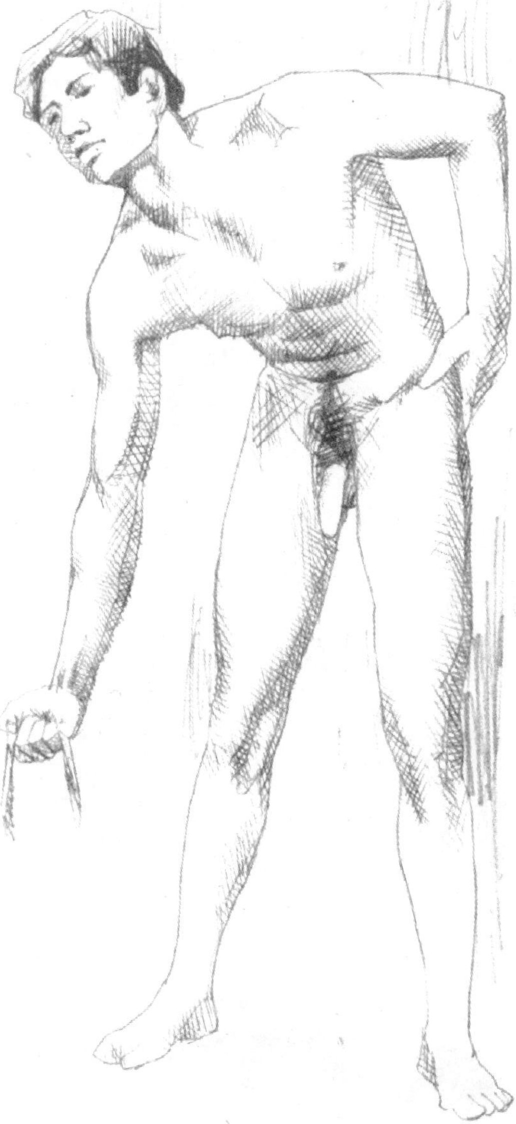

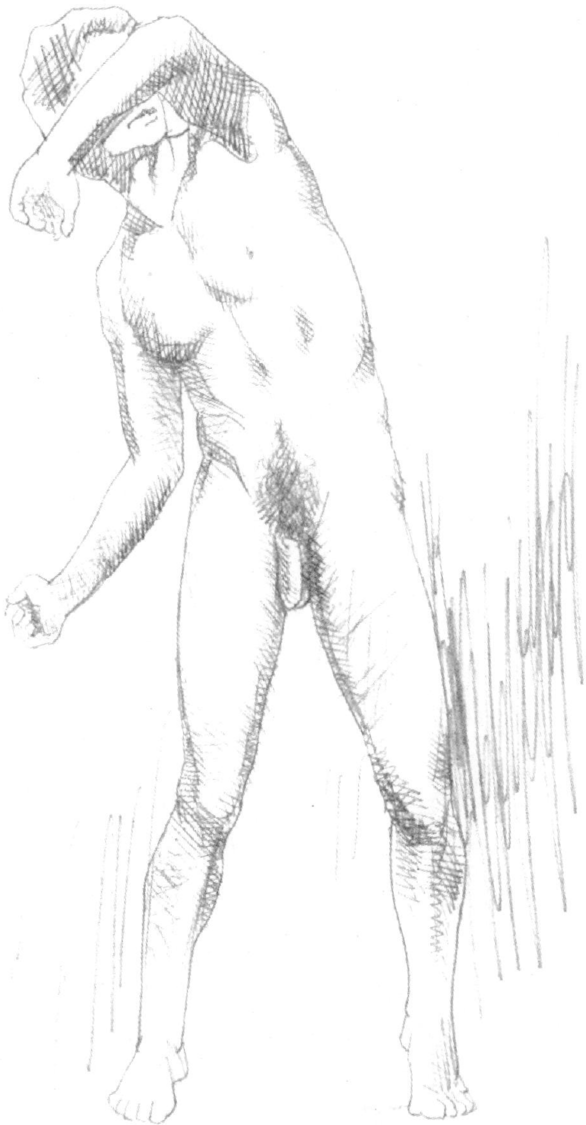

In this drawing the flexion of the trunk, together with a light torsion causes tension in the musculature of the legs, used to find and maintain balance. Observe the lower edge of the thoracic cage, defined by the costal arch.

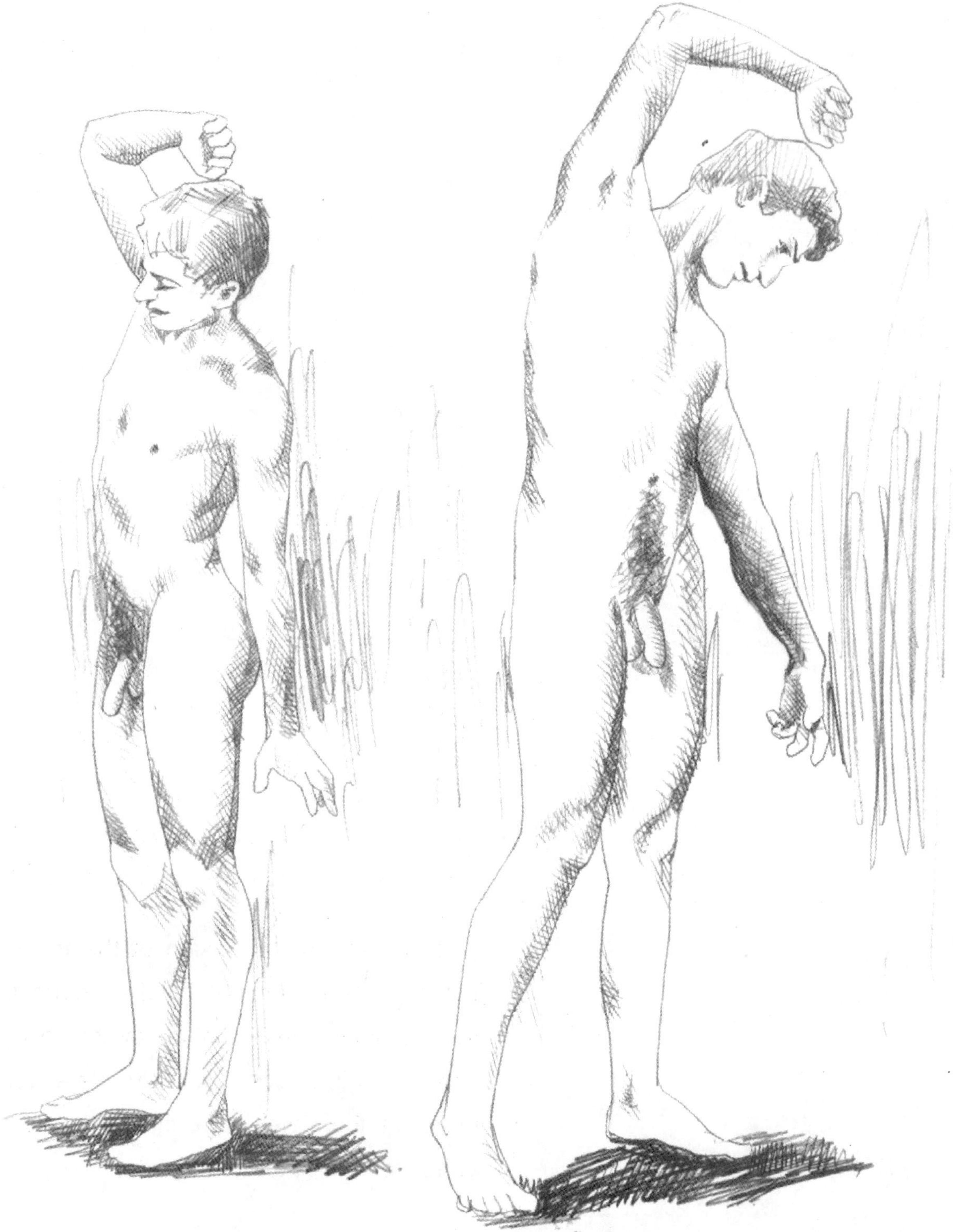

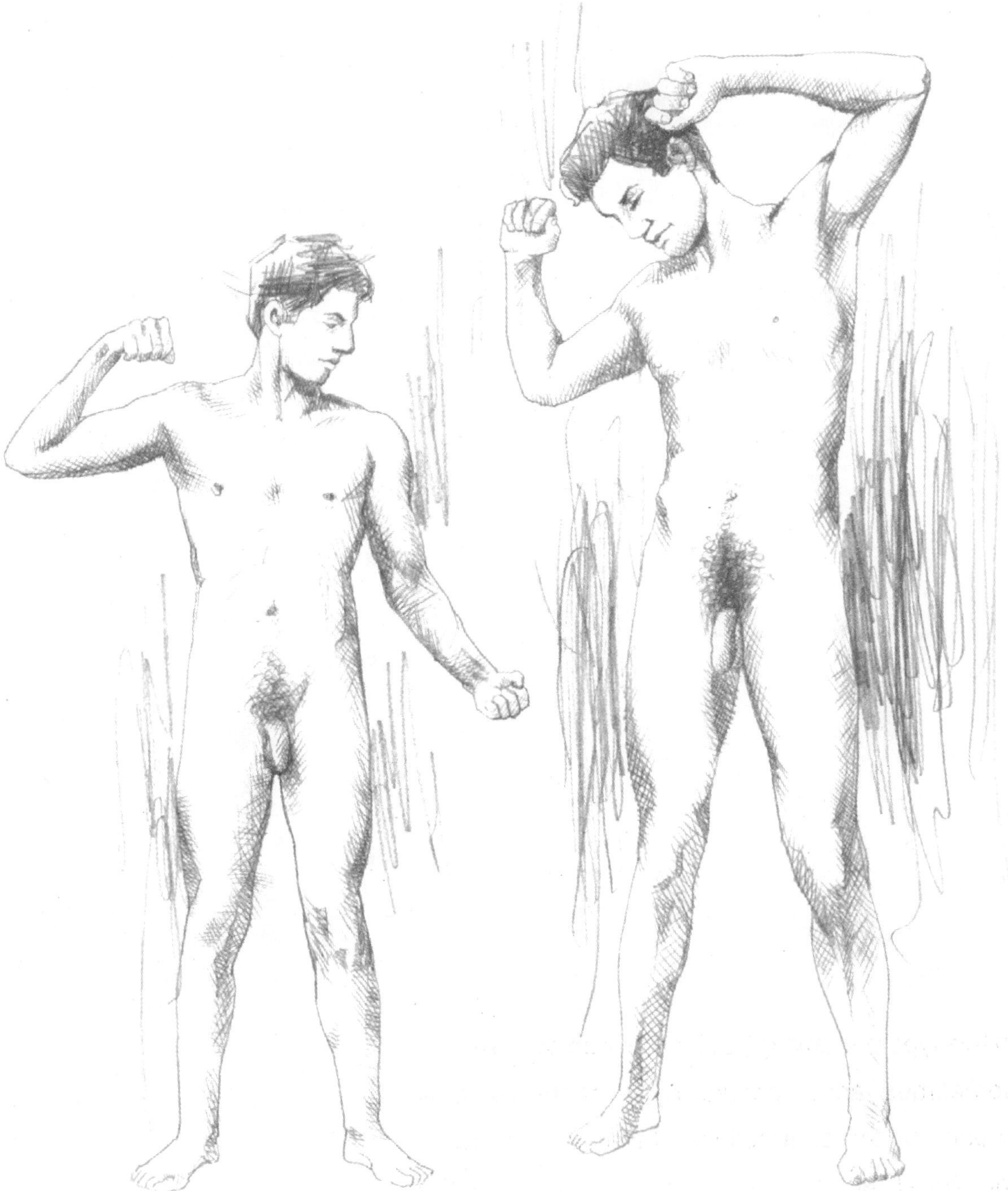

When the arm and shoulder clearly demonstrate movement, the lower half of the body is set firmly on the ground; the legs and feet, somewhat apart, bear the weight equally, in these type of poses in which only half the body seems to move.

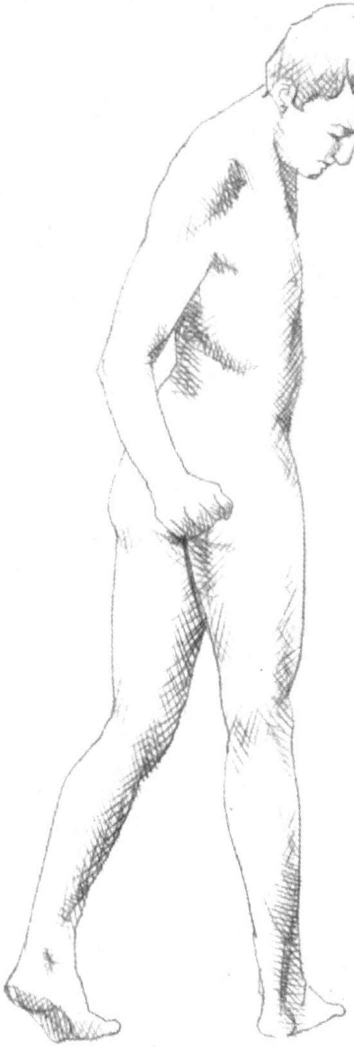

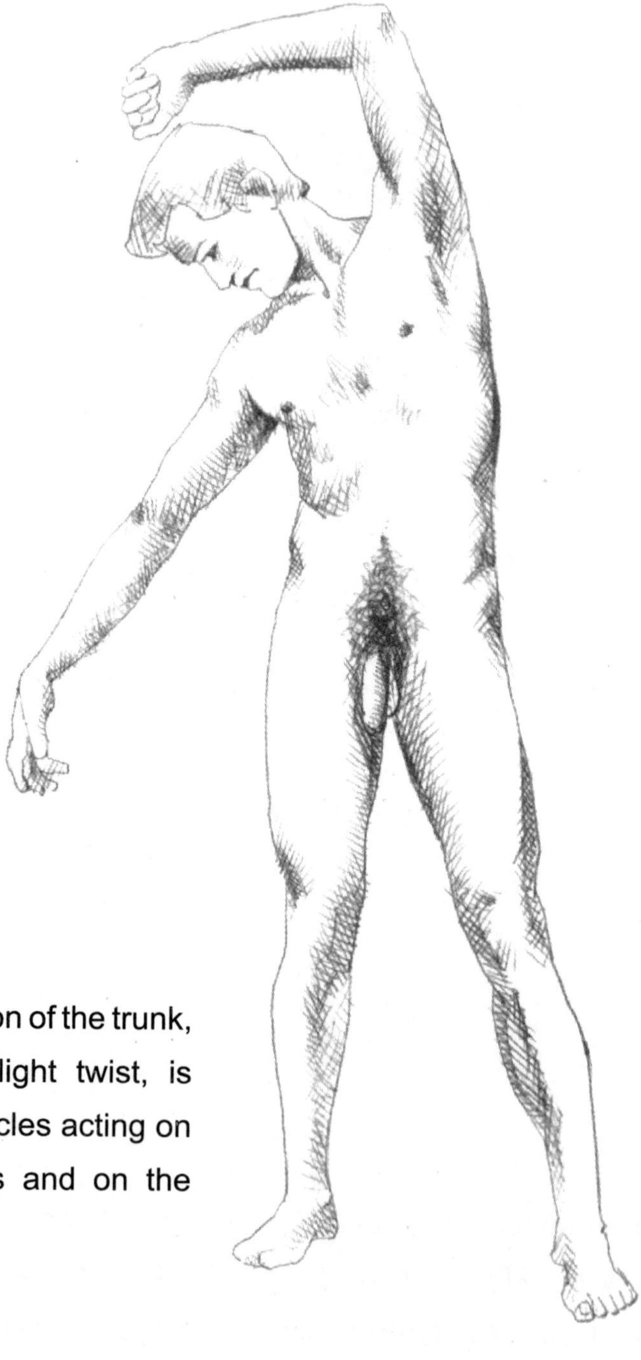

In this type of drawing position flexion of the trunk, sometimes accompanied by a slight twist, is caused by the contractions of muscles acting on the vertebral column, on the ribs and on the pelvis.

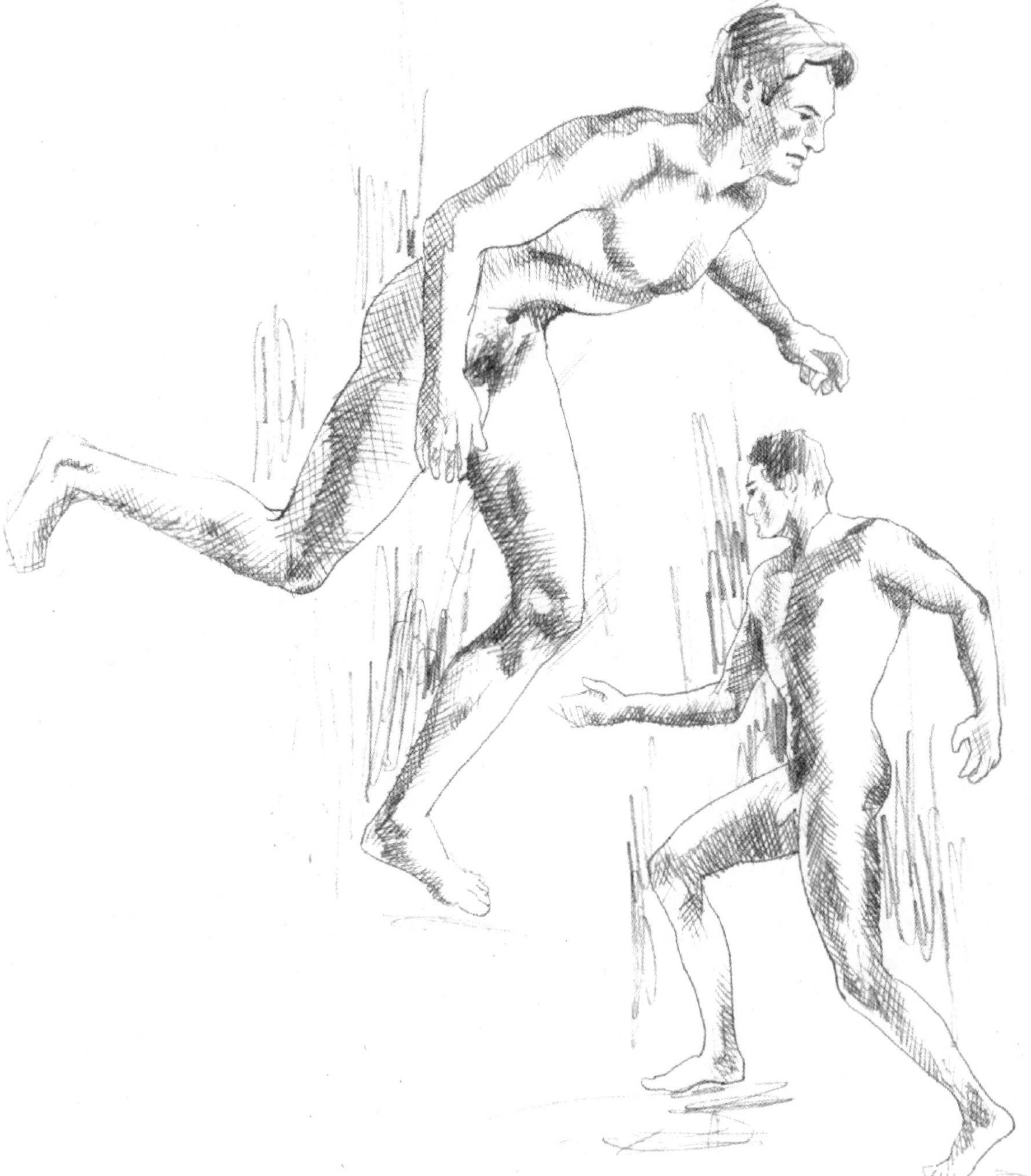

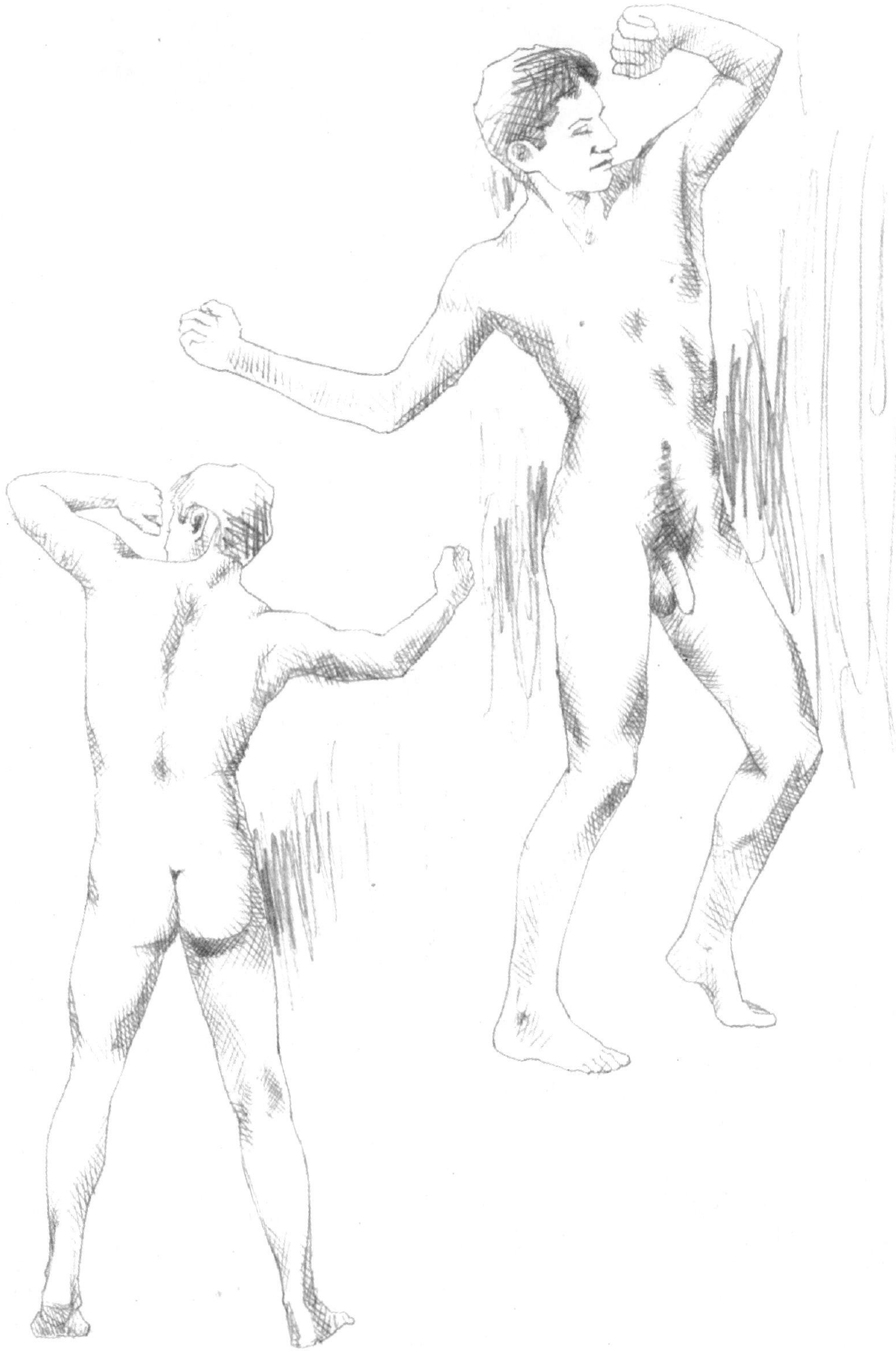

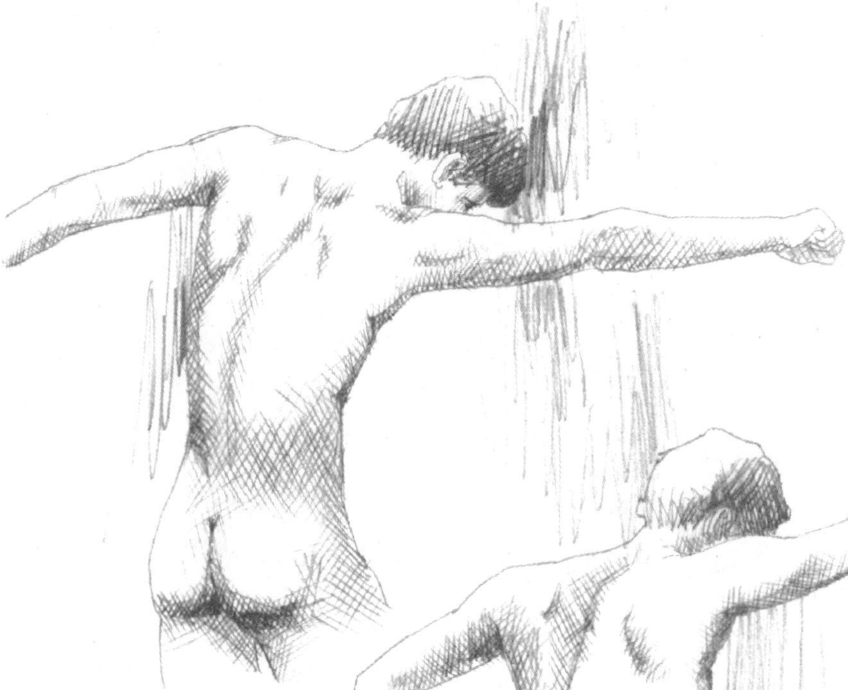

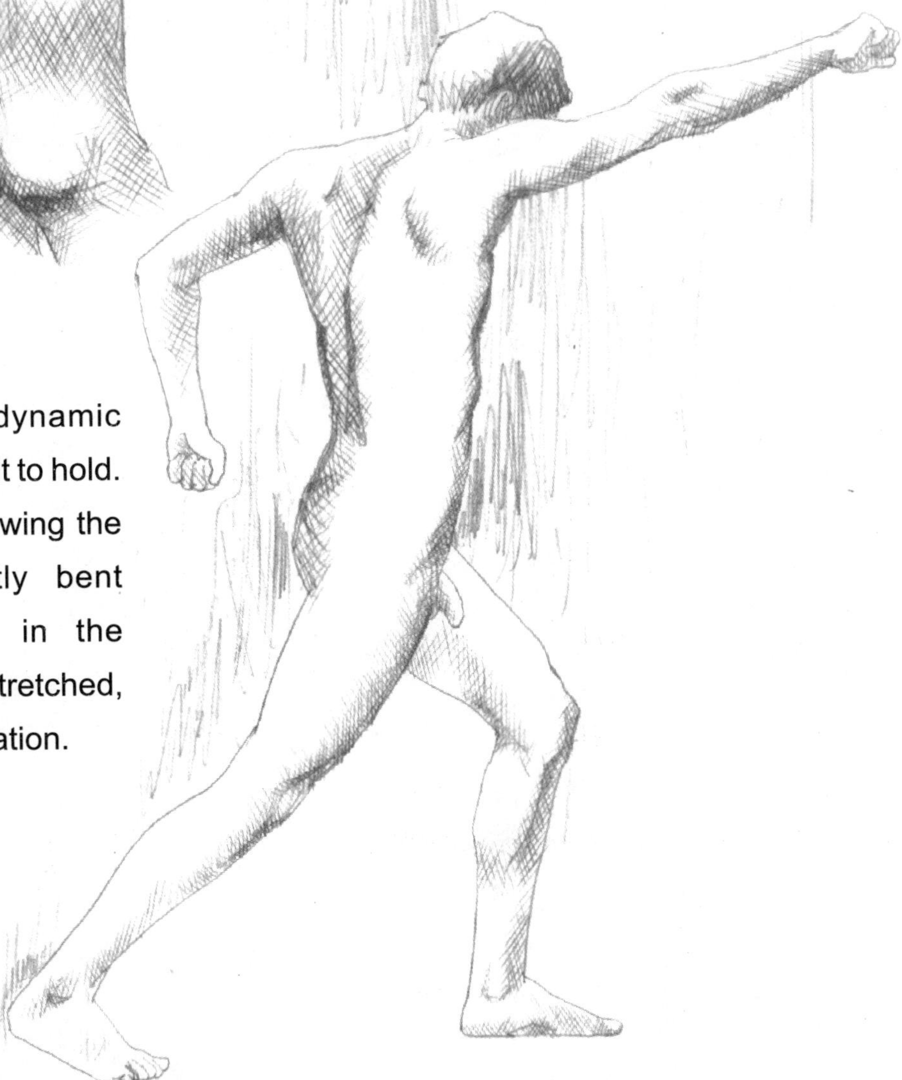

These more dynamic poses are difficult to hold. In the upper drawing the trunk is slightly bent forward, while in the lower it is more stretched, though still in rotation.

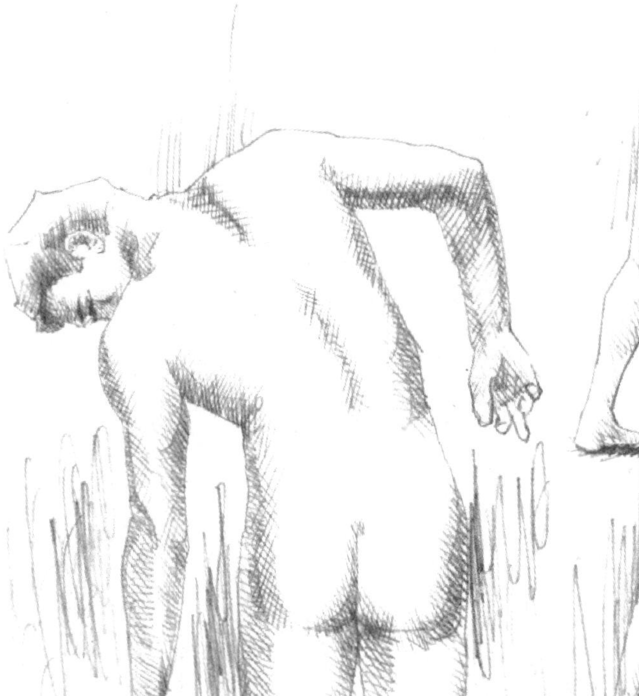

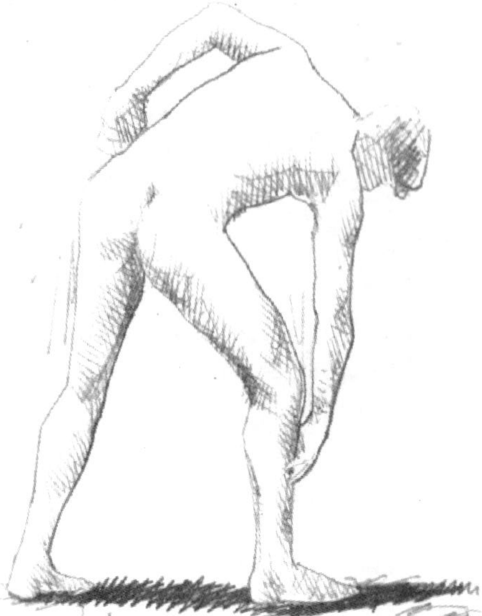

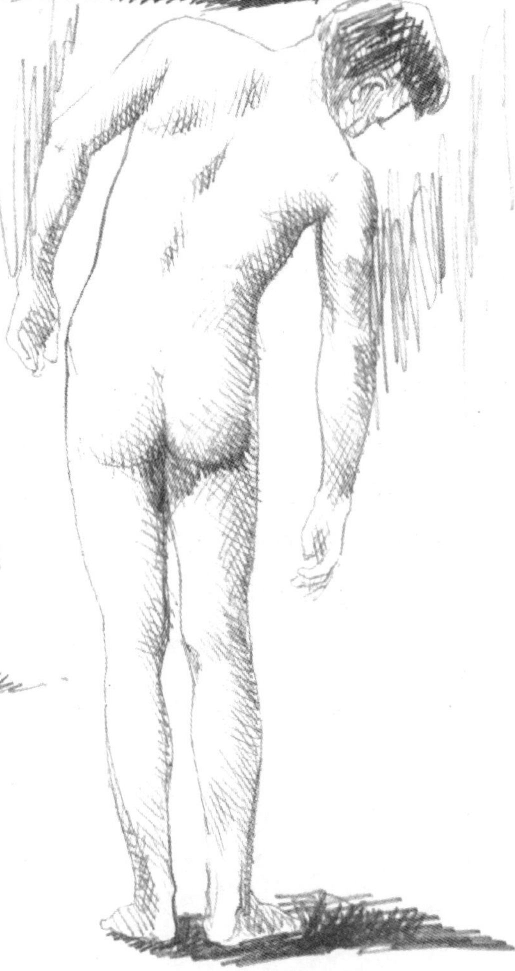

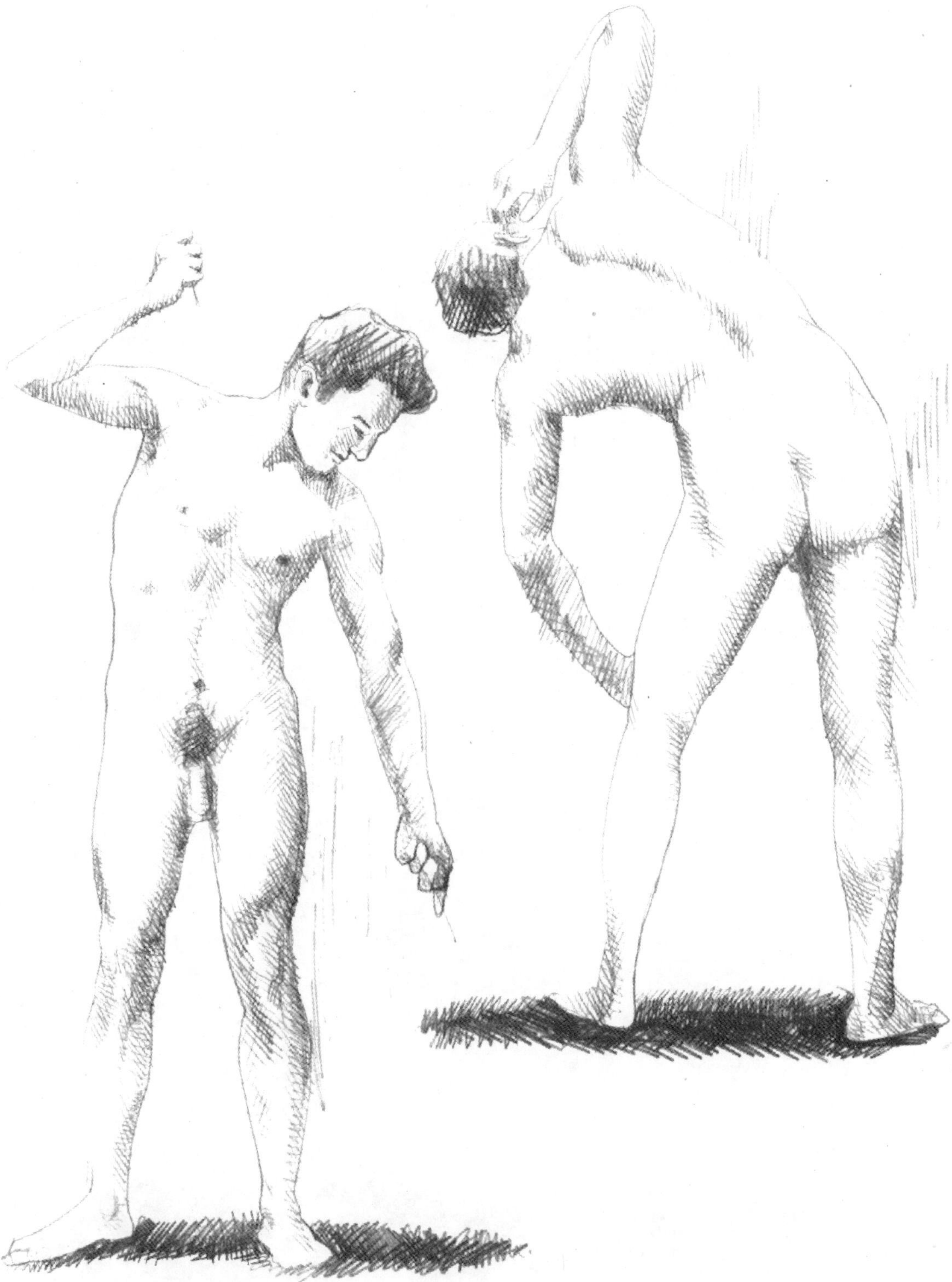

In this drawing thrusting forward from a support, the muscles of the back and shoulders move energetically, assisted by those of the legs, one foot rests firmly on the ground and the balance of the body is contrasted by the firm support of the walls. It depends on the amount of strength in the surface of the wall against which hands are pressing.

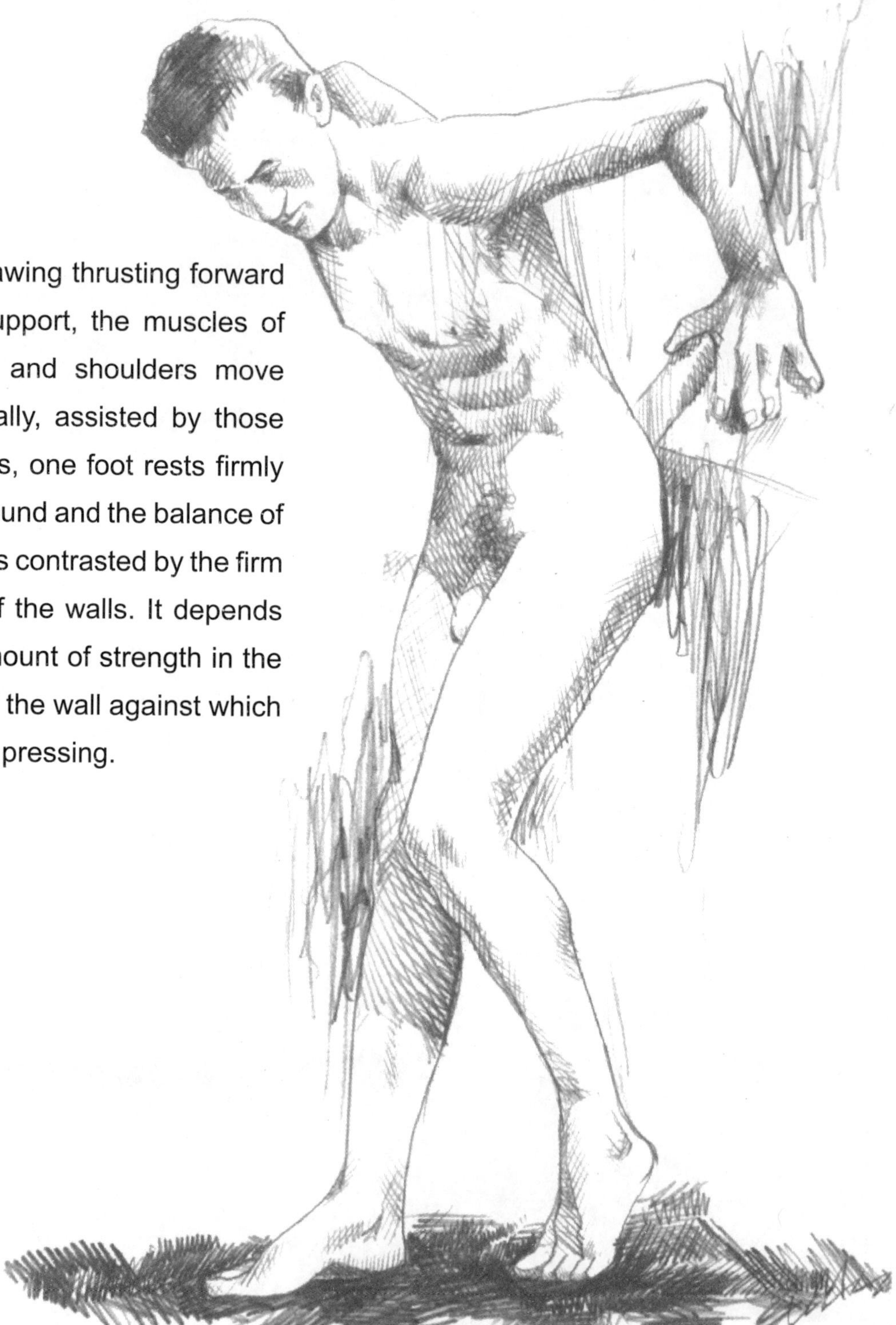

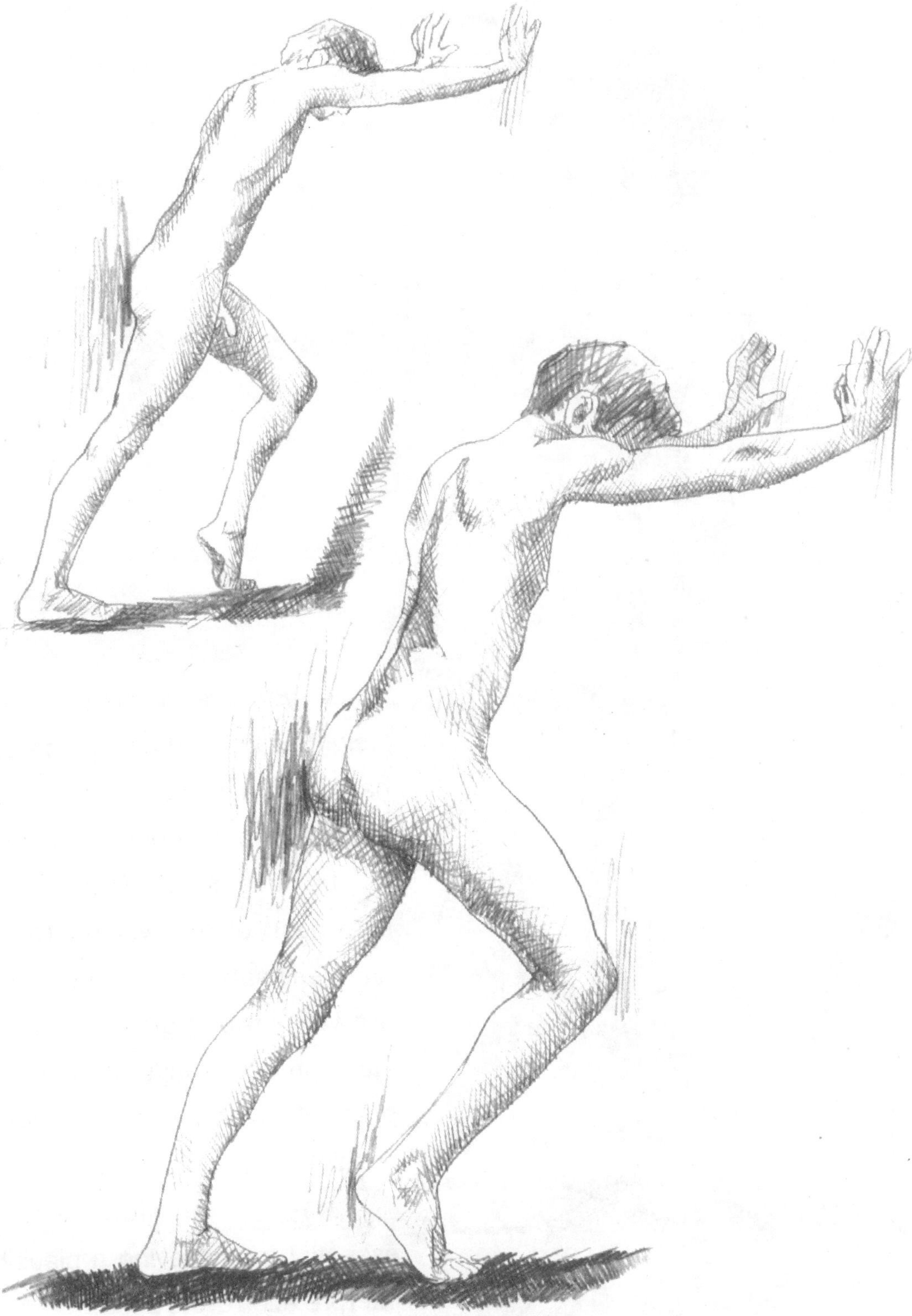

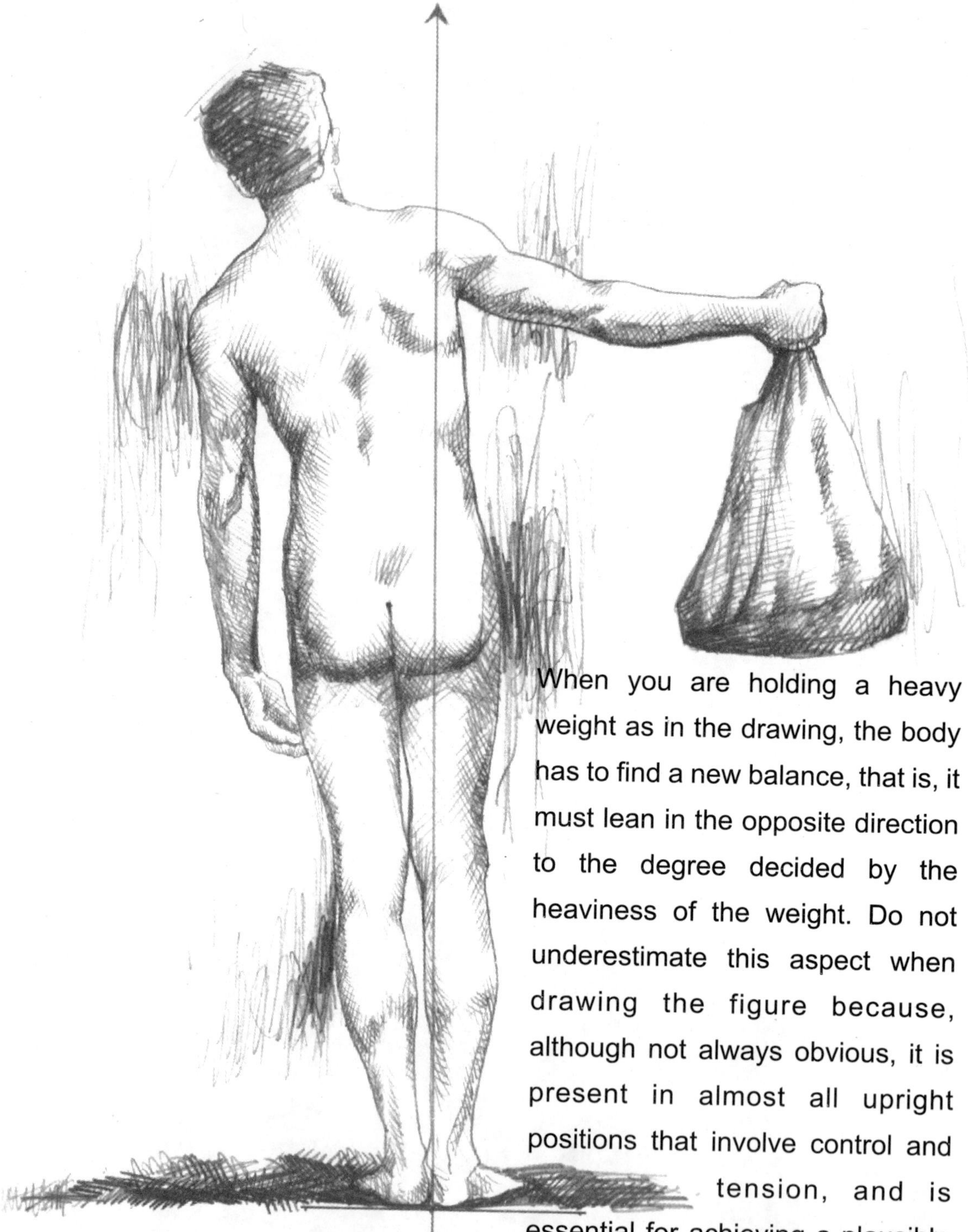

When you are holding a heavy weight as in the drawing, the body has to find a new balance, that is, it must lean in the opposite direction to the degree decided by the heaviness of the weight. Do not underestimate this aspect when drawing the figure because, although not always obvious, it is present in almost all upright positions that involve control and tension, and is essential for achieving a plausible interpretation of the pose.

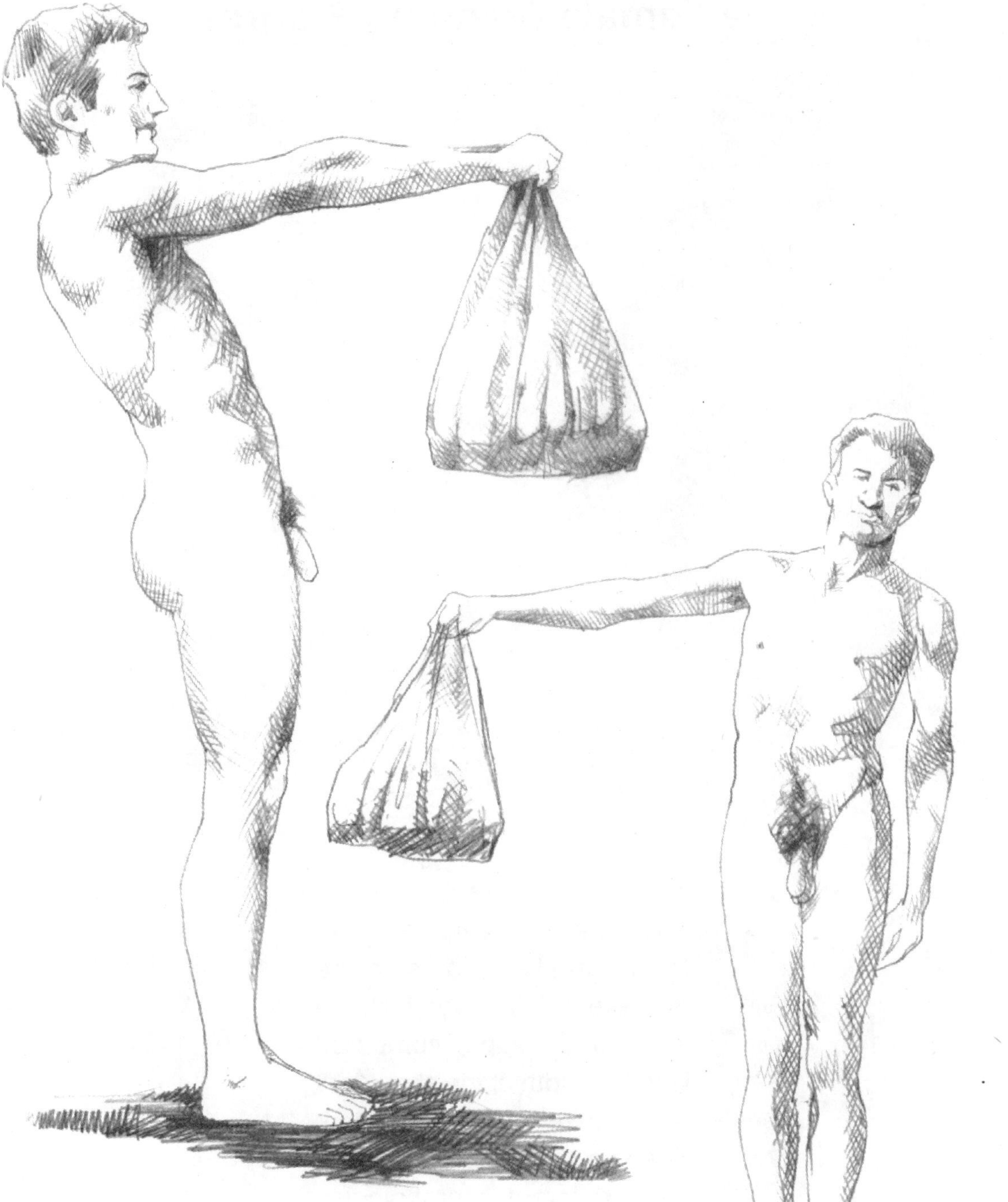

The Female Standing Figures

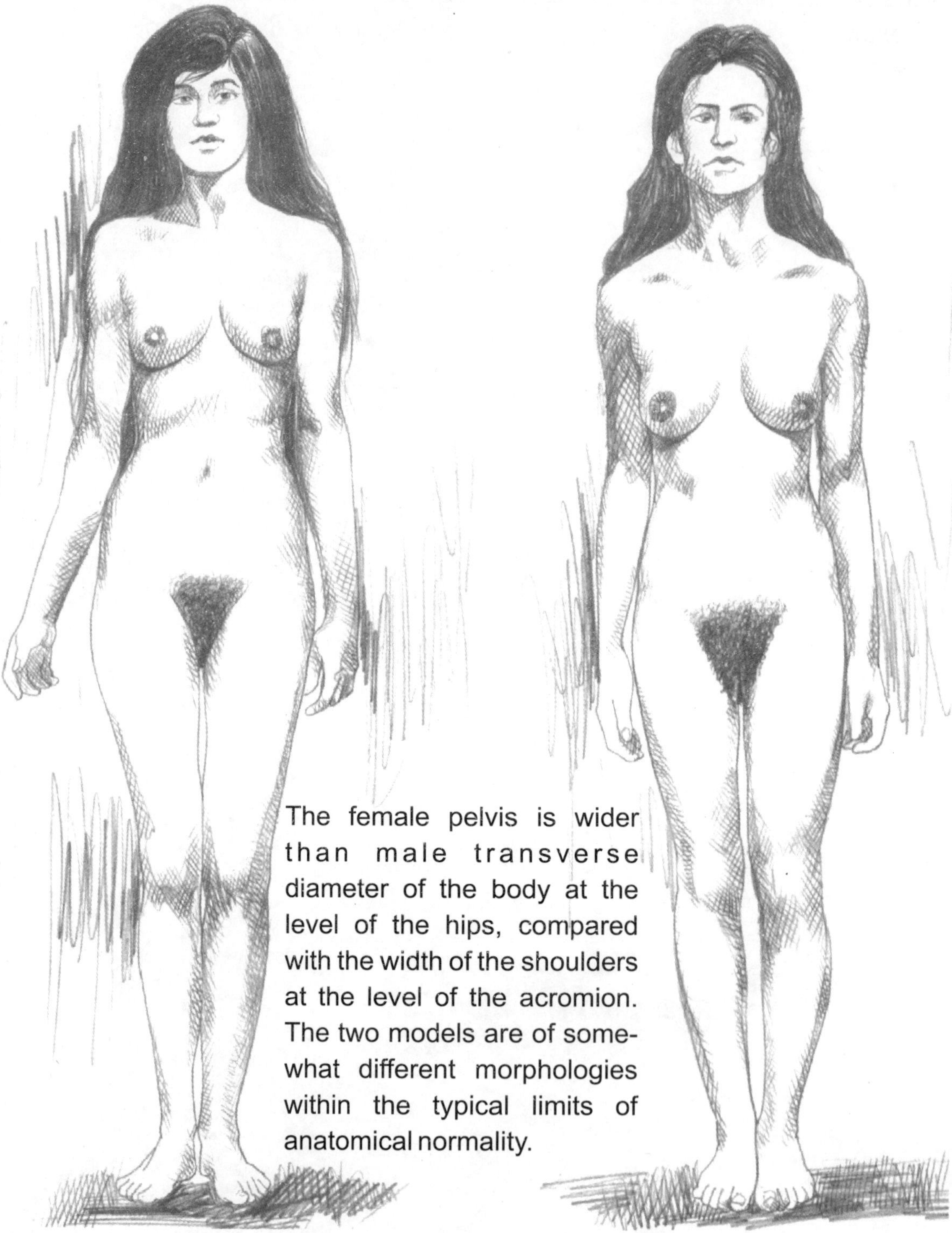

The female pelvis is wider than male transverse diameter of the body at the level of the hips, compared with the width of the shoulders at the level of the acromion. The two models are of somewhat different morphologies within the typical limits of anatomical normality.

Develop the habit of observing individual physical characteristics, especially those of the skeletal structure, but also those of adipose and subcutaneous muscles. Note, for example, in the two models shown, the difference of form and volume in the breasts, the different protrusion of the belly and the different angles formed by the axis of arm and forearm.

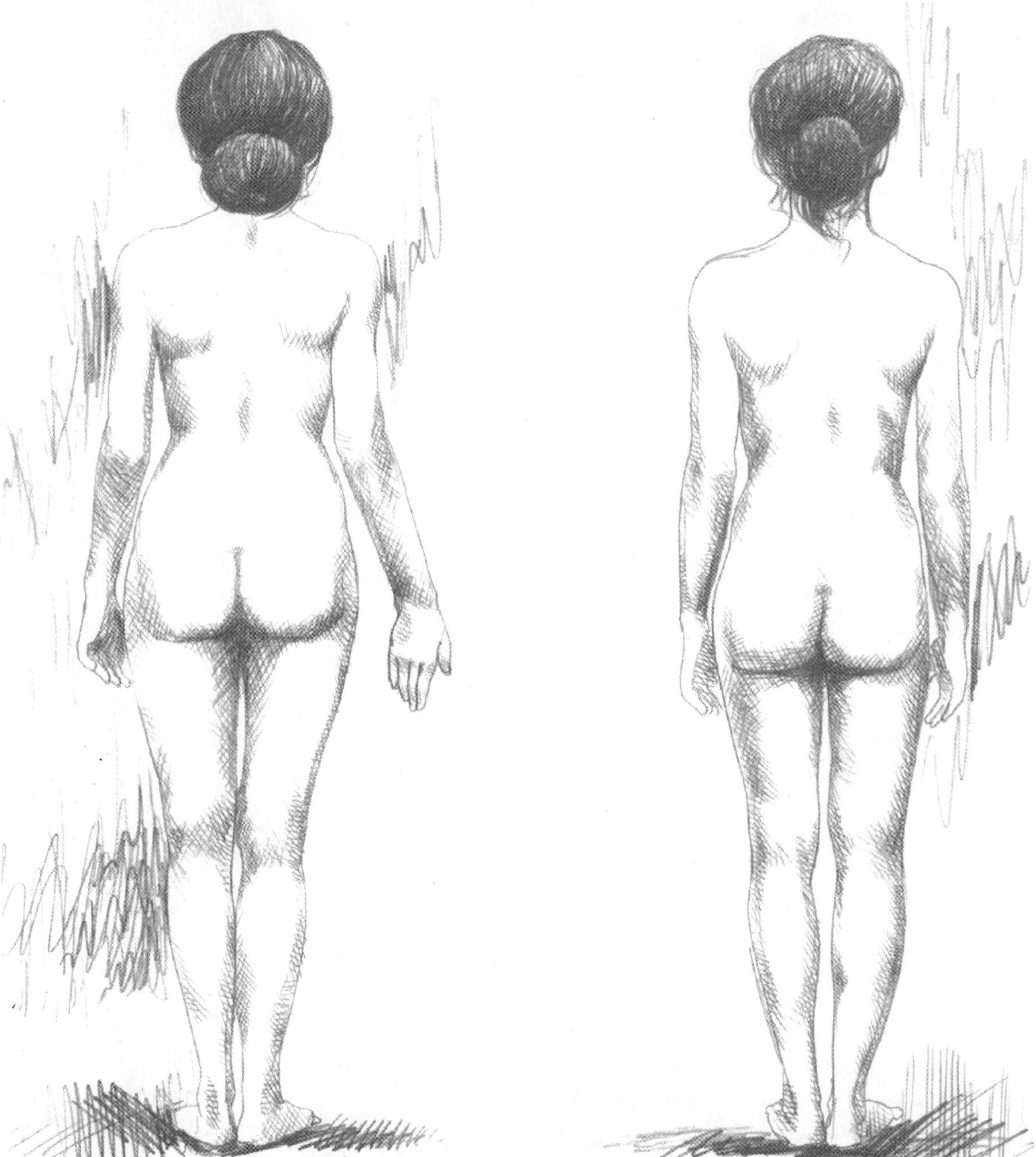

In the model on the left, the axis of the femurs converges sharply at the level of the knees so that with the legs together, three typical apertures appear, while in the other model the shorter distance between the femurs at approximately at the level of the pelvis, reduces the angle of convergence of the axis so that even the knees remain slightly apart.

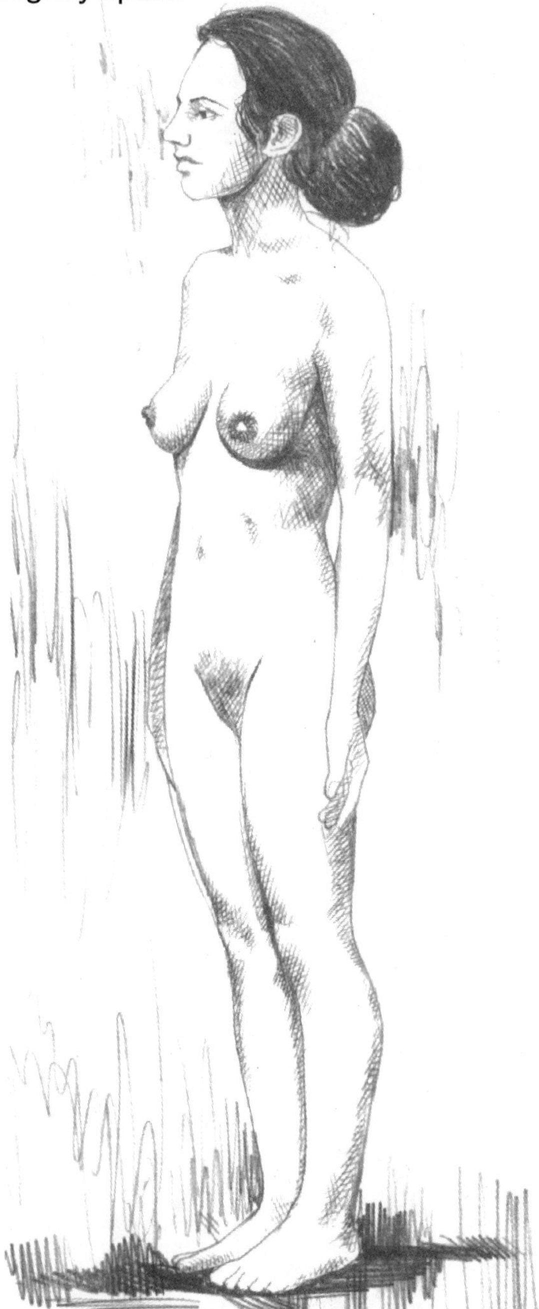

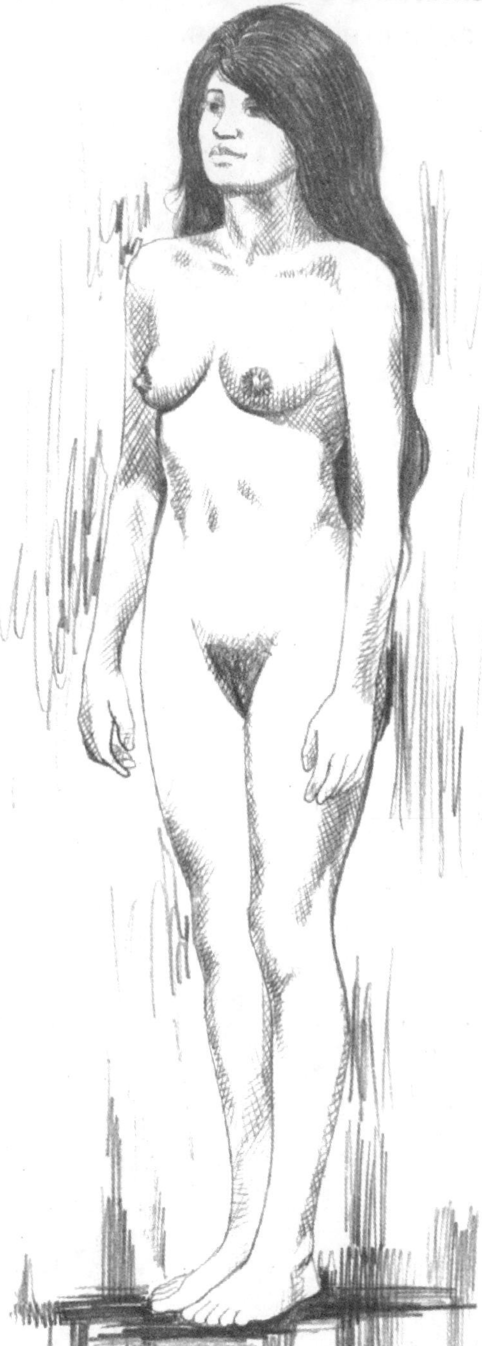

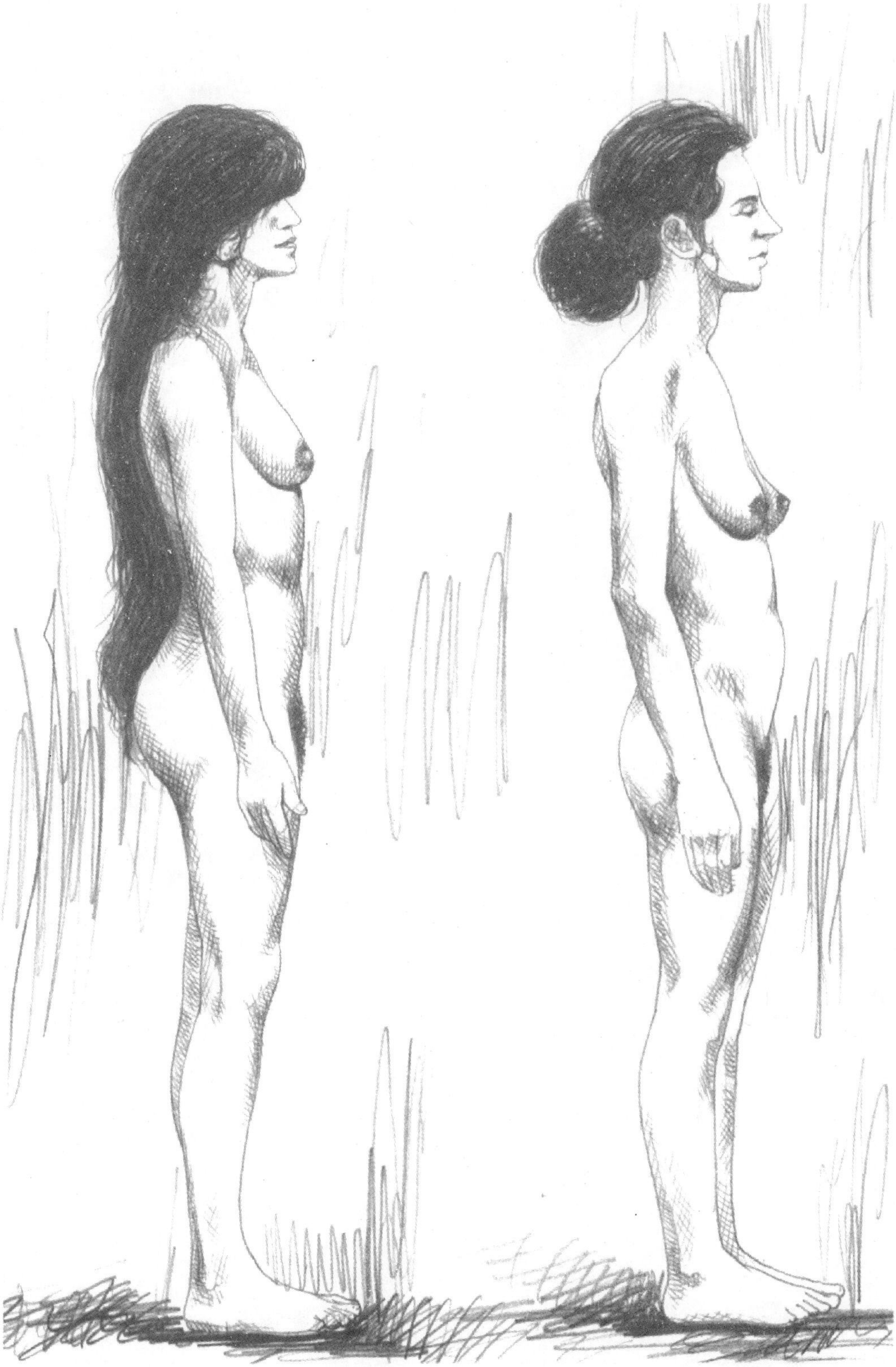

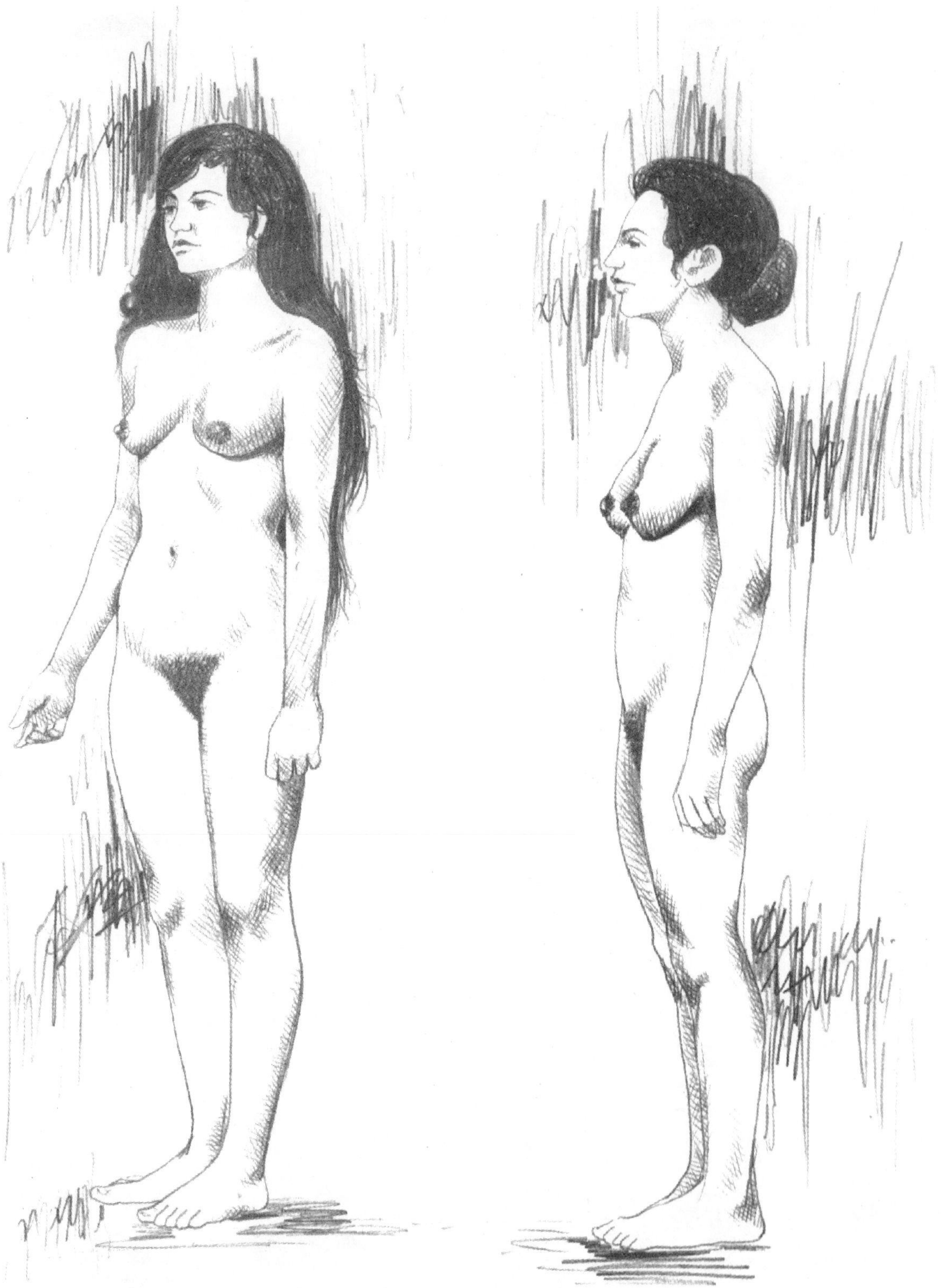

The both models pose in anatomical position, in which it is easy to note the individual morphological differences.

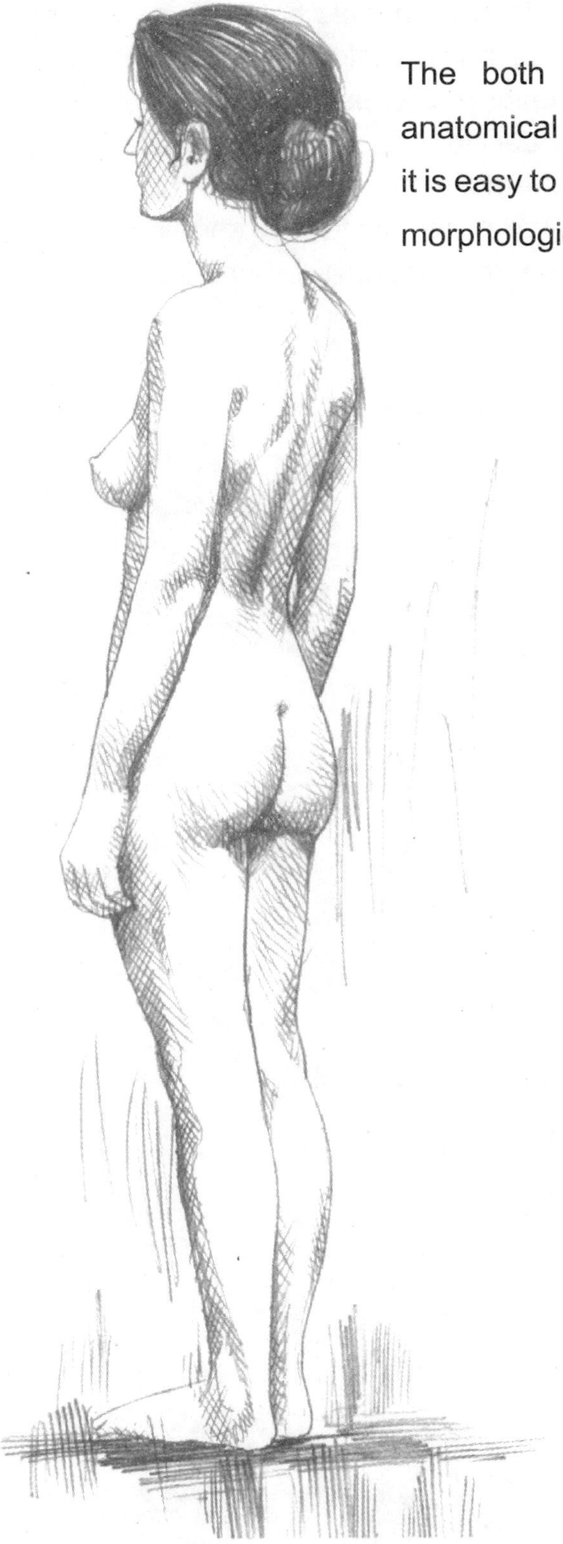

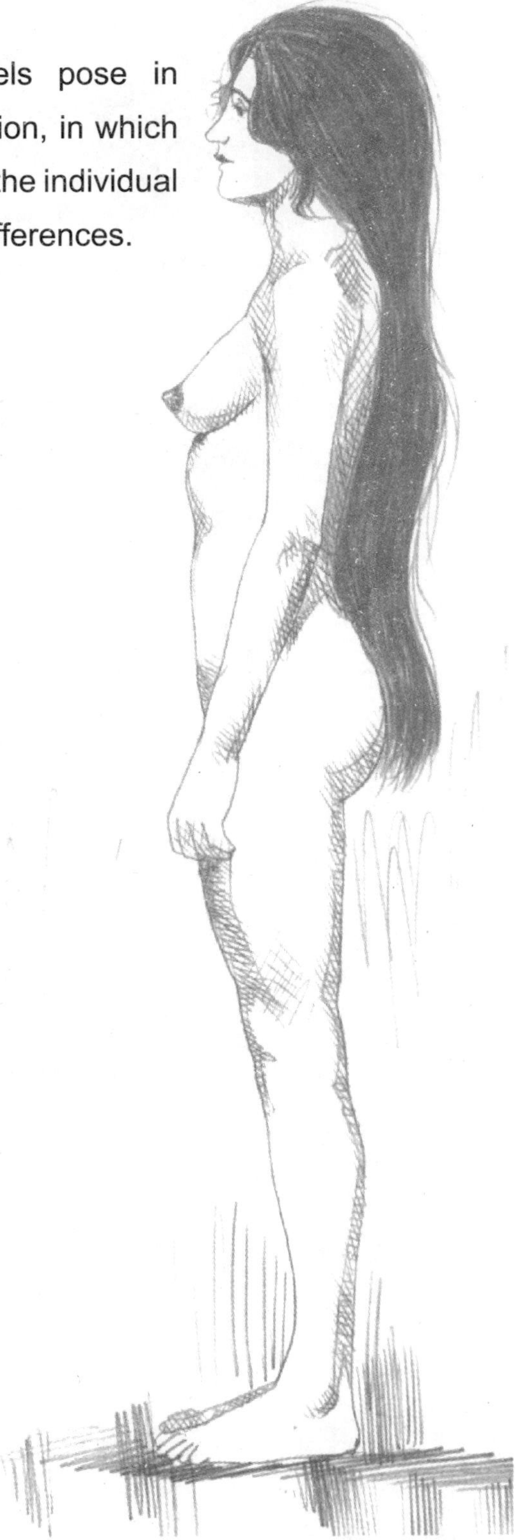

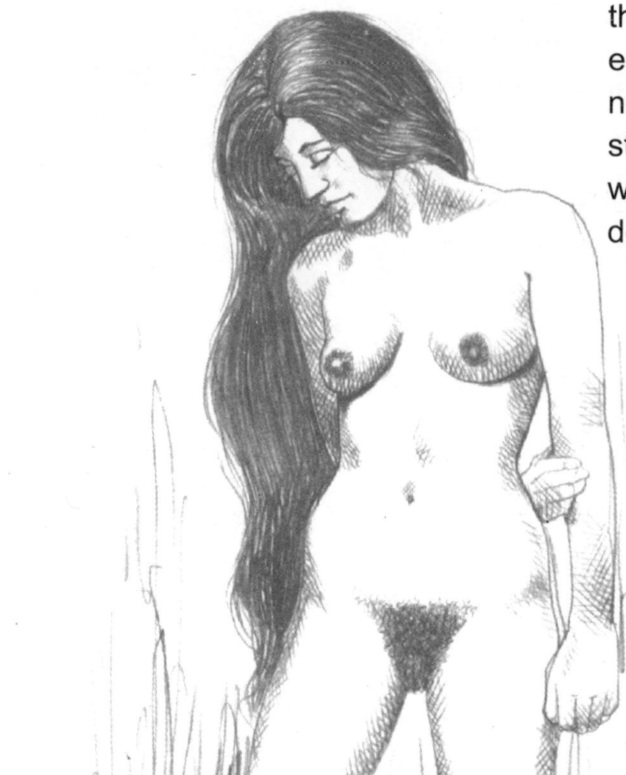

Both the models bending arms behind the back, make the thorax look very enlarged, especially in the upper part near to the shoulders, therefore the sternum and the costal arch show up, while the clavicle in certain cases, is depressed onto the thoracic cage.

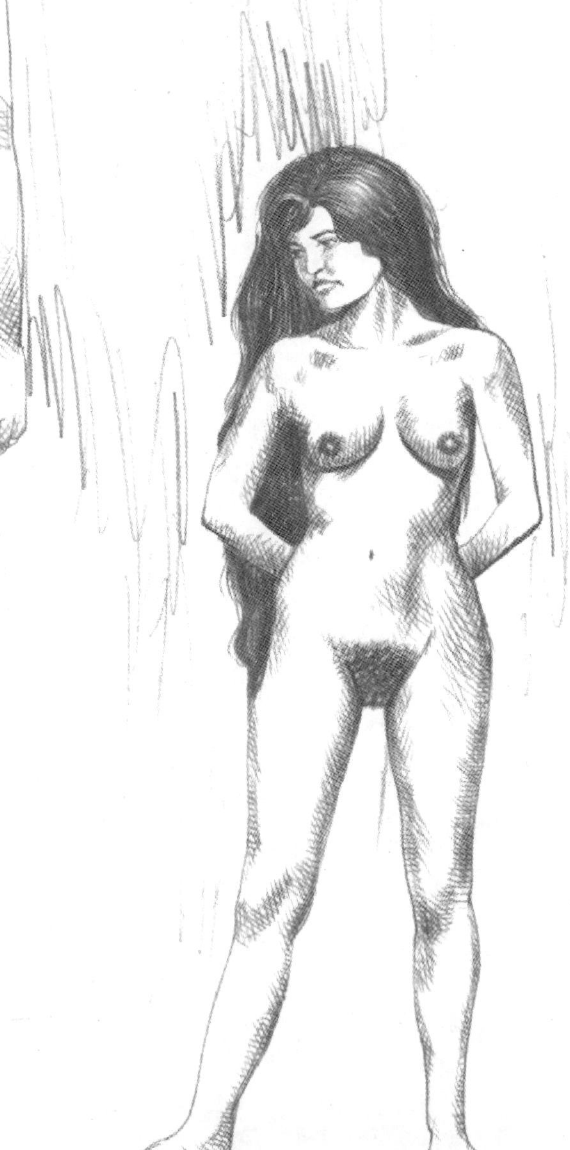

Look at the model closely at the body's line of gravity which must fall into the area of support bounded by the feet. The hands resting on the hips, push the arms away from the body and the slightly stretched pectoralis major is seen like cords from the thorax to the shoulder, helping to outline the armpit. Pay close attention to levels of some parts of the body (breasts, hips, head, trunk, limbs and foot).

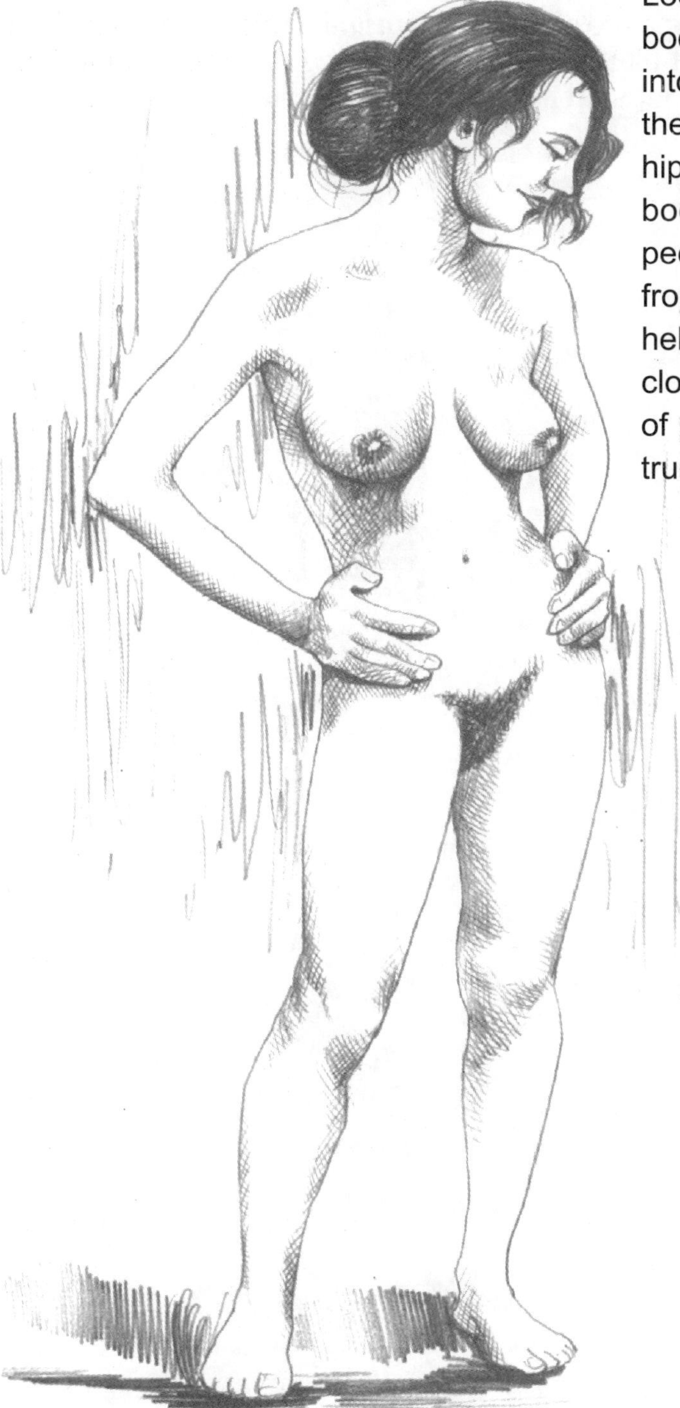

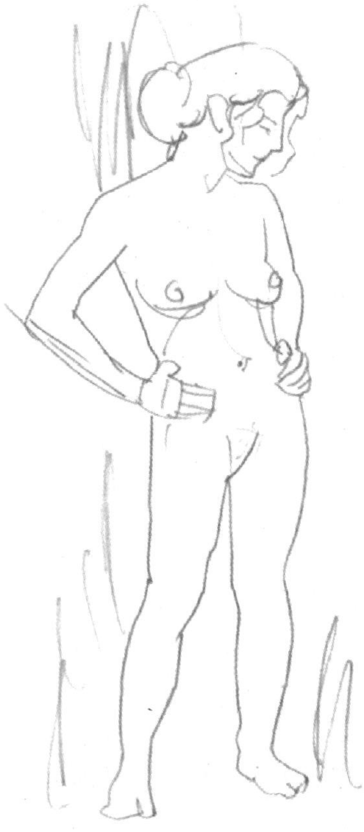

When model bears the weight on only one leg, the pelvis of the body inclines sideways, dropping down on the opposite side to the taut limb. This position is called contrapporto and occurs in almost all upright positions except those in which the body is perfectly balanced on both legs. In the figure with the arm raised, note how the breast is move upwards.

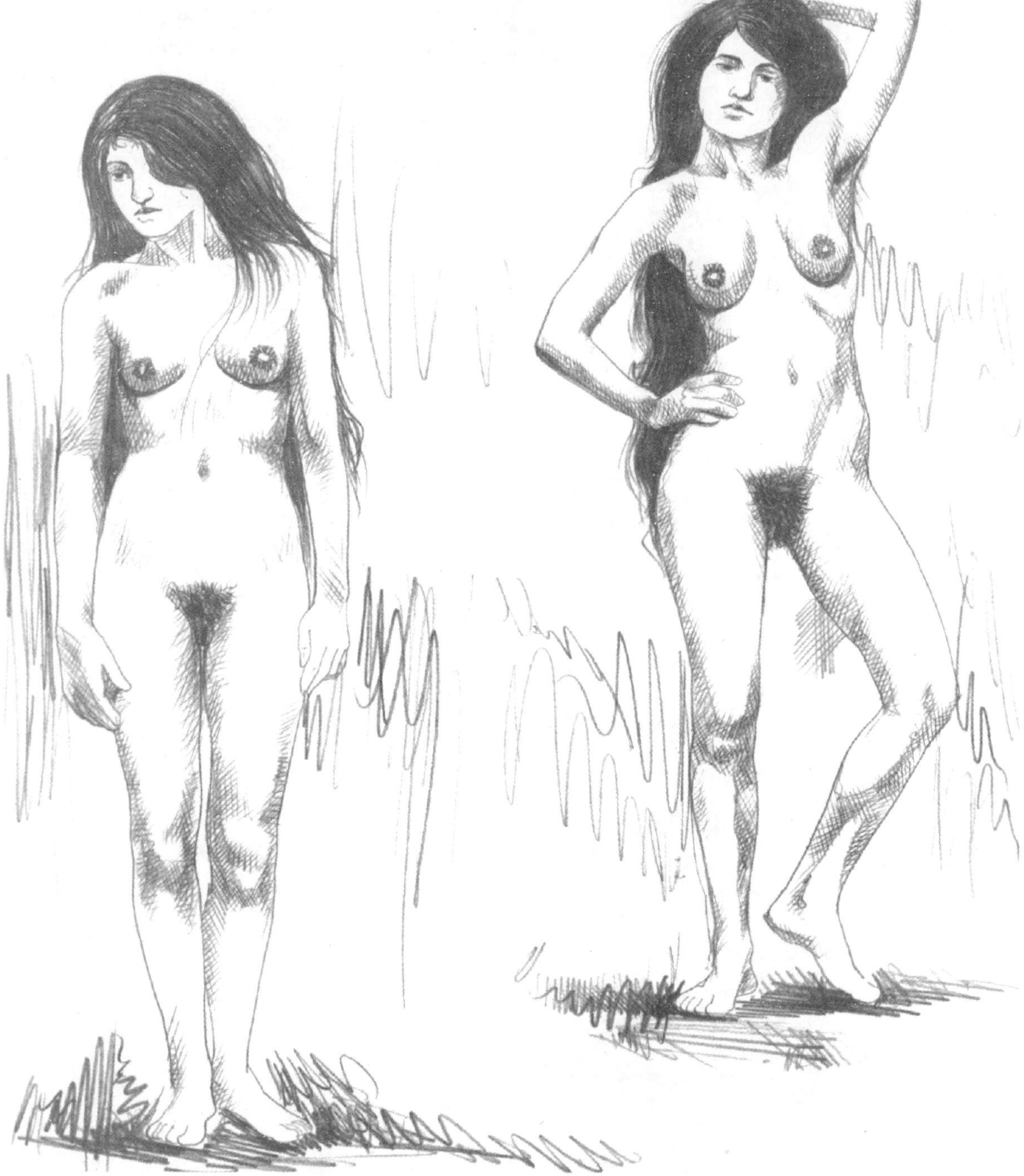

Constrictive Drawing

This technique uses the human body by separating the parts of the framework, that is, the masses of the head and the upper and lower parts of the torso. A constrictive drawing is achieved by sketching in an almost geometric way the various sections of the body highlighting the arrangement of masses. The process is useful in memory drawing.

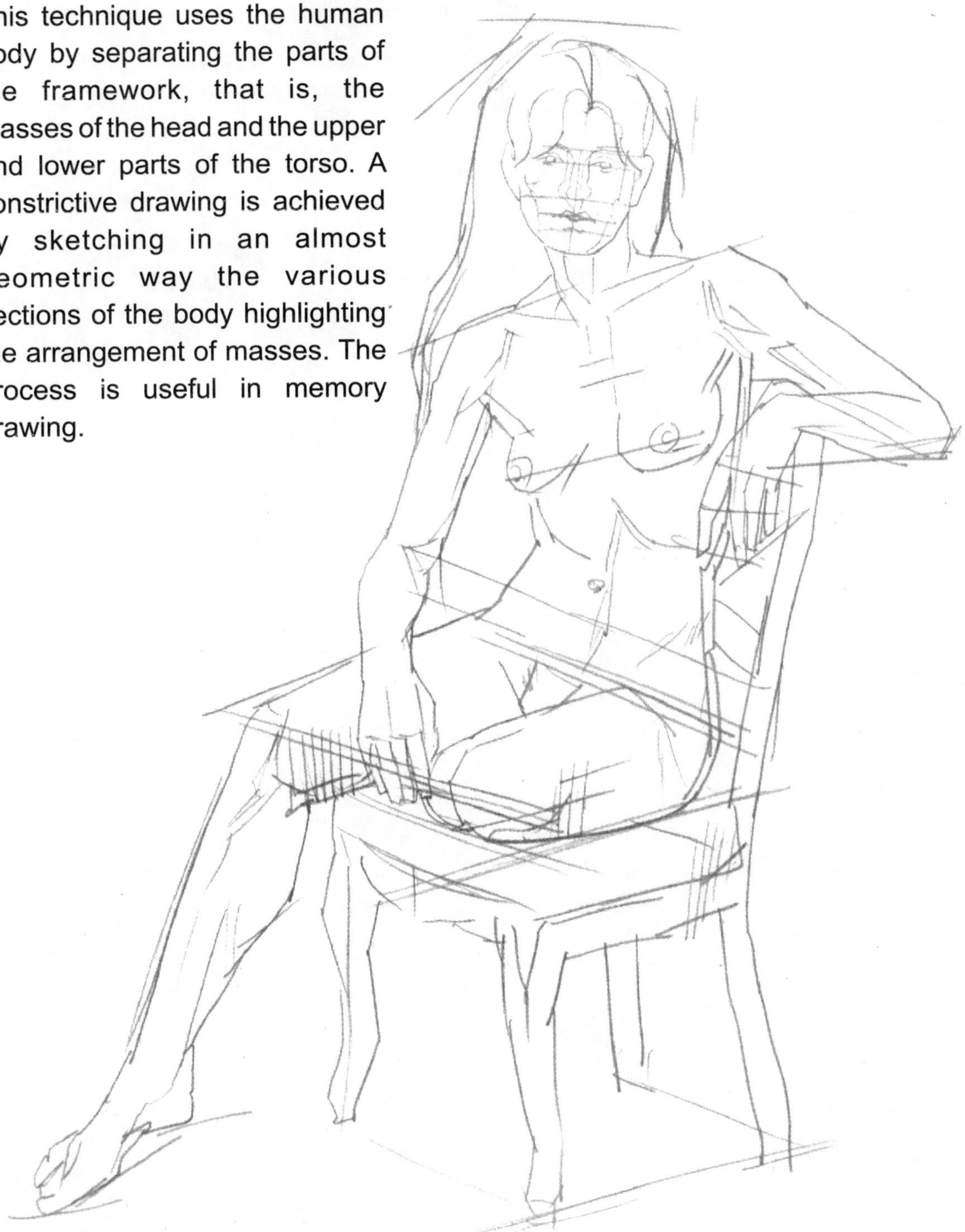

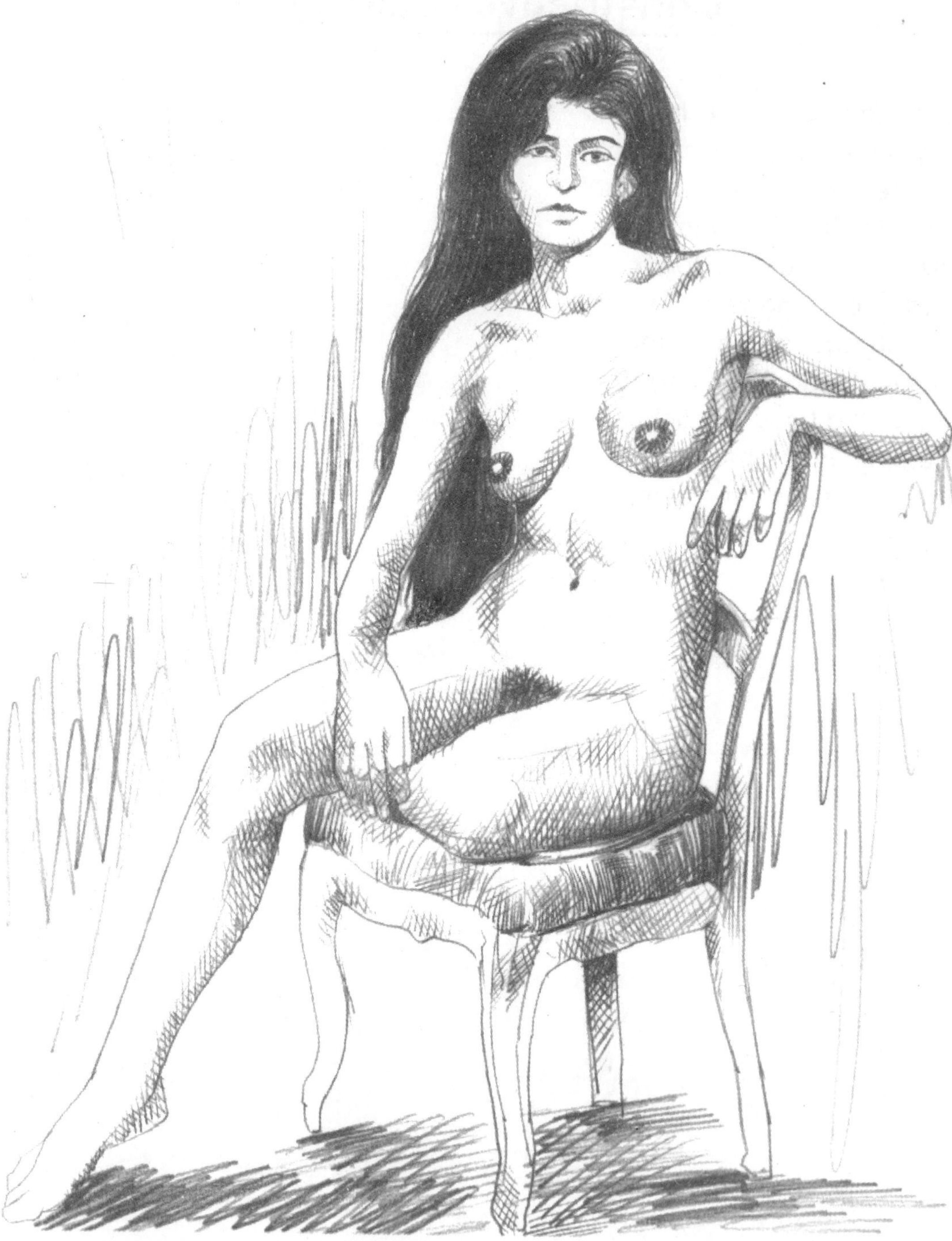

The Female Seated Figures

The longest bone is femur in the skeleton. You must take care when drawing a foreshortened thigh and its proportional relationship with the lower leg. Crossing the legs causes compression and strain in various parts where the limbs come into contact with one another or are resting against a supporting surface. The patella and tibia run under the skin of the length of the lower leg.

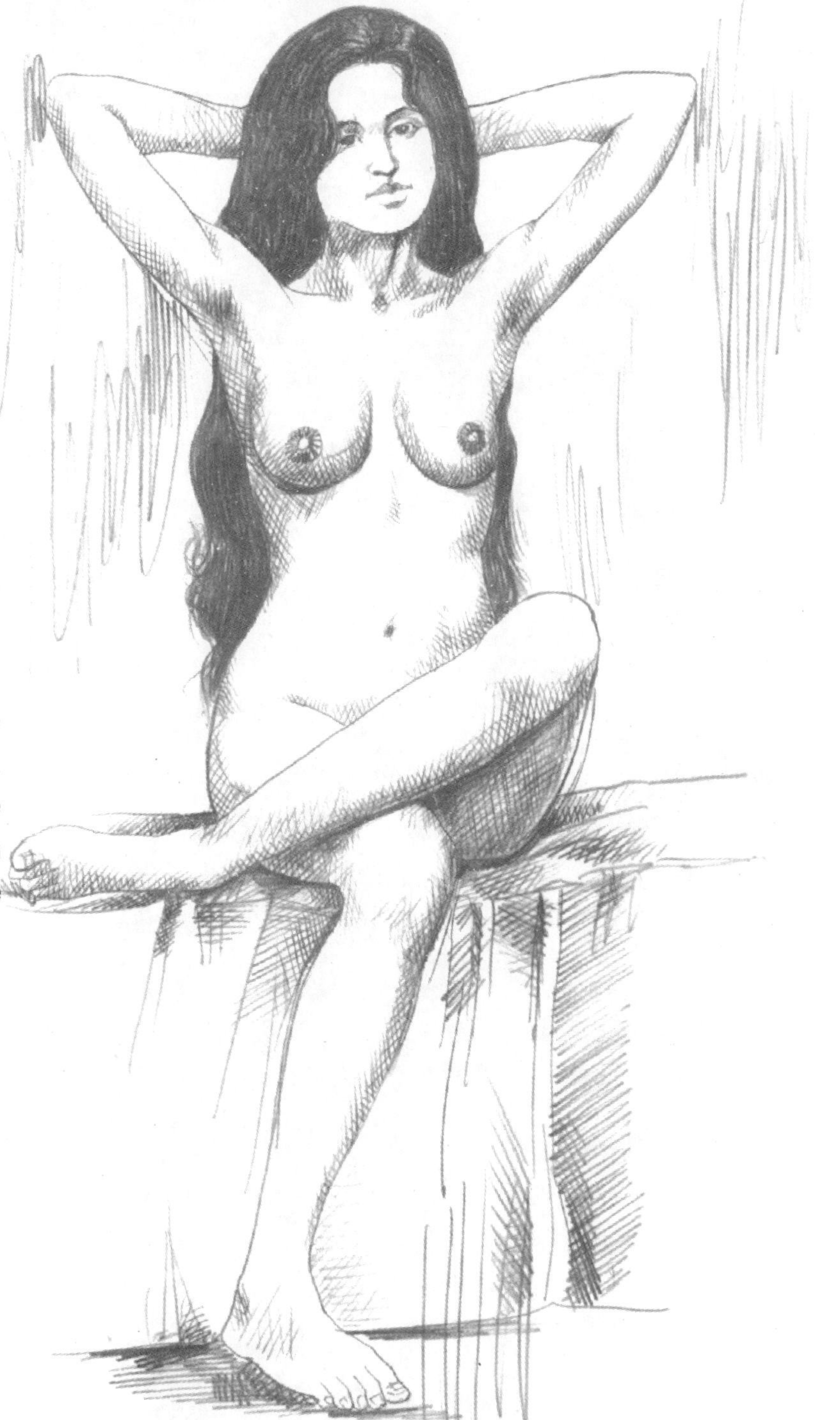

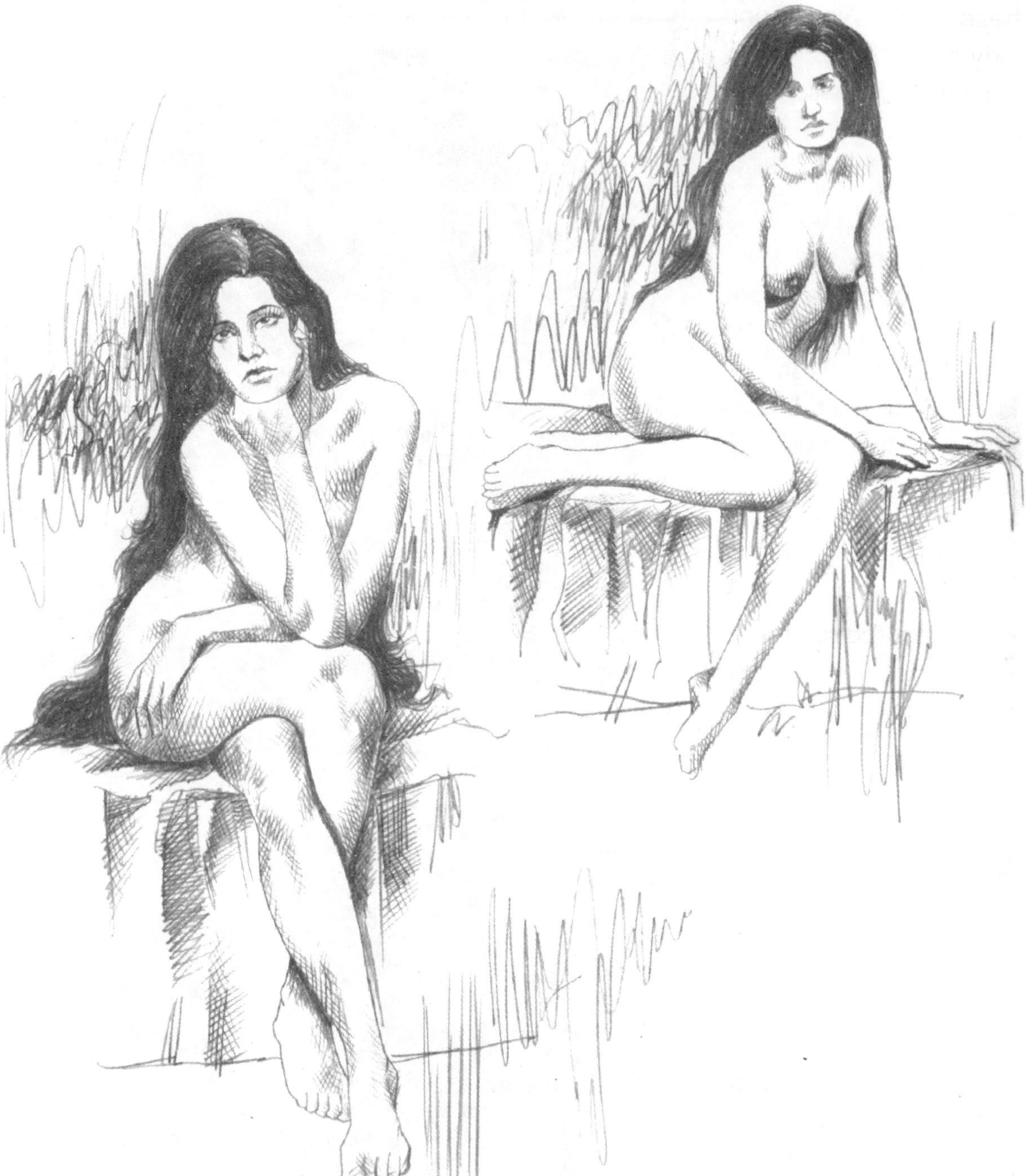

These models' positions are helpful in the study of the relationships of proportion and positioning of the upper and lower limbs.

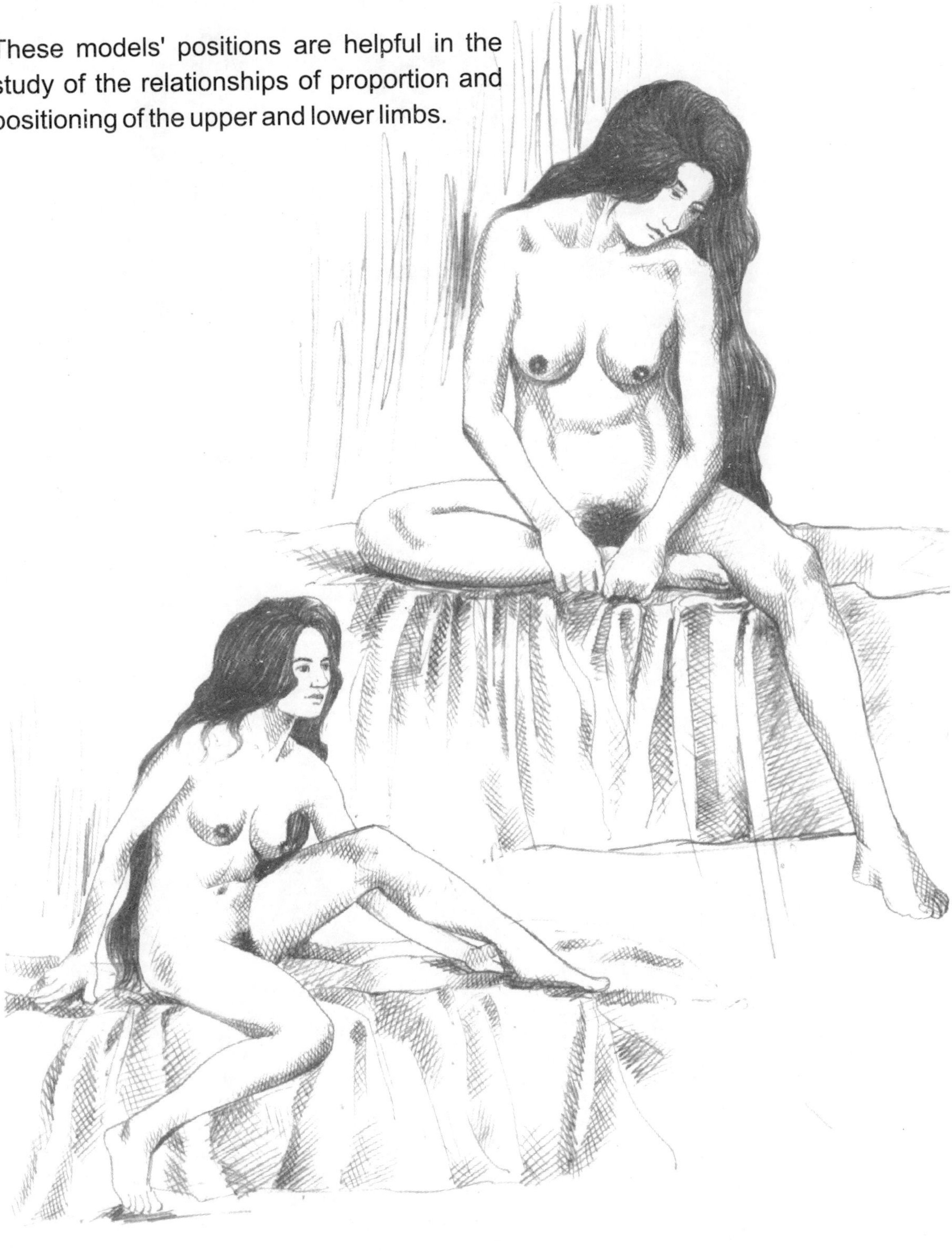

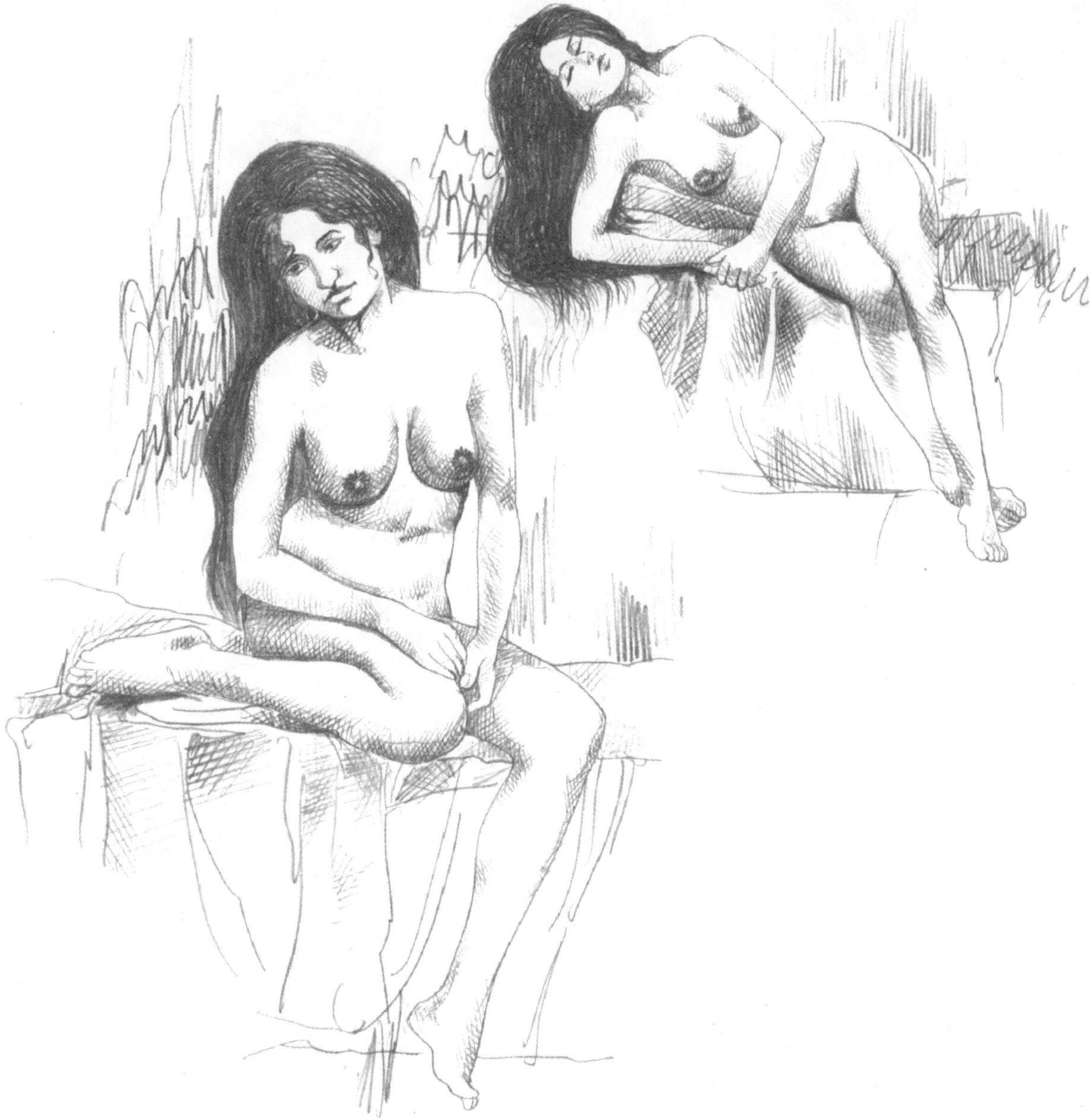

The poses used here are, in fact, particularly well suited to observing change in the fleshy parts as they are flattened against the solid surface. Estimate, on the seated female body, the proportional relationships between the lower limbs and the trunk.

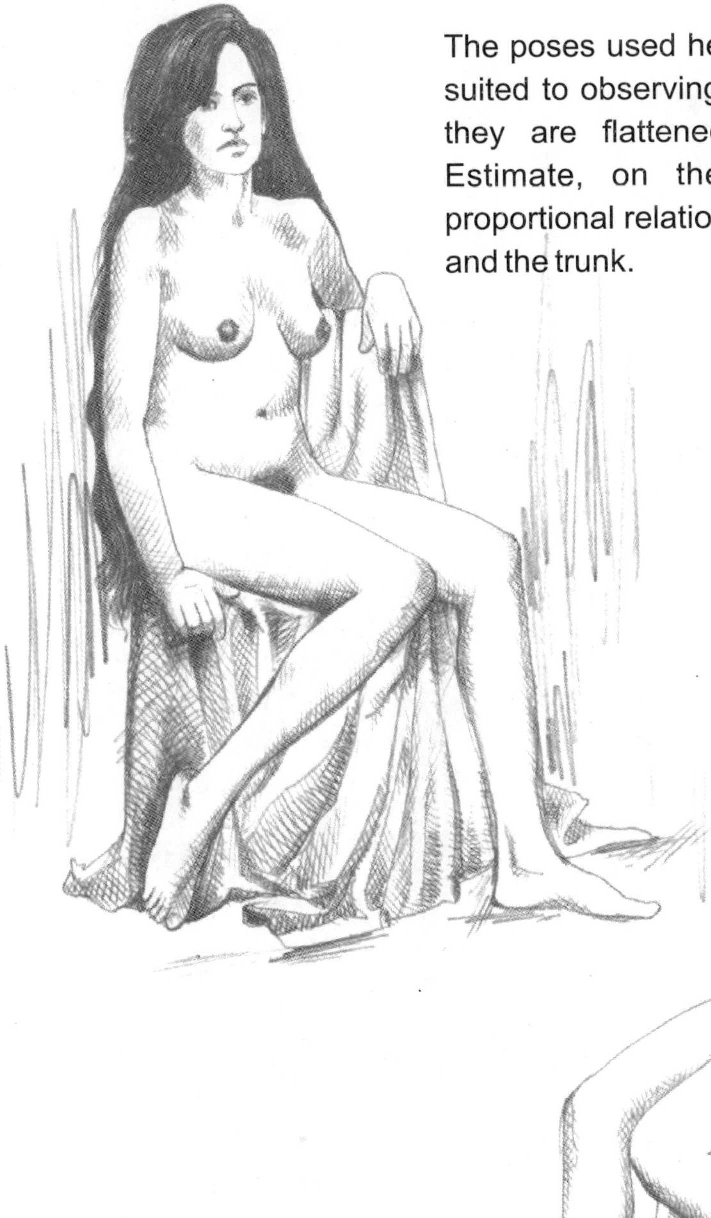

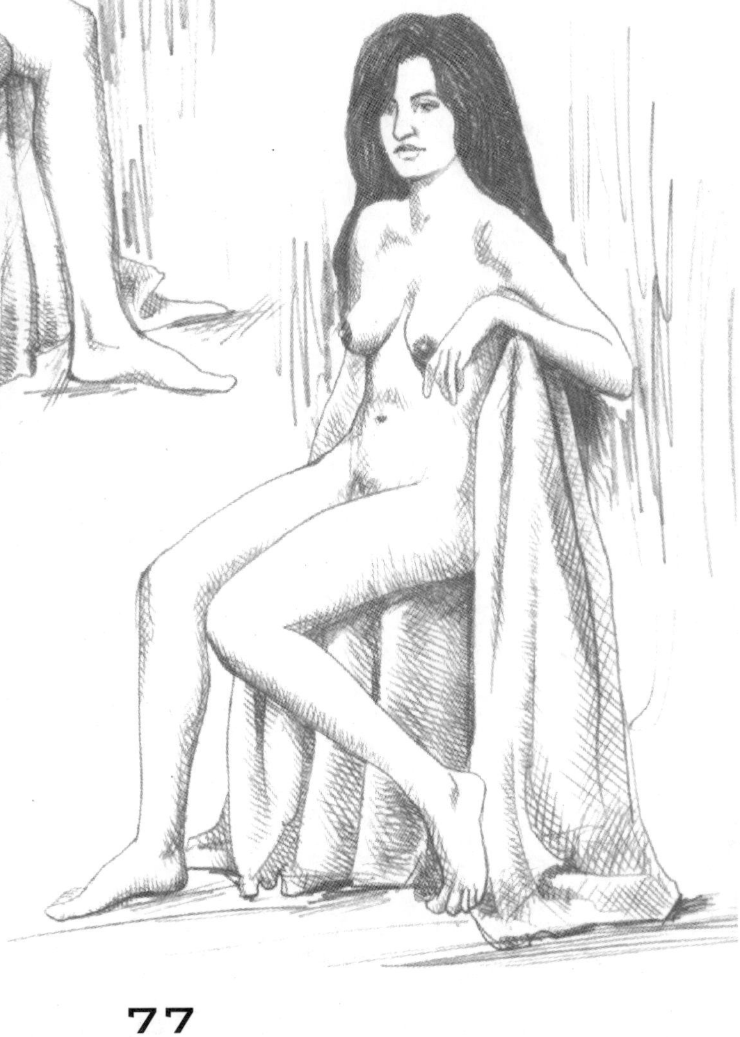

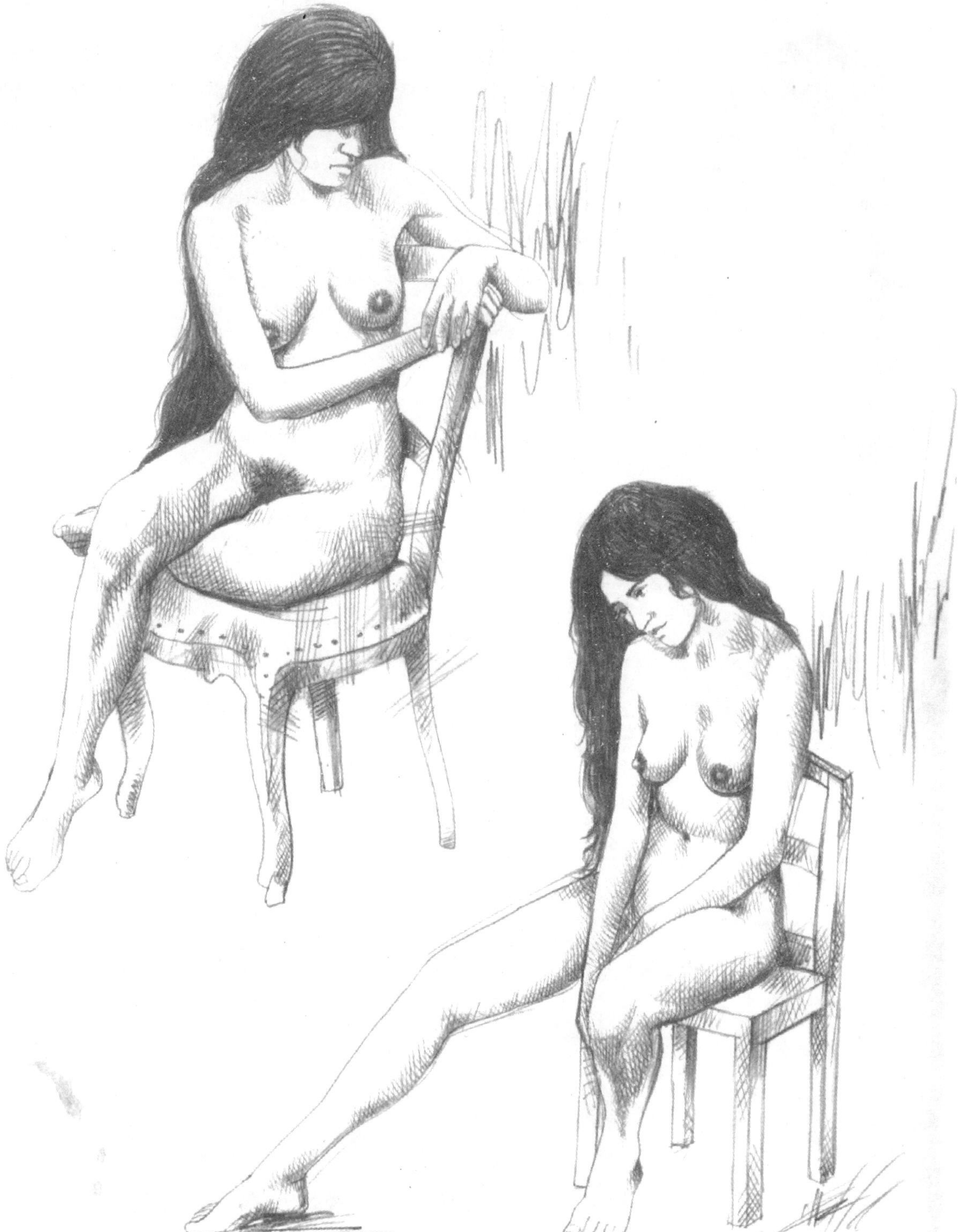

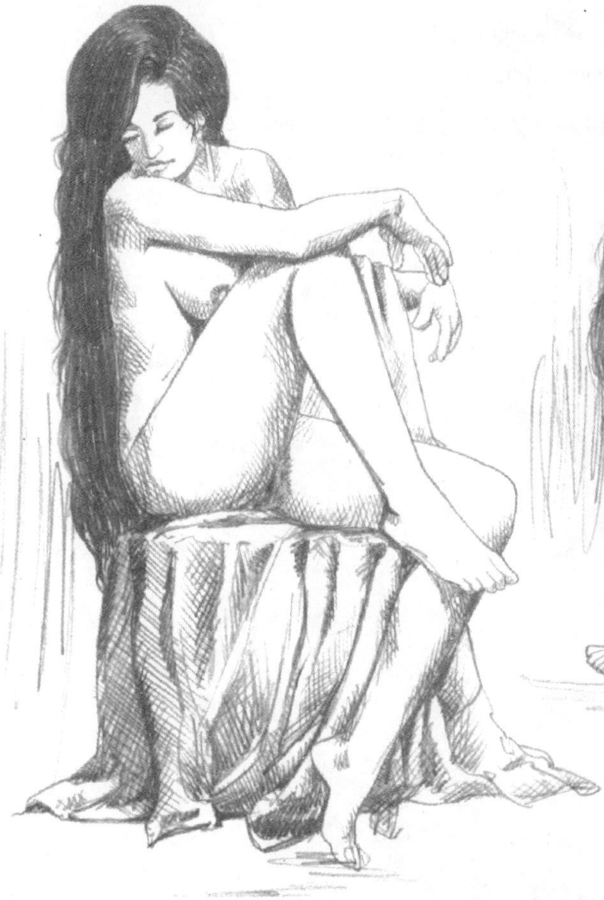
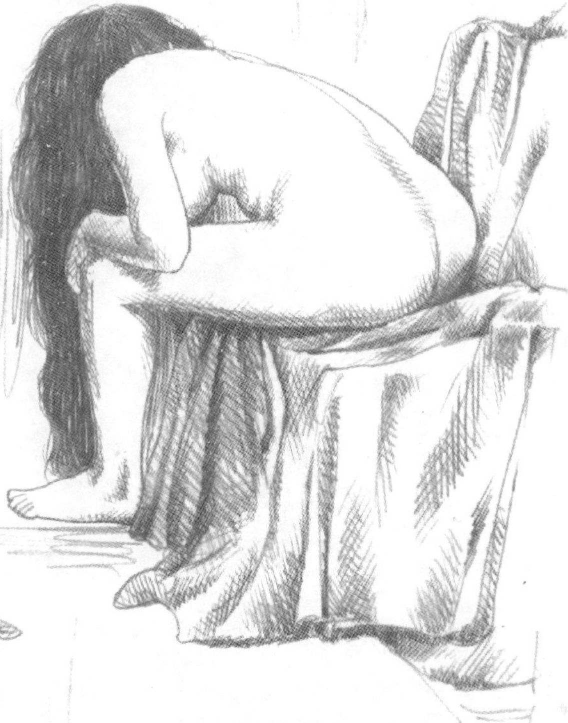
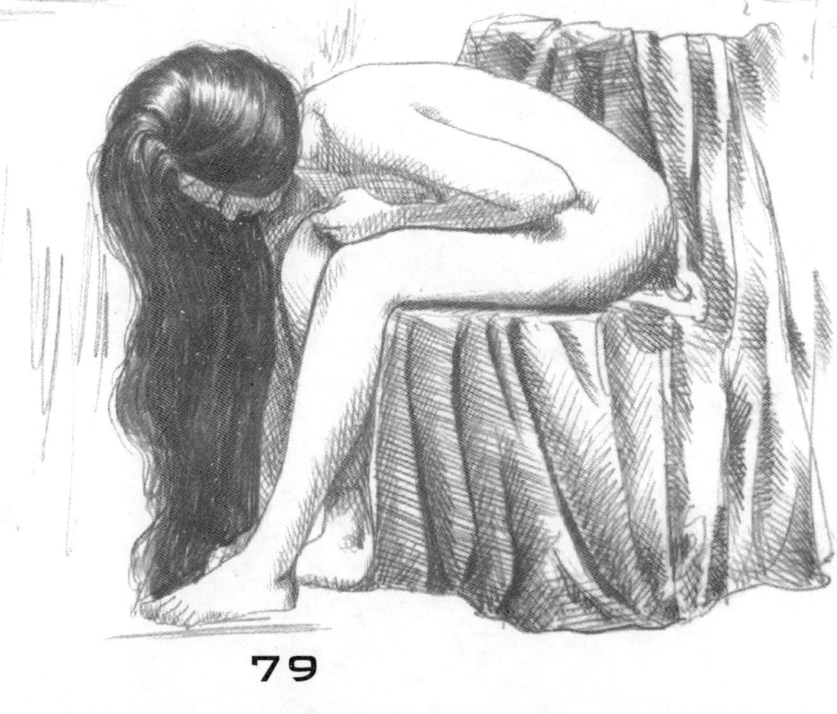

In these type of seated positions of the model, the body posture balances itself by appropriate positioning of the head and limbs, making use of supporting surfaces. Observe the sitting positions of the model from different viewpoints.

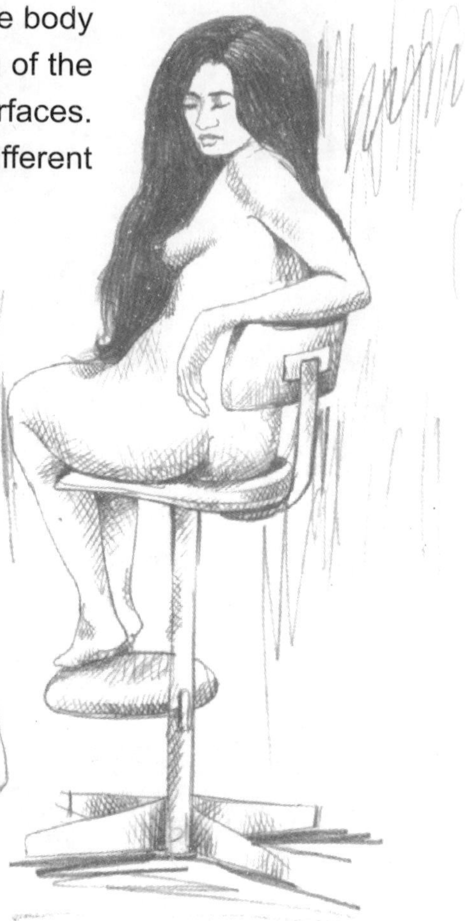

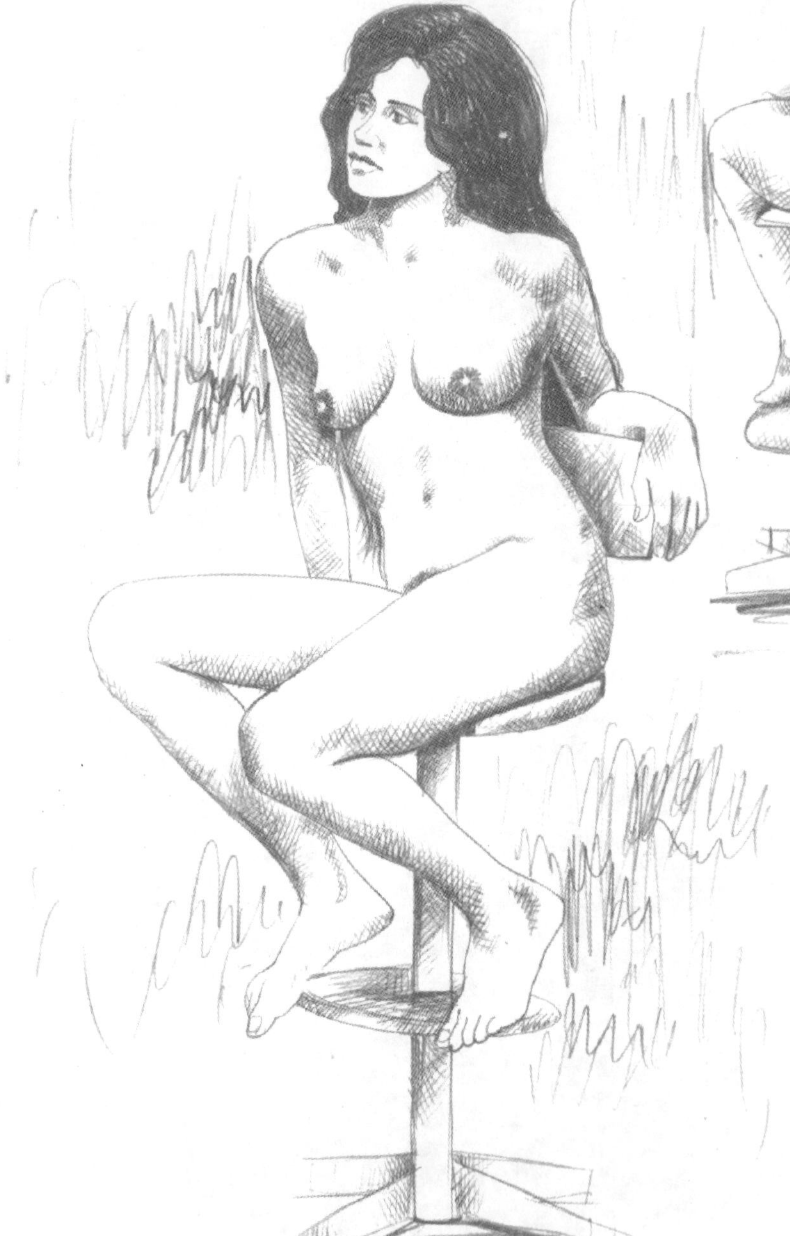

The Kneeling Figure

You can observe various kneeling positions in these figures. The model has let the weight fall on one or both of her knees. The model's trunk may be flexed, extended or rotated; the arms may balance the body or act as supports. Observe the contractions of the straight muscles of the abdomen. The navel appears slightly dilated, because the abdominal wall is stretched and is pressing against the internal fasciae and organs.

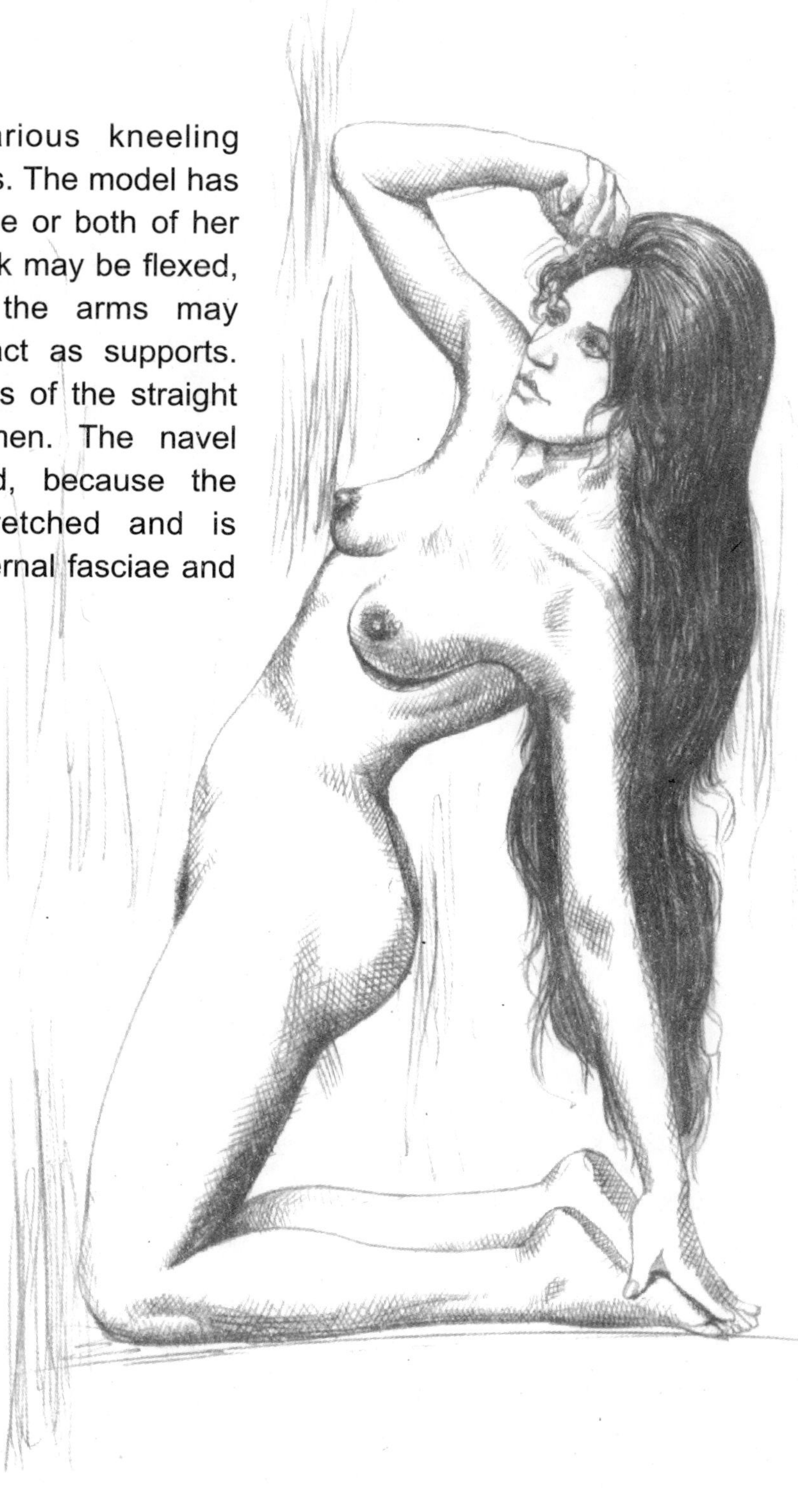

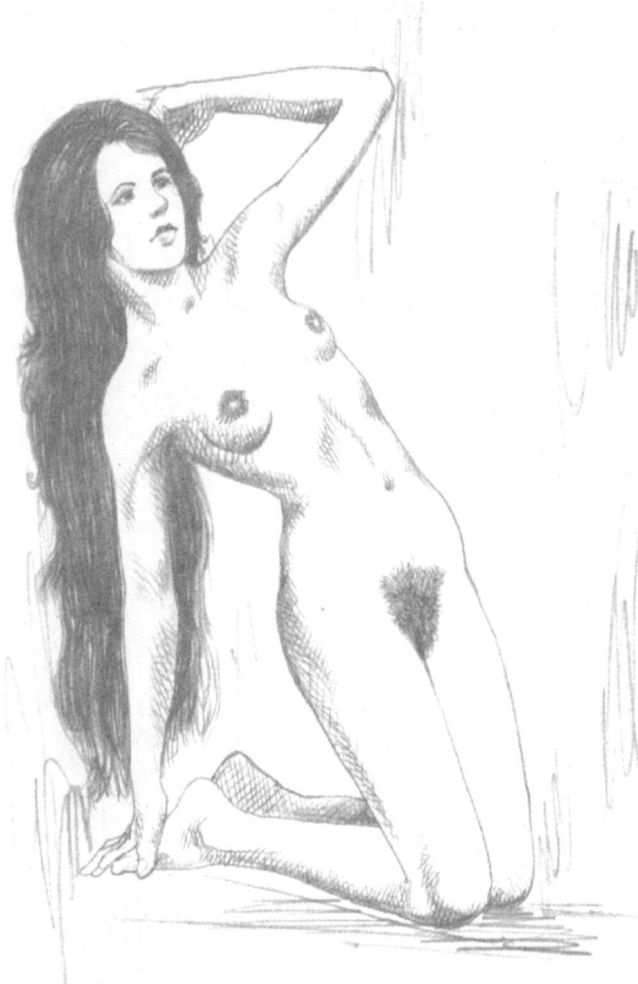

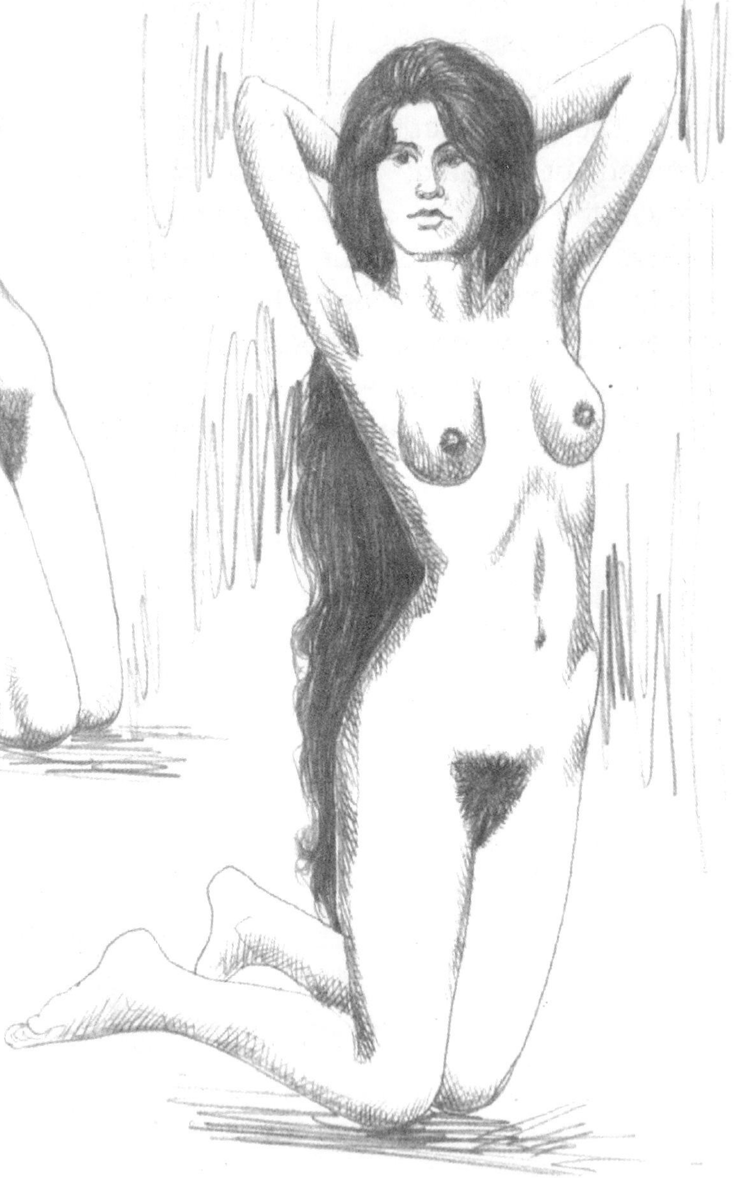

Look at the models' displaying kneeling position of partial torsion of the trunk, together with lateral flexion. Observe the view of the models both from the side and from the front, so as to see exactly the axis of equilibrium of the principal bodily parts: the trunk, the head and the limbs.

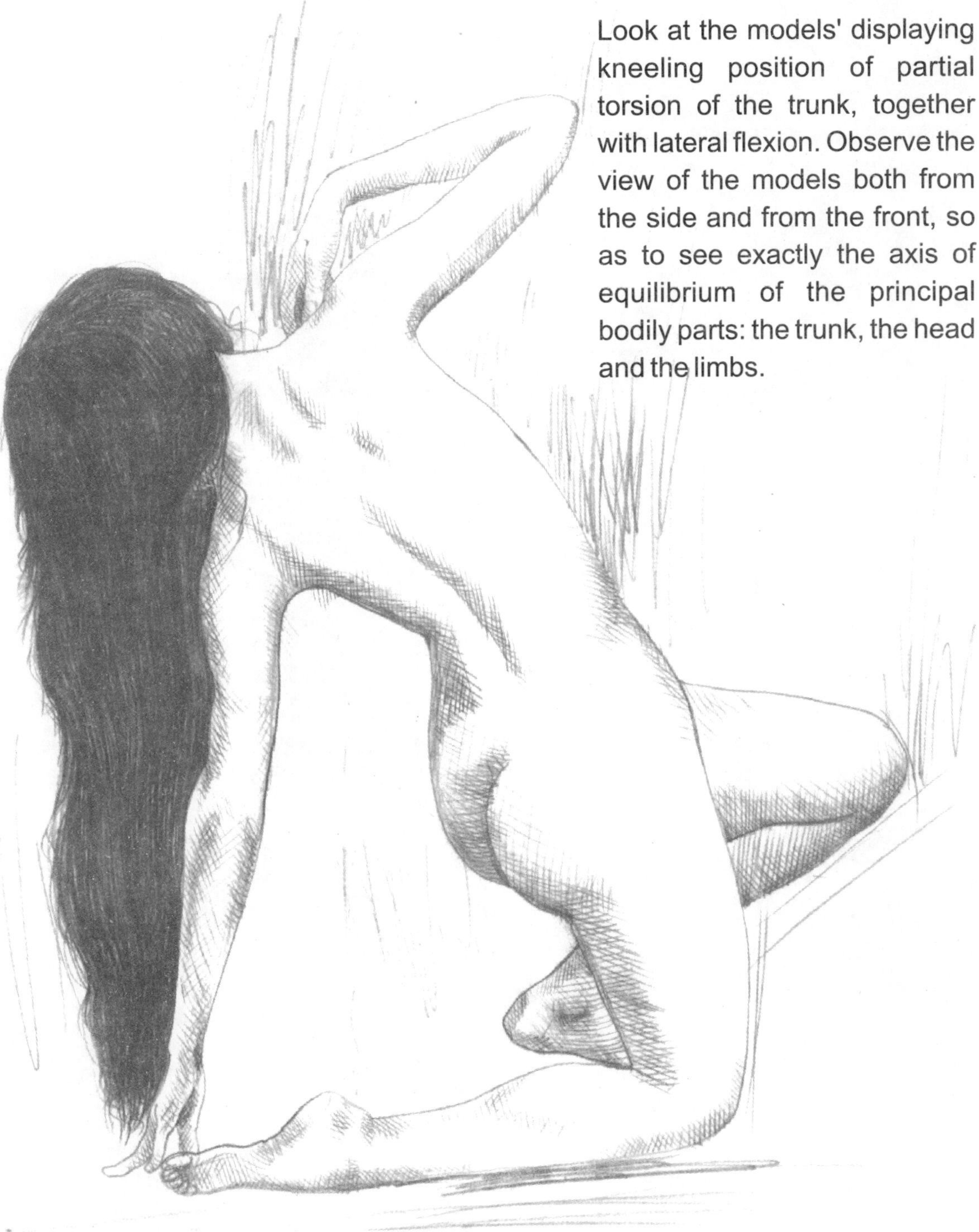

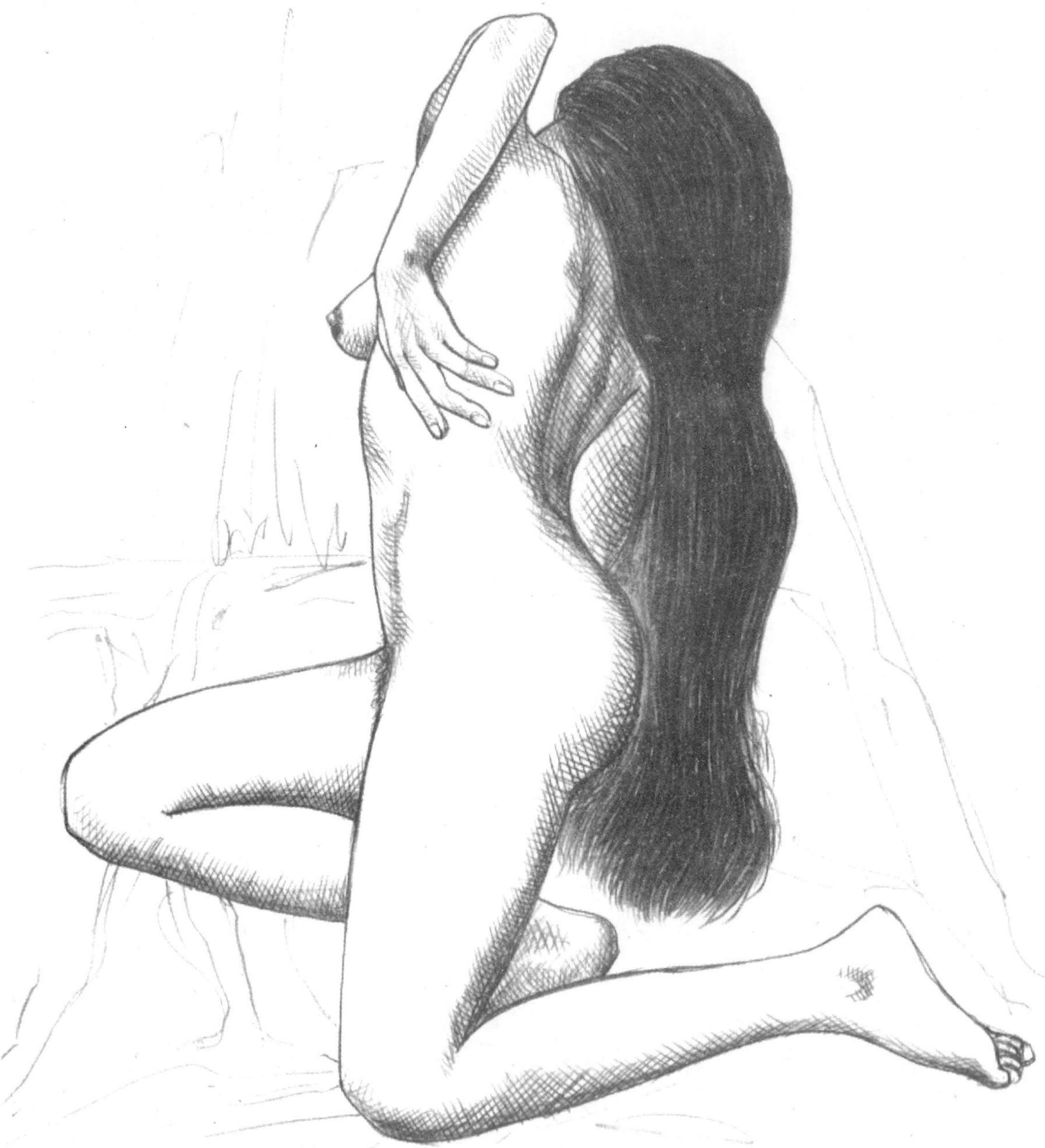

Look at these models seated on all fours, with her weight carried on her knees and through her arms. The shoulders are pushed upwards and the shoulder blades pushed away from the thoracic cage. The vertebral column forms an arched bridge from the pelvis to the head or may, especially in the lumbar tract display a downward curve. The breasts fall free, taking a conical shape.

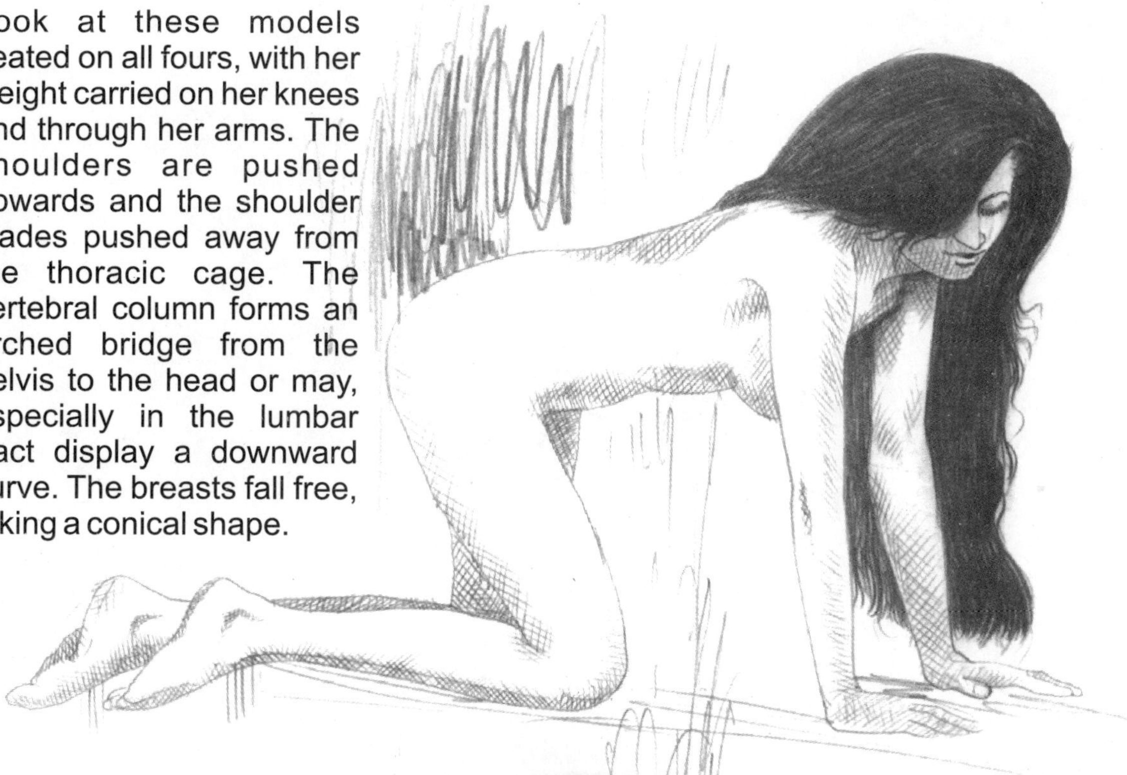

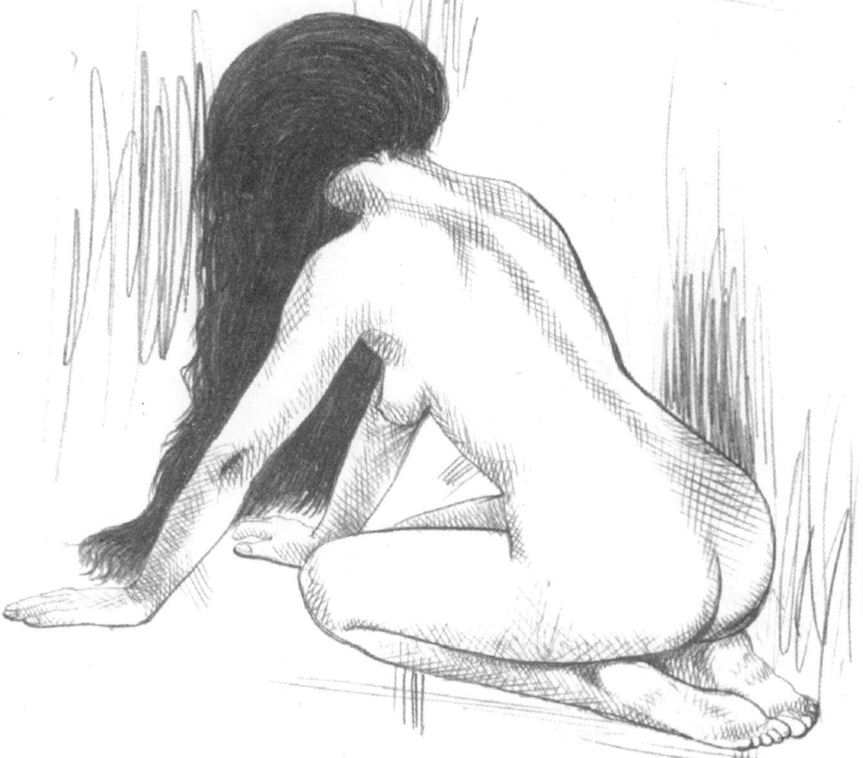

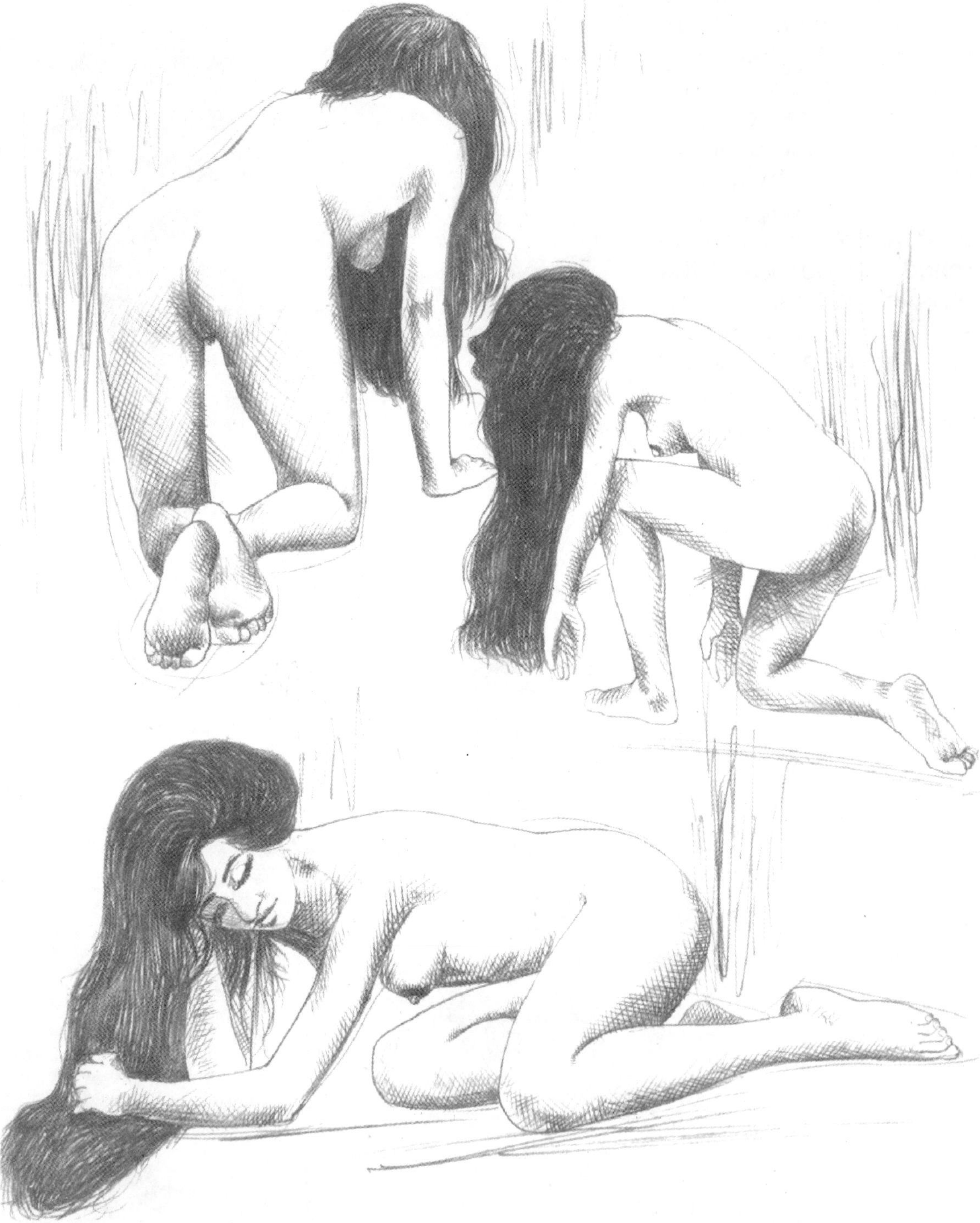

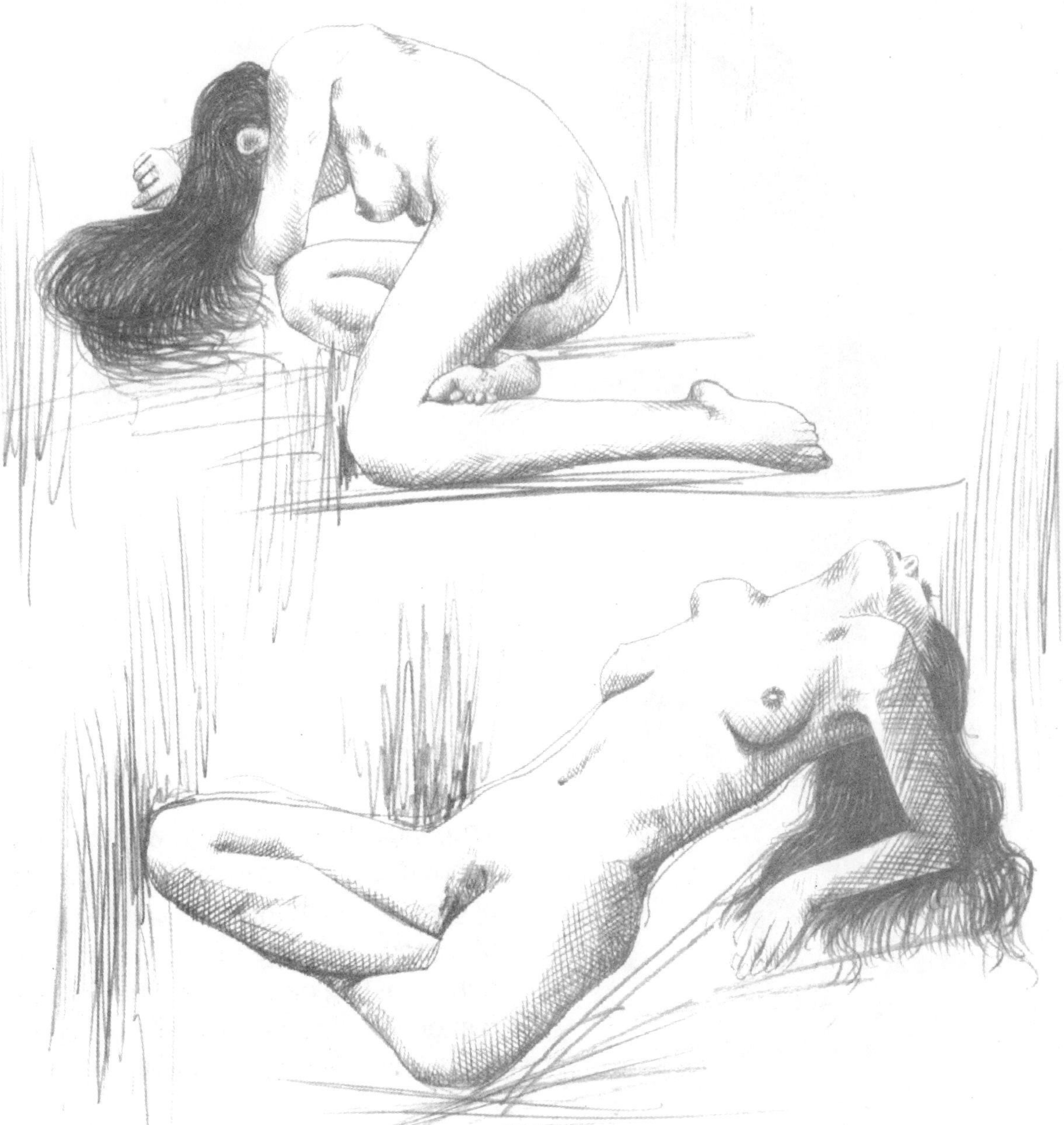

The Female Upright Position

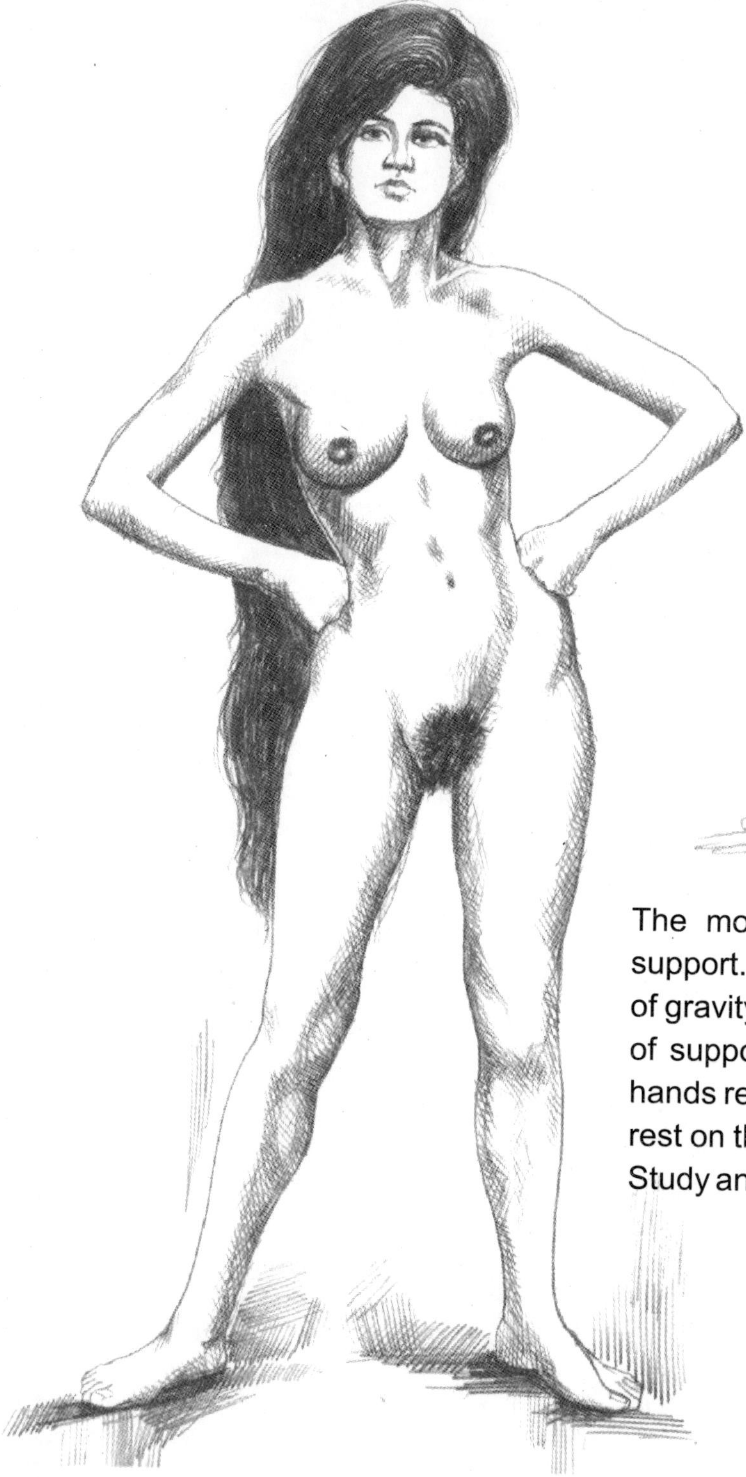

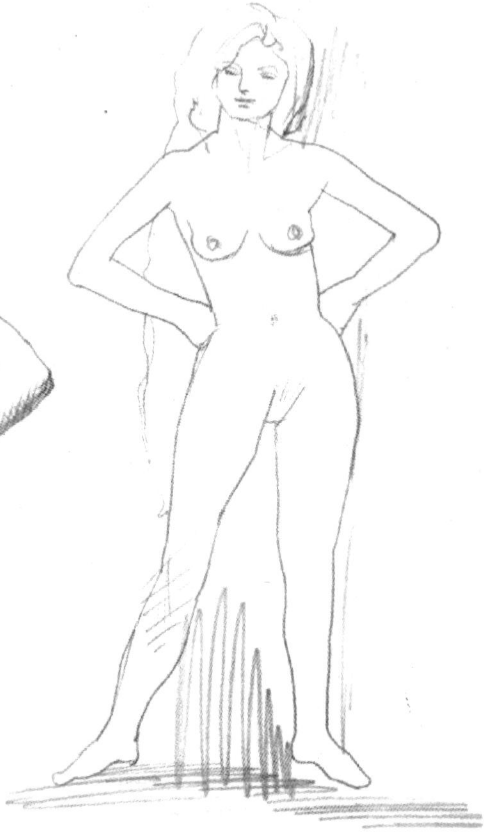

The model is standing without any support. Look closely at the body's line of gravity, which must fall into the area of support bounded by the feet. The hands resting on the hips. The breasts rest on the anterior part of the thorax. Study another standing posture.

In this pose the model is standing firmly on both legs even though the weight is unequally distributed. In this pose model's hands are raised and the head and trunk inclined. The wide lateral flexion of the spinal column and protuberance of the ribcage and costal arch are clearly observable.

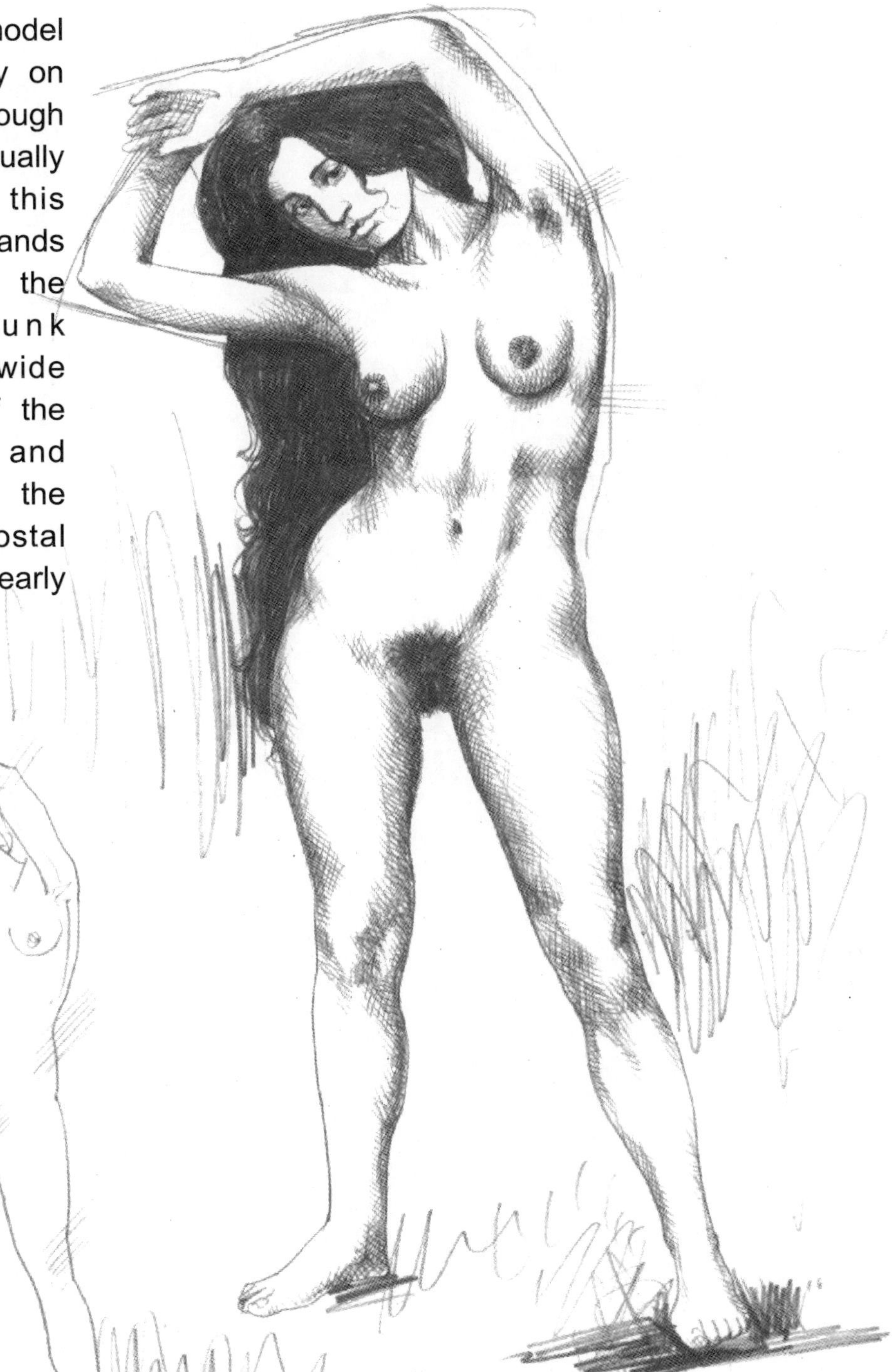

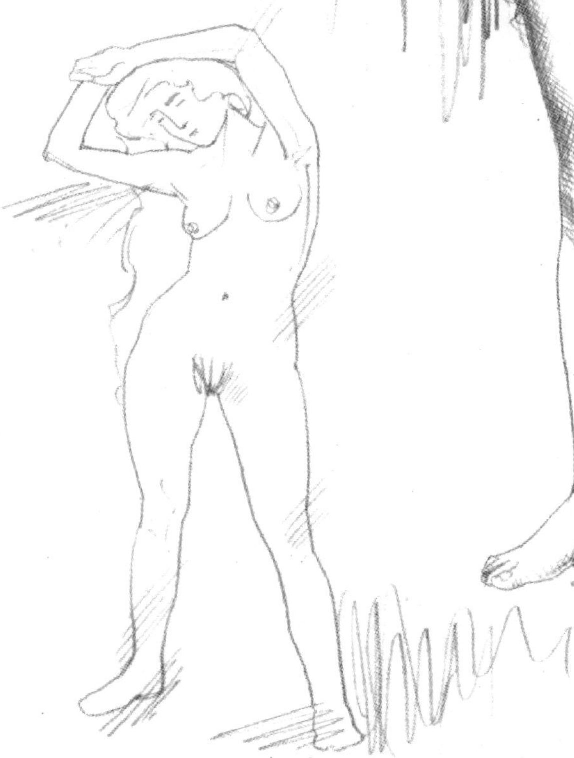

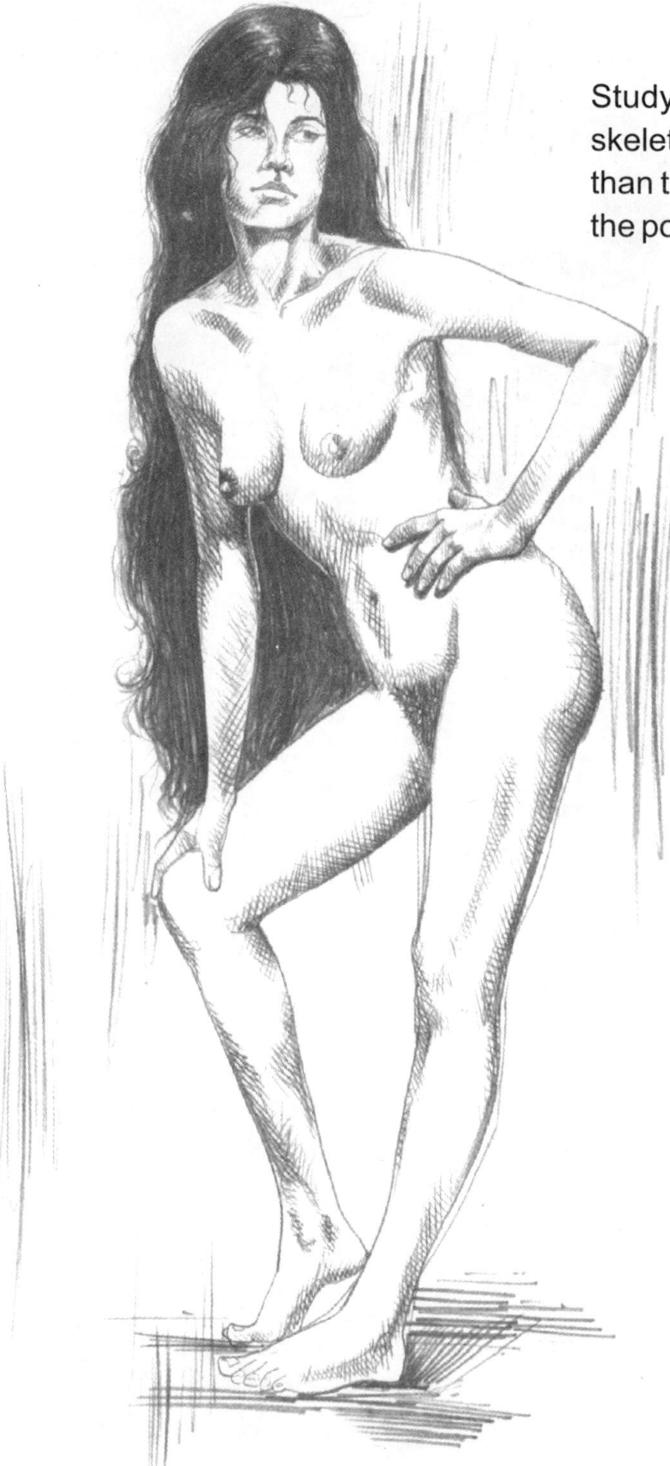

Study closely the model's entire skeletal structure that, in fact, rather than the muscular system, determines the postural attributes of the body.

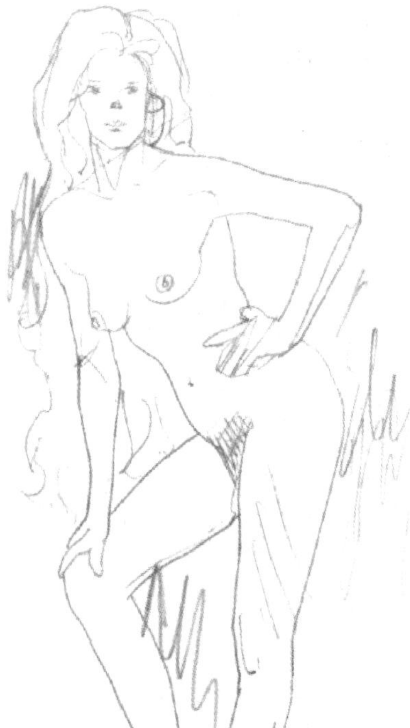

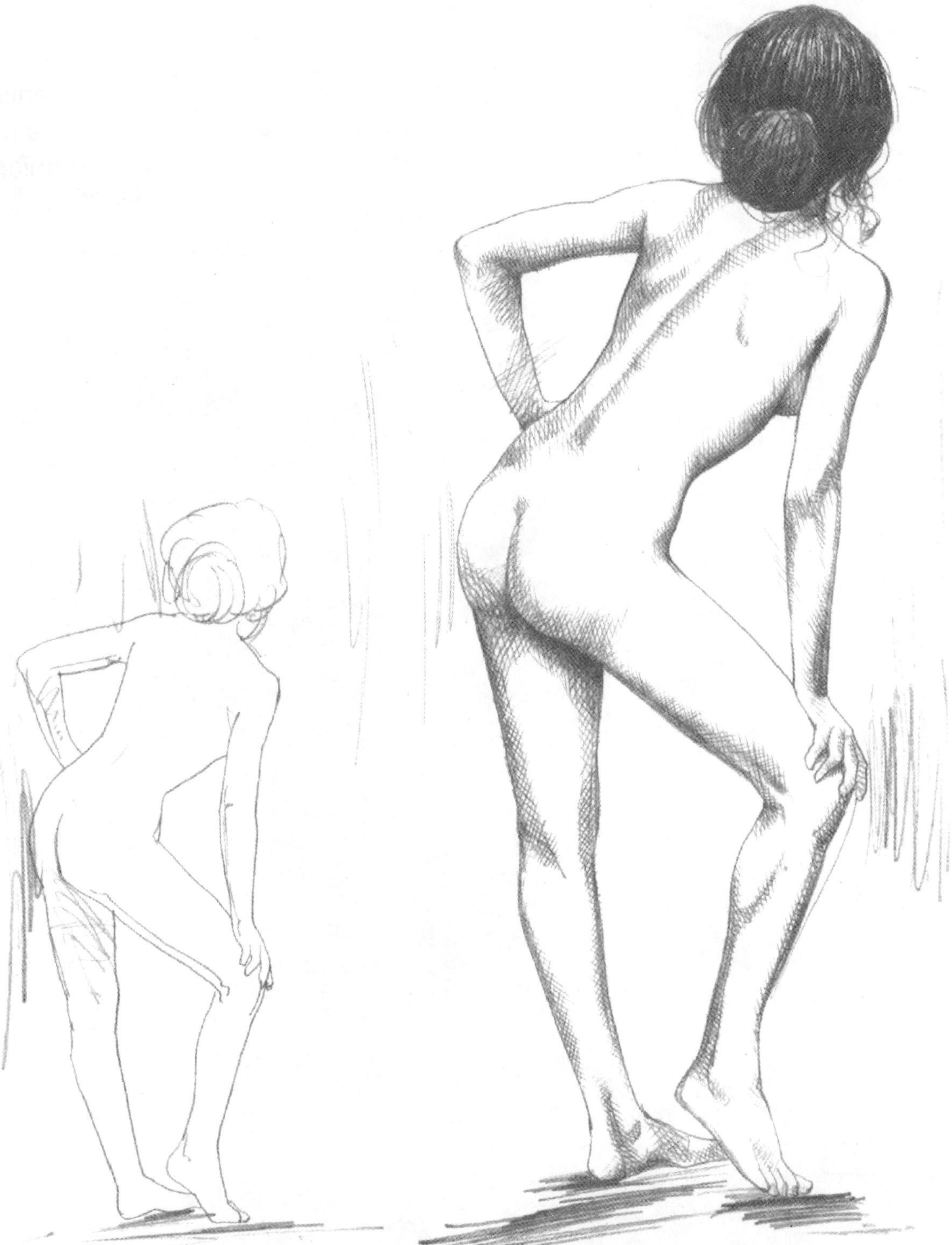

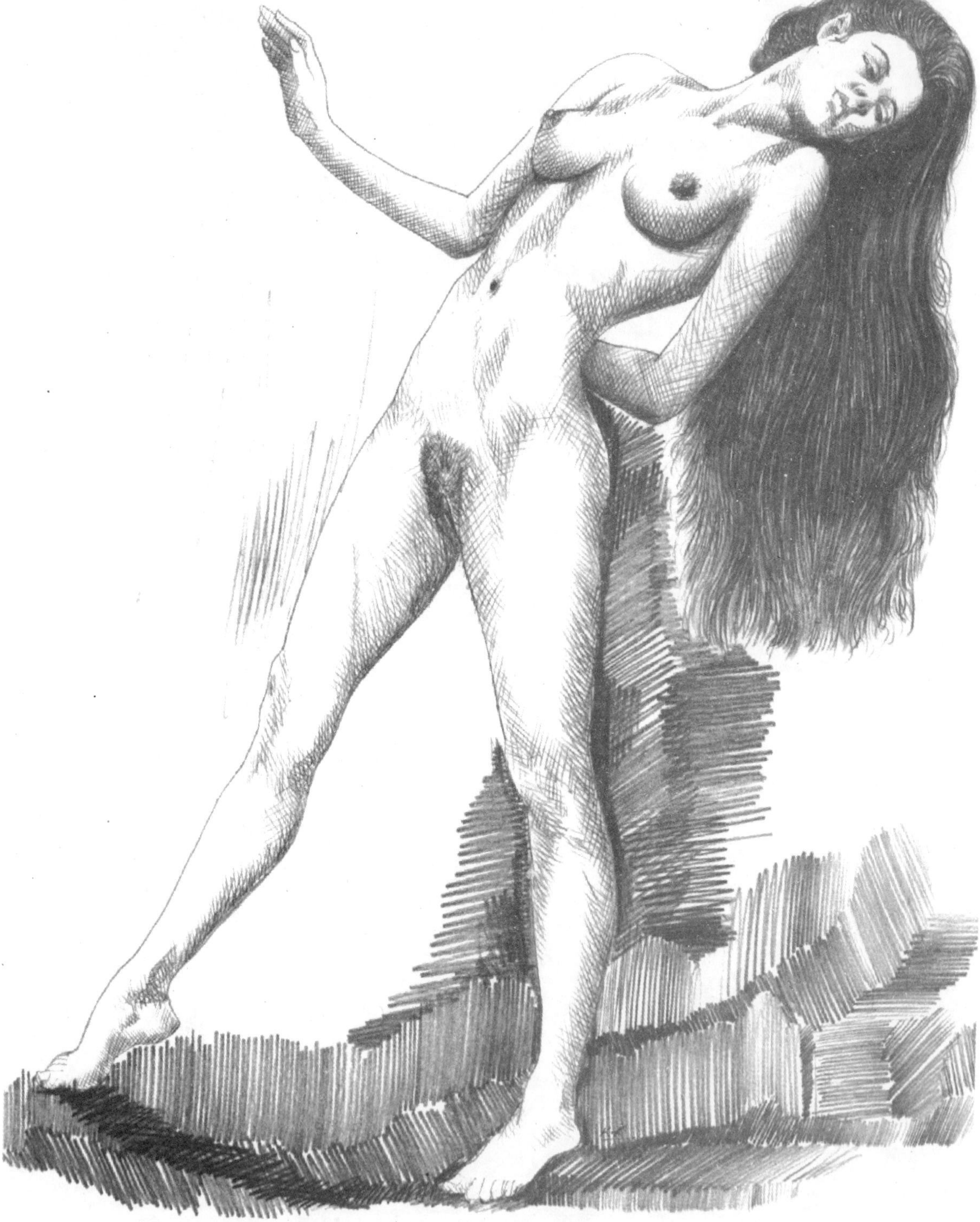

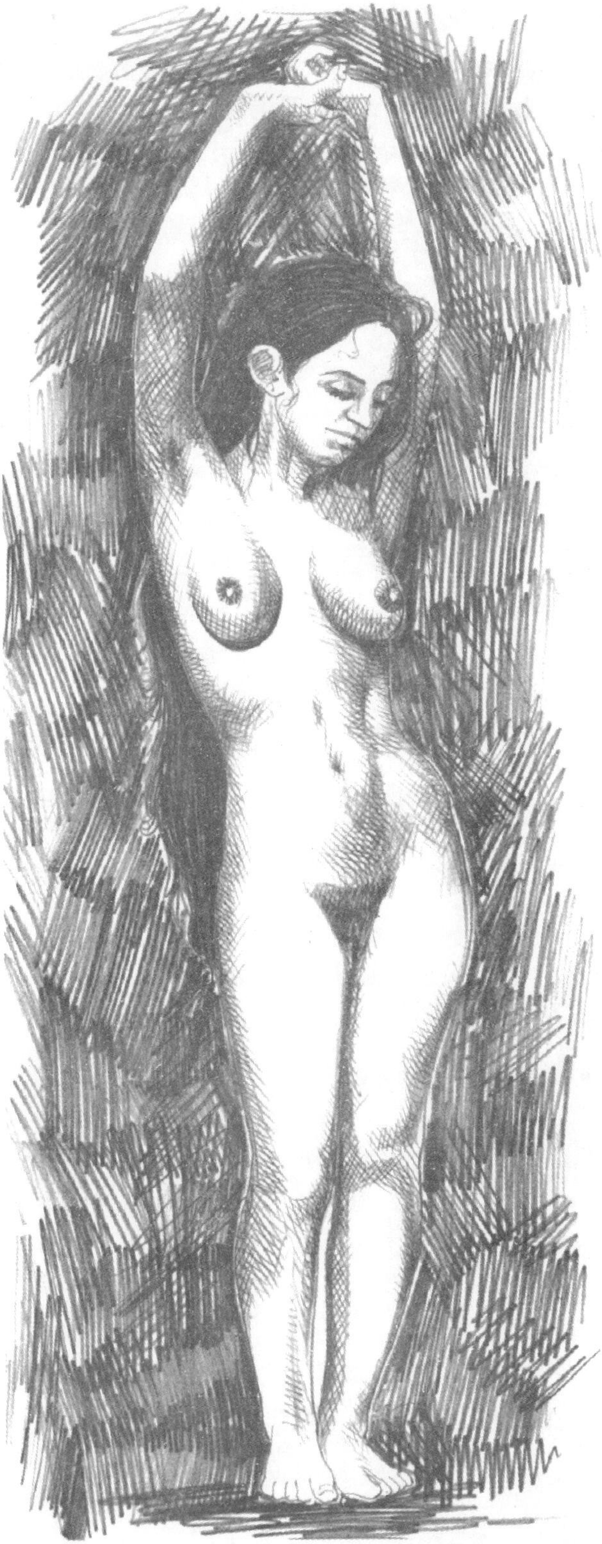

The model has raised her arms above the head. Observe the hollows of the armpits and their anterior and posterior walls formed by the muscles coming form the trunk and inserted near the head of the humerus. The tilt of the pelvis then allows a correspondingly different dislocation at the knees.

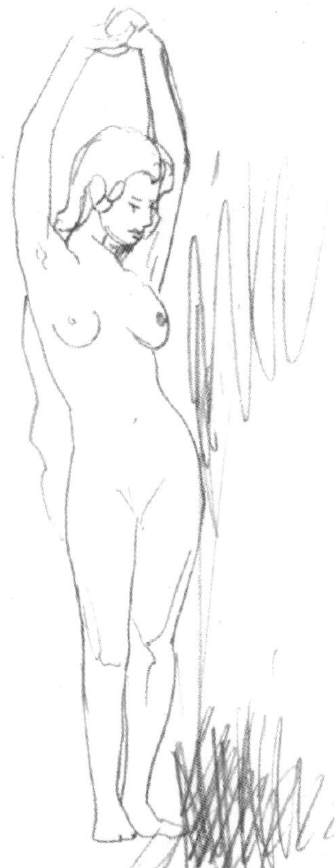

The model is drawn from front and back viewpoint. The aim is to show the complex working of the skeleton.

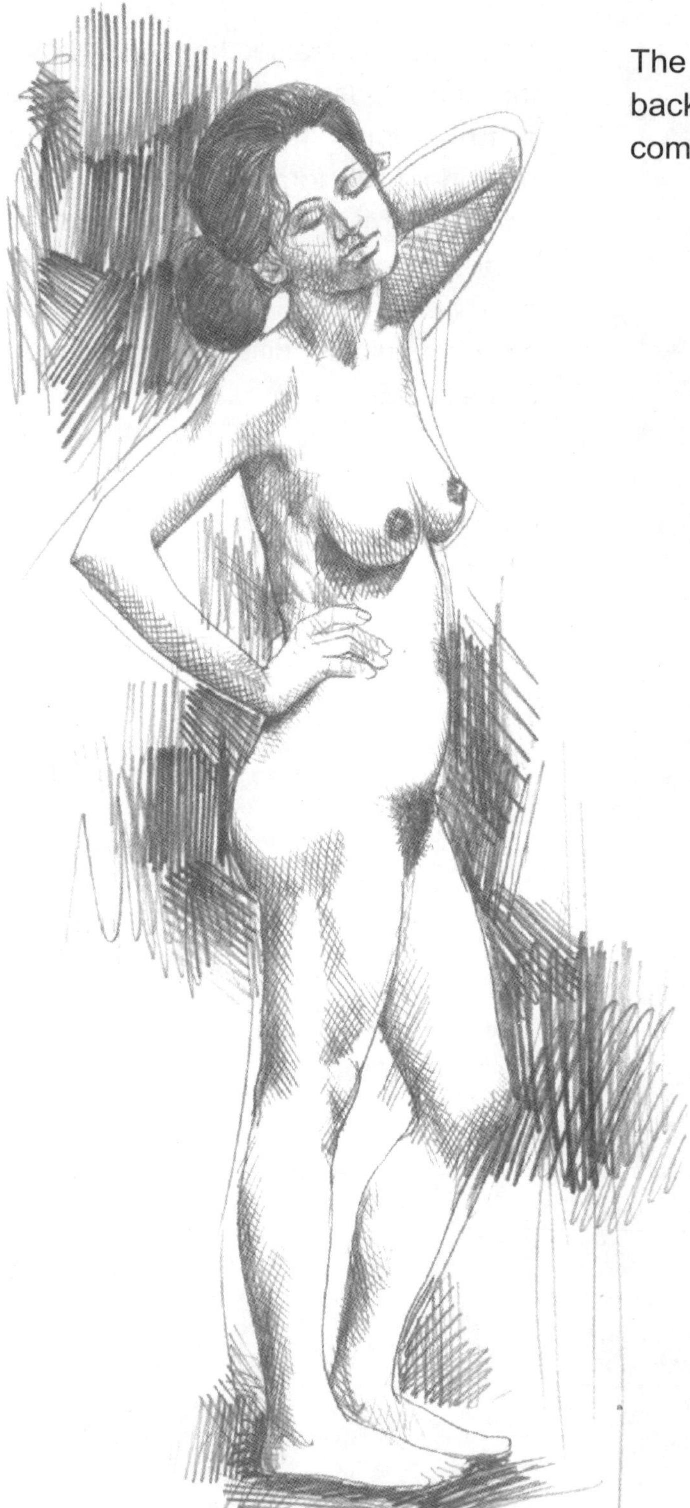

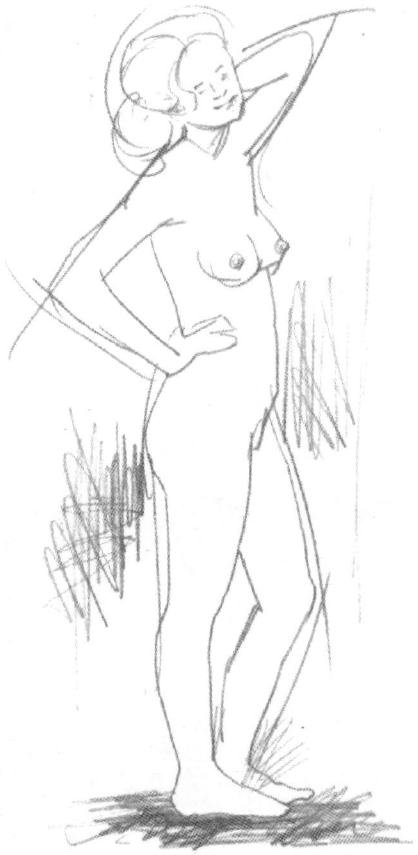

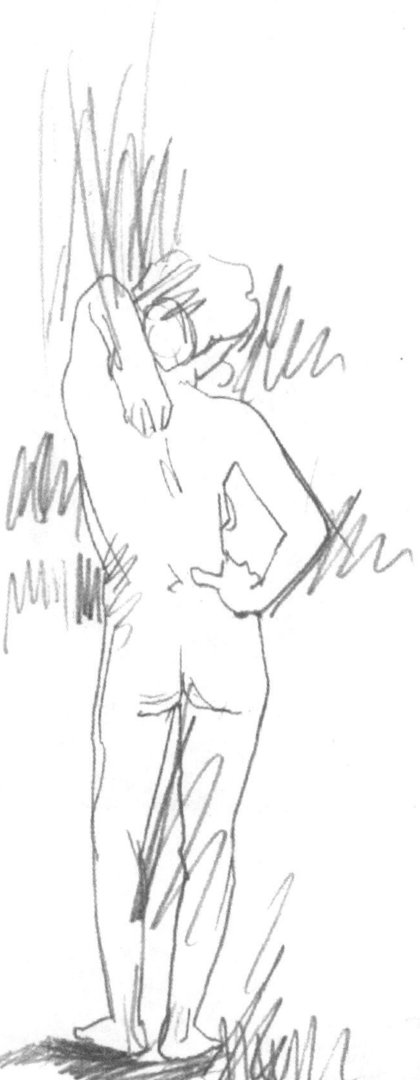

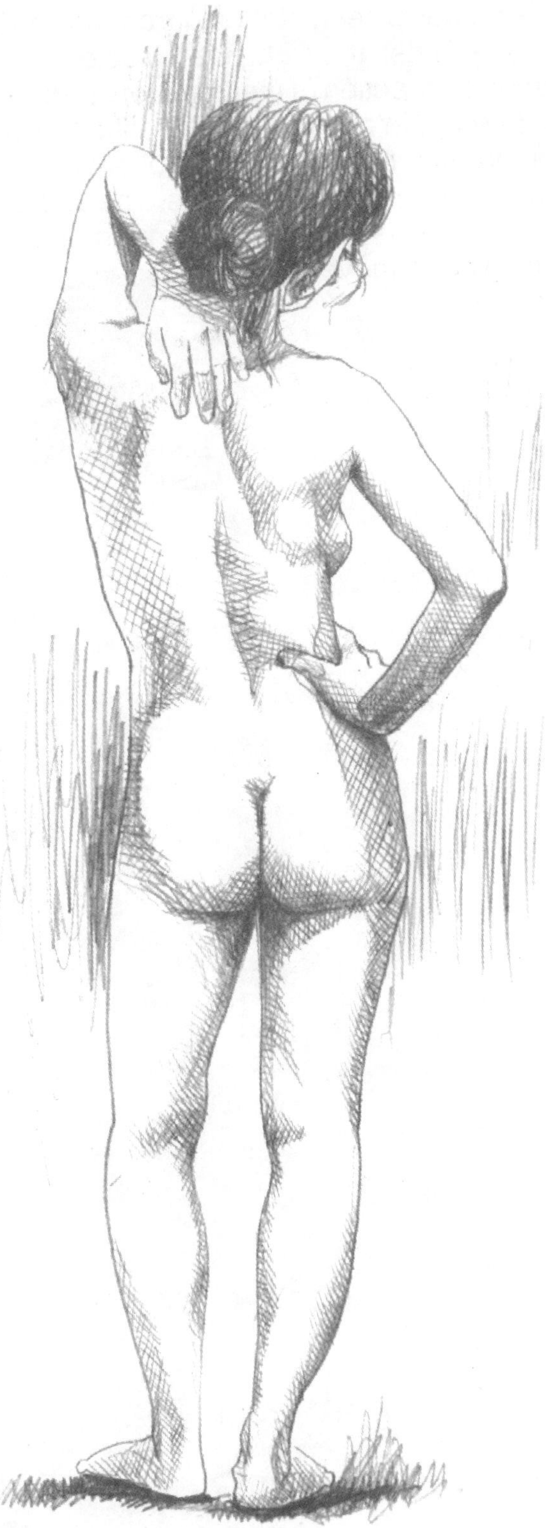

The model is seen standing from her back, showing her body against the light that displays most clearly the opposite direction of the transverse axis of the shoulders and pelvis. In relation to the postero superior iliac spine two prominent symmetrical hollows are visible and give the greater width of the pelvis. The spinal column makes a wide sideways curve to compensate or turns on itself with twisting movement.

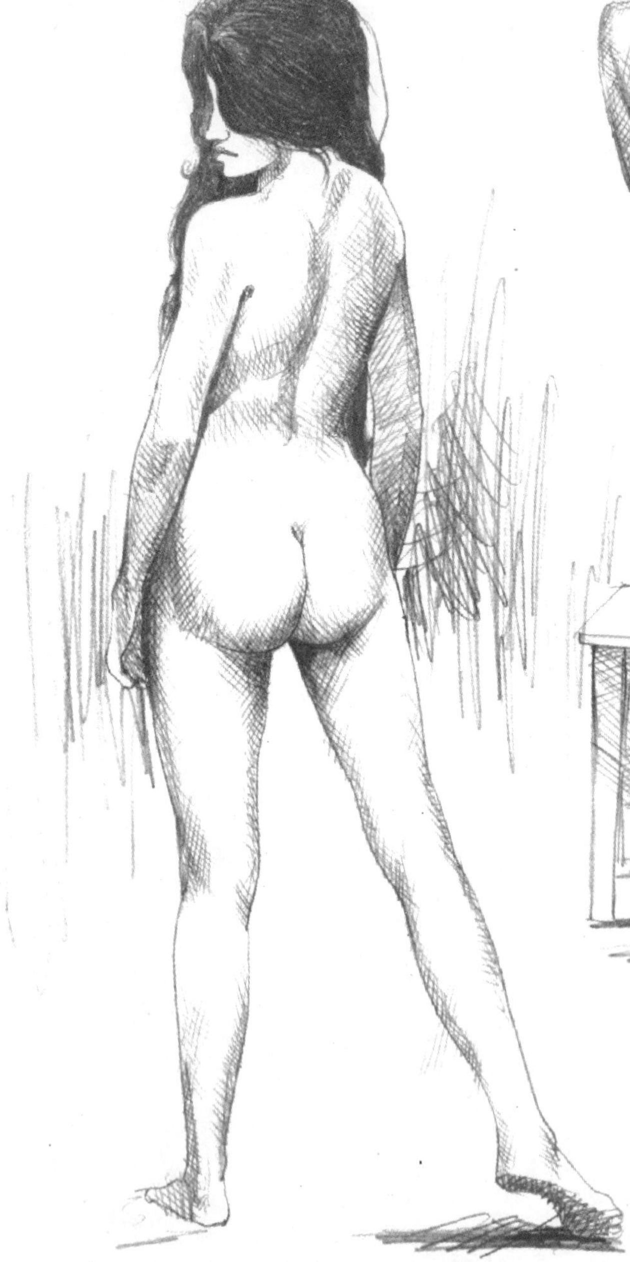

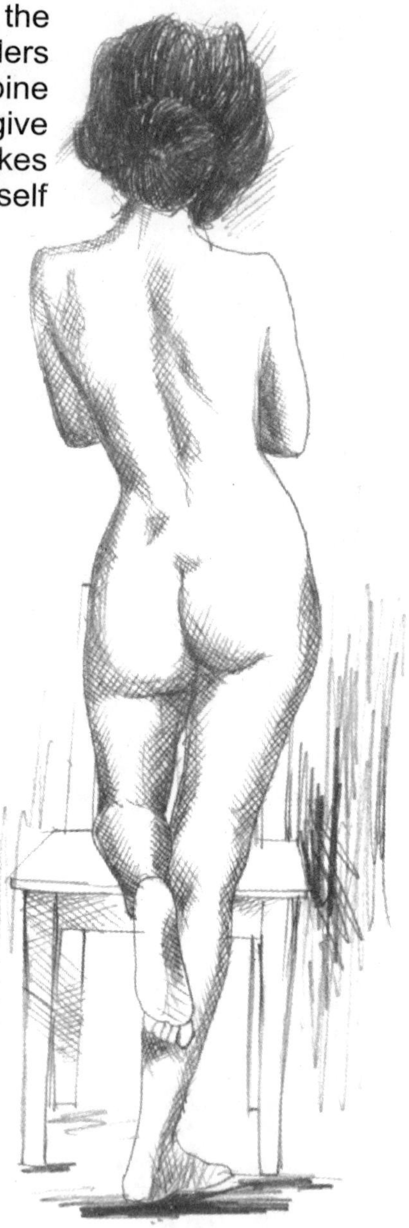

From the front view, the model's weight of trunk falls on the right lower limb. But note the left lower limb that carries the weight.

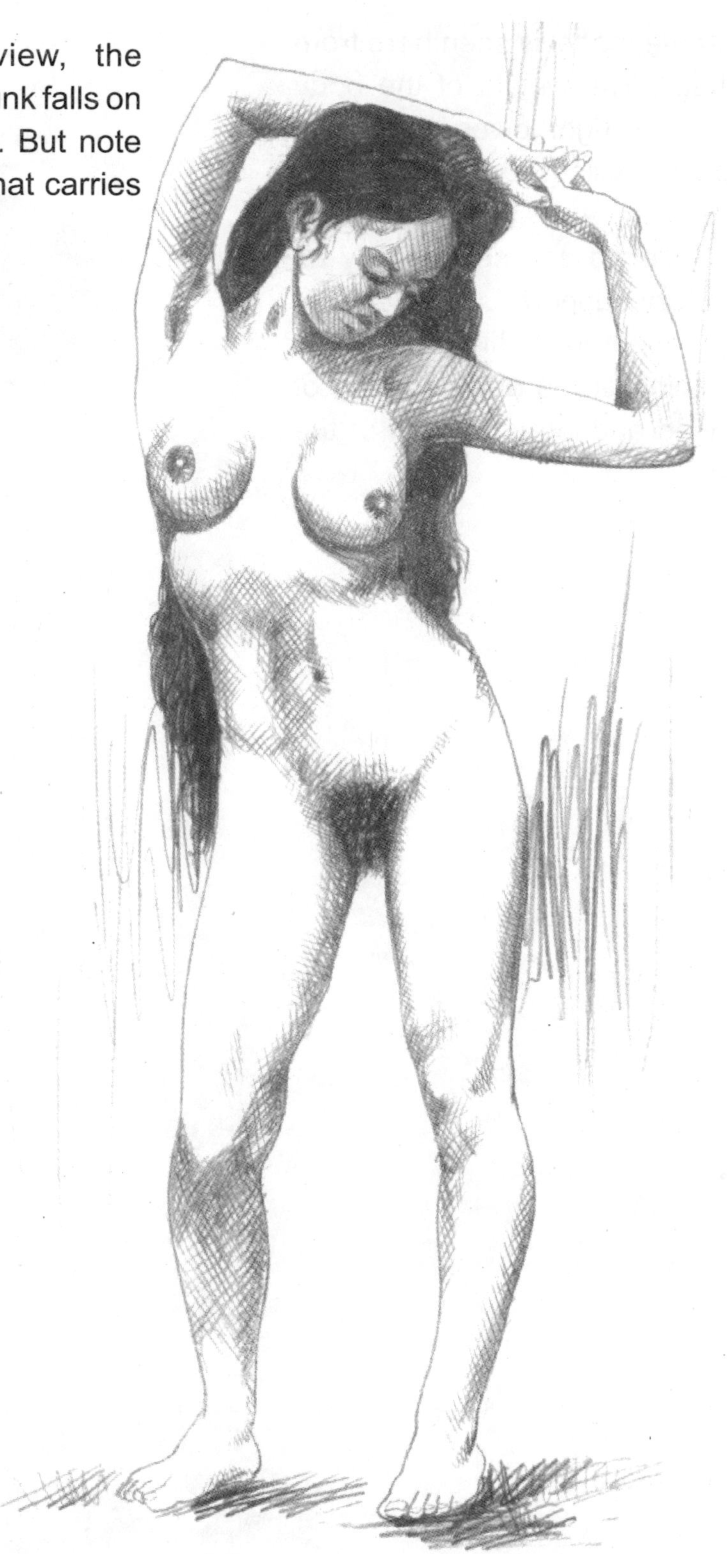

The same model is seen here from the back. The weight of the body falls on the right lower limb, while the pelvis inclines, dropping on the left side because the left limb is slightly flexed and serves only as subsidiary support. Lateral shift of body weight is achieved by the positioning of the arms, turning of the head and lateral flexion of the thorax.

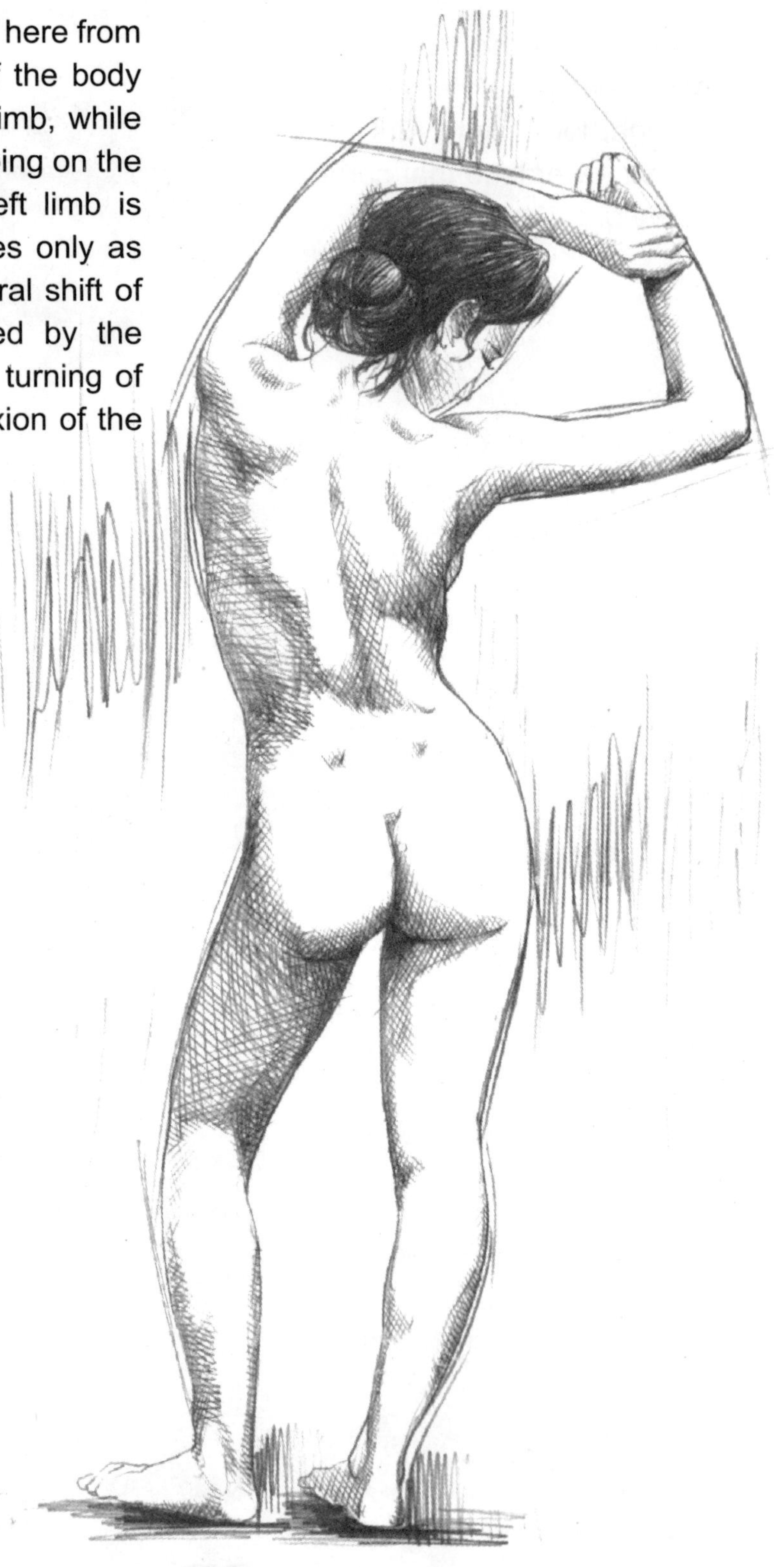

The Moving Figures

Even though the model is static, look at the interesting movements of torsion, flexion in rotation and extension derived from vertebral column, the supporting unit of the trunk.

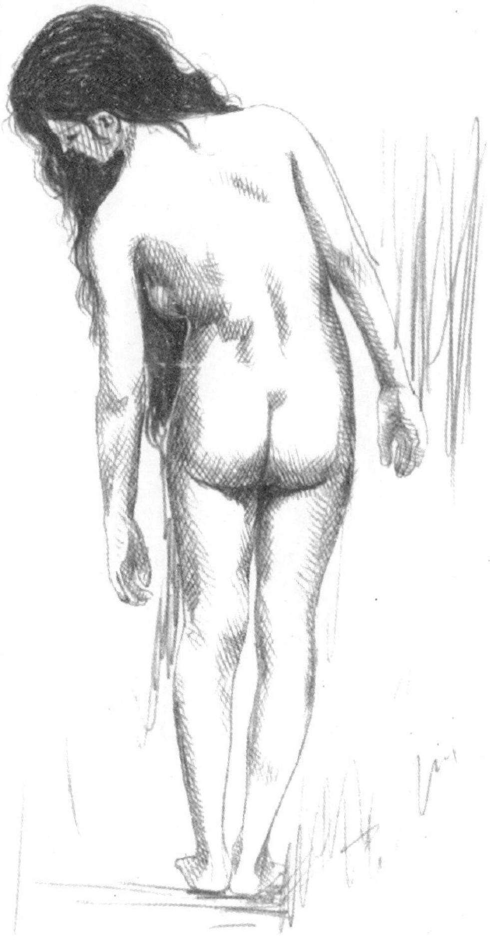

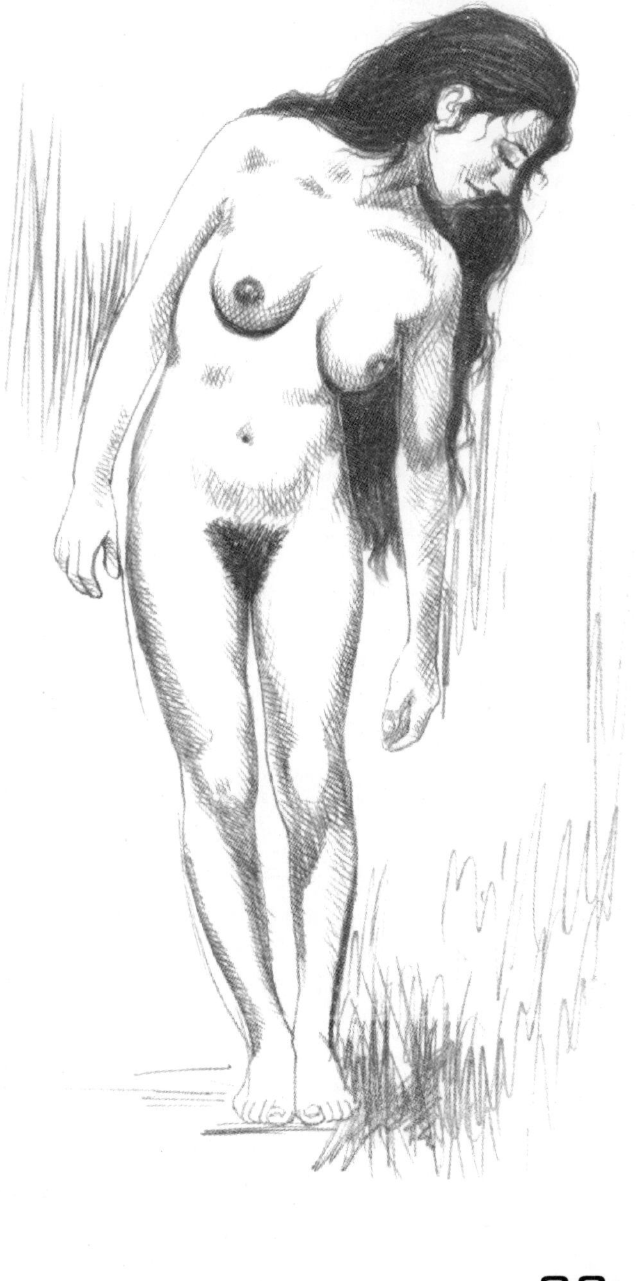

The model's literally 'dynamic' action can be studied by looking carefully at her when she is doing something, identifying the sequence of movements and selecting the important one.

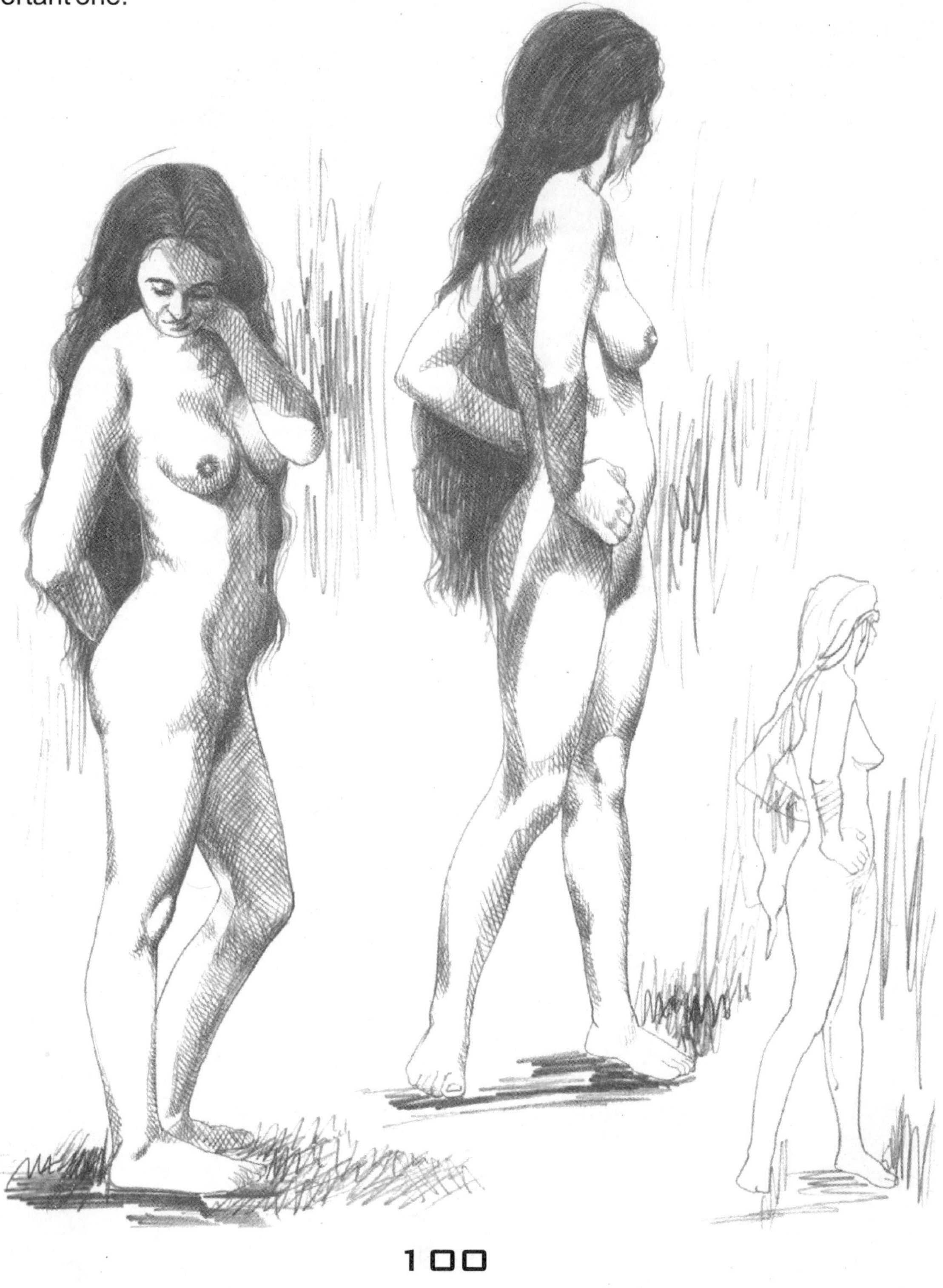

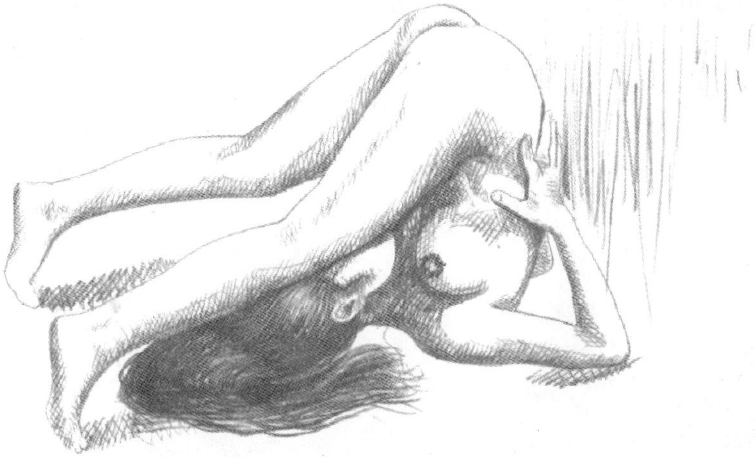

These models are in yoga positions. These positions are interesting to study. Flexion of the trunk with the shoulders on the ground and the pelvis moving freely, require strong contraction of rectus abdominis and, successively, of the gluteal muscle and biceps femoris, to maintain an arched position.

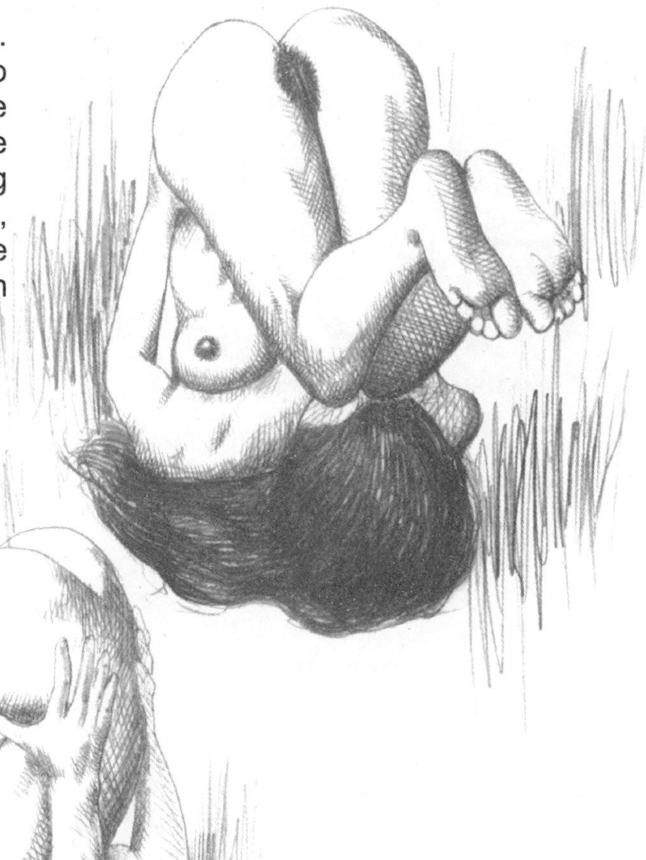

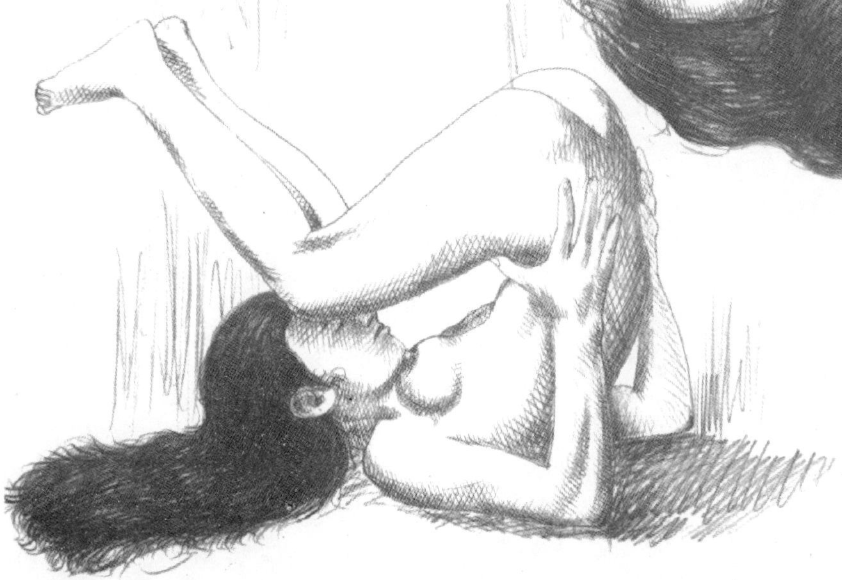

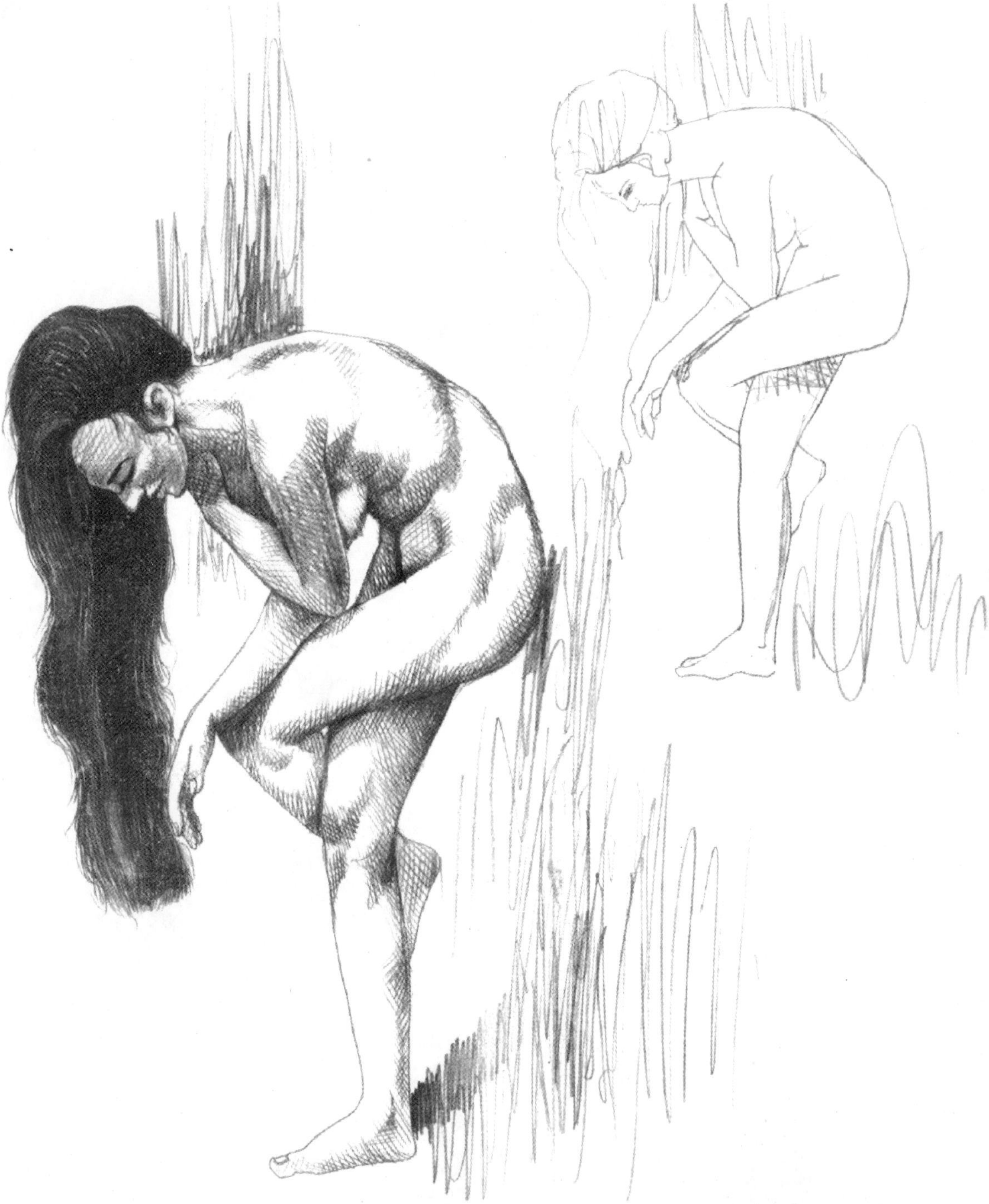

The Figures in Depth

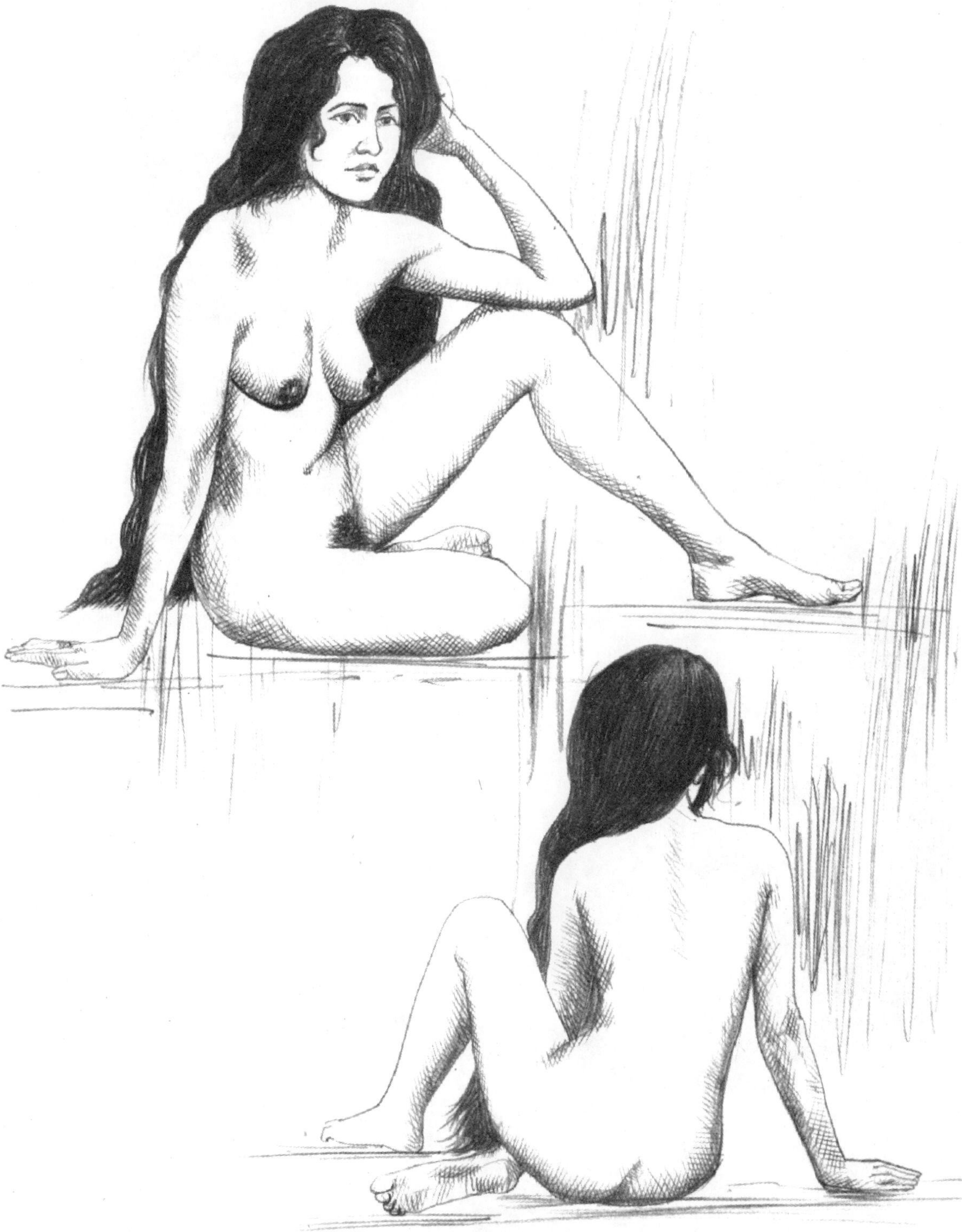

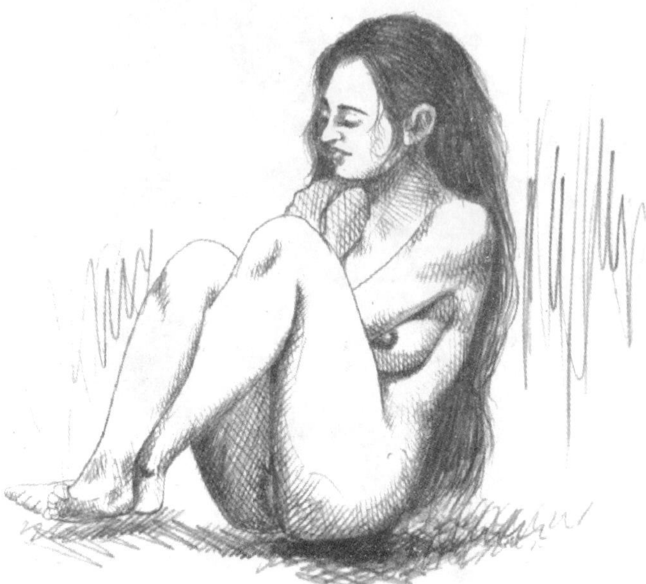

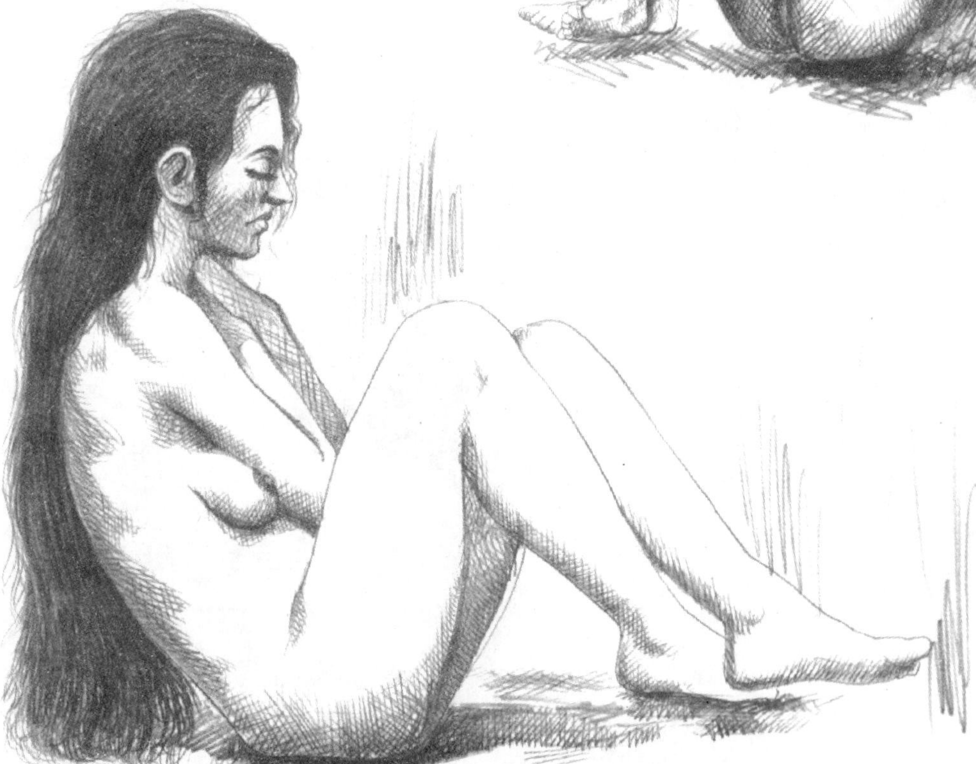

The Figures in Depth

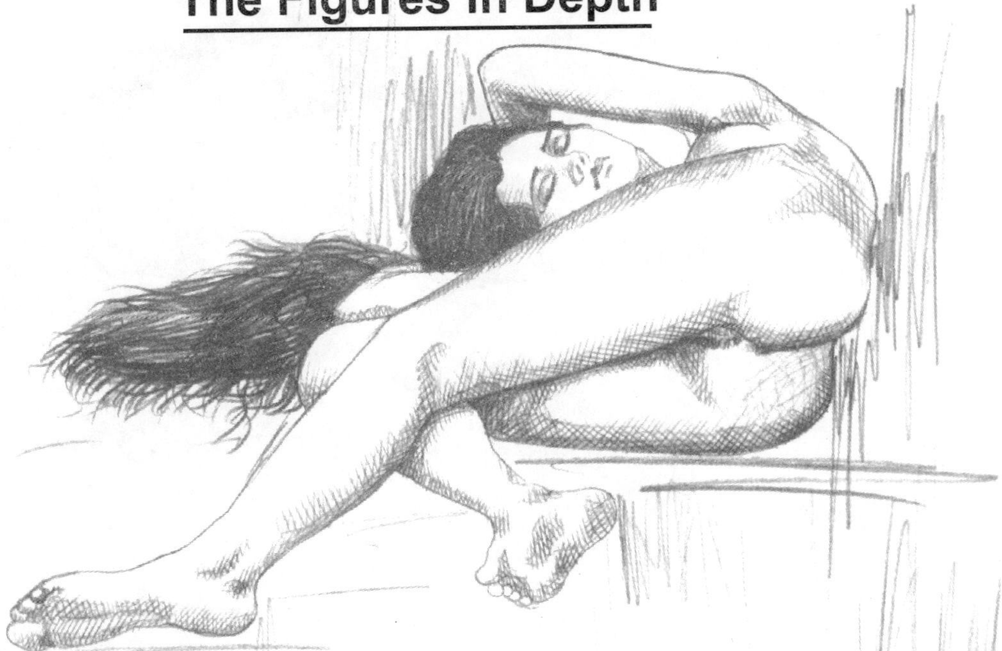

Even though positions are rare in which some parts of the body are not in depth. To draw the figure in exaggerated perspective presents a few difficulties. It may help you to place the figure in space by considering it a geometric solid, such as cubes and cylinders, which are easier to put into perspective.

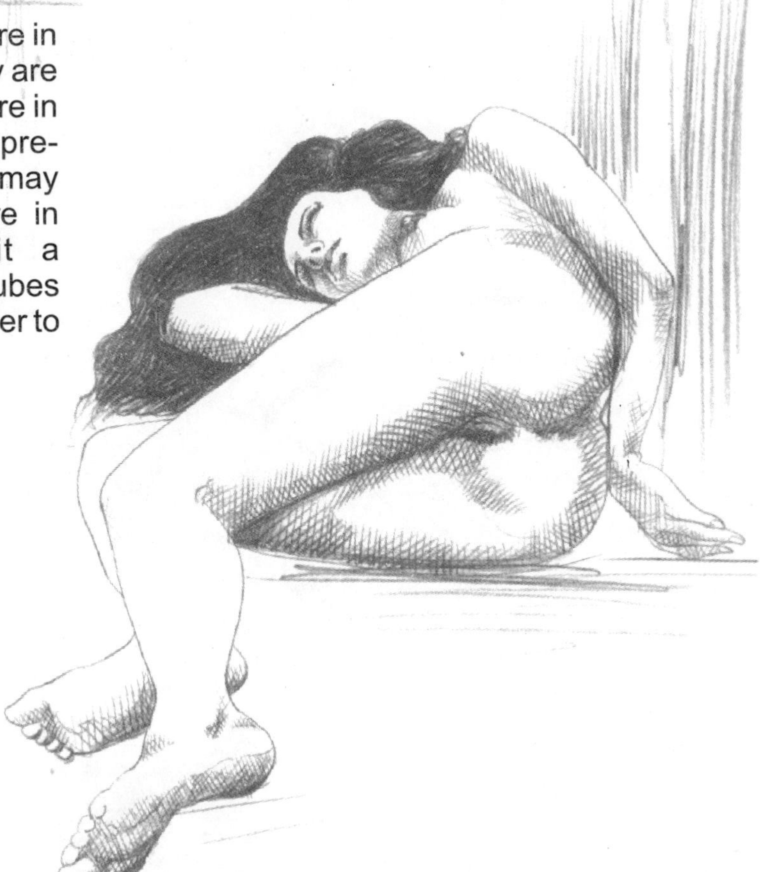

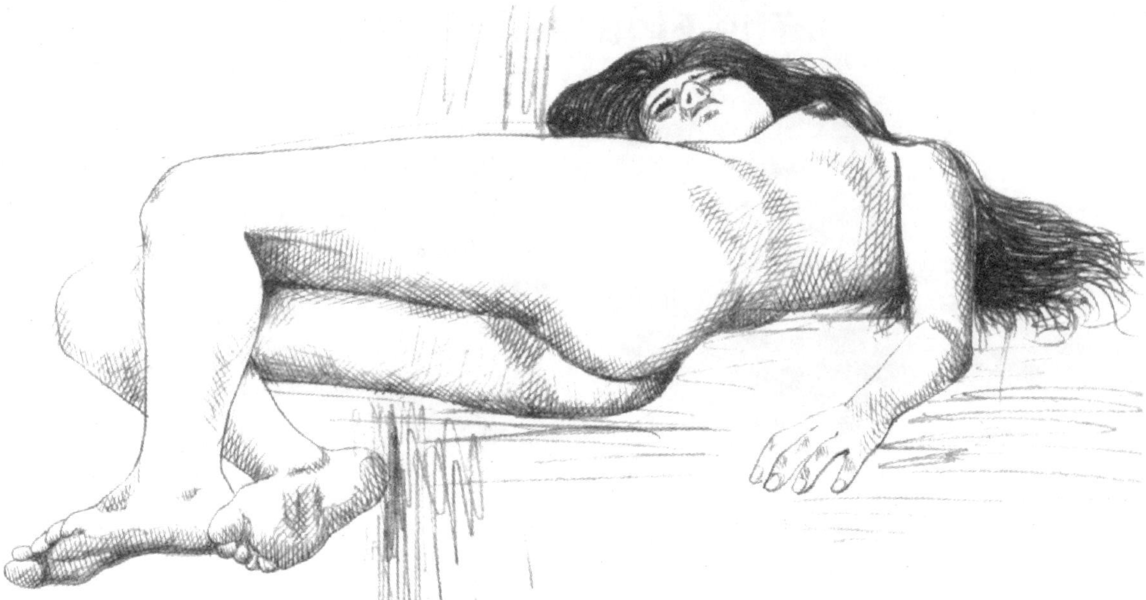

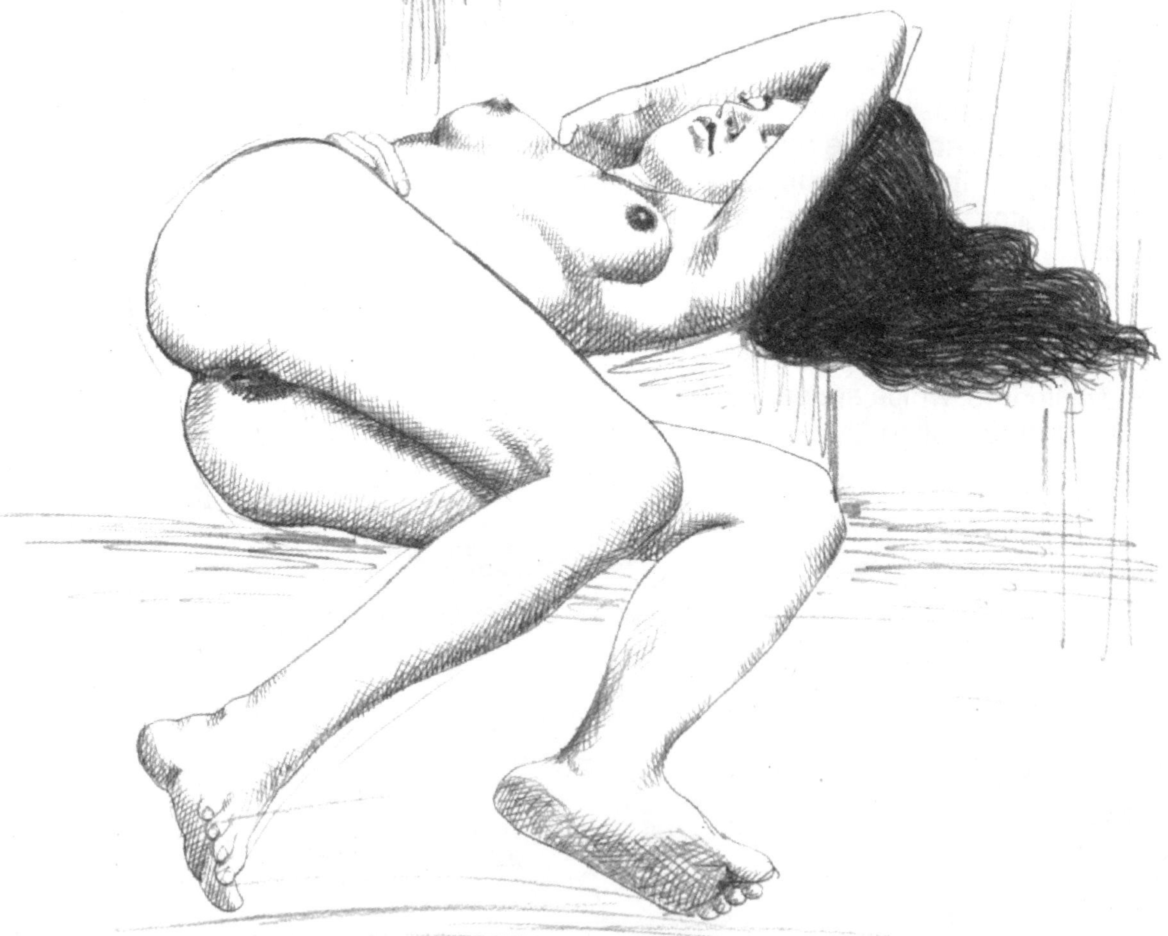

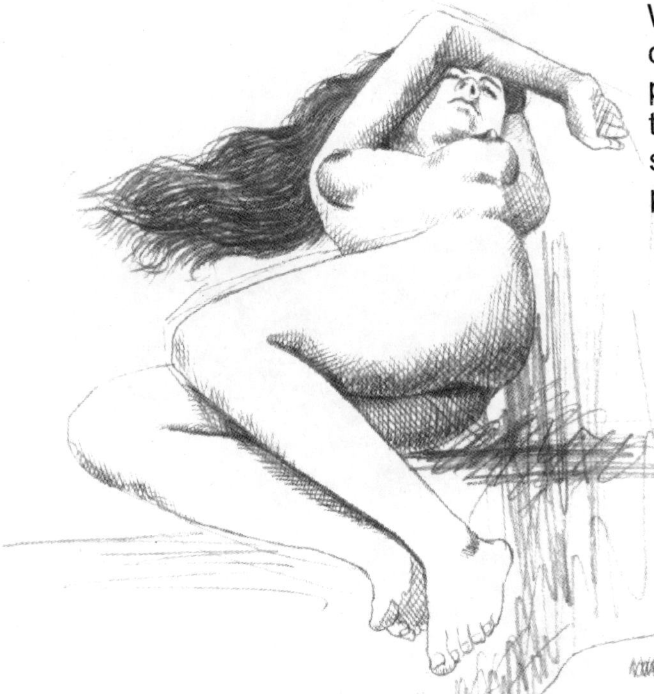

When the body is outstretched, it can naturally take up spontaneous positions in which the torsion of the trunk is very accentuated, sometimes to the limit of the articular process.

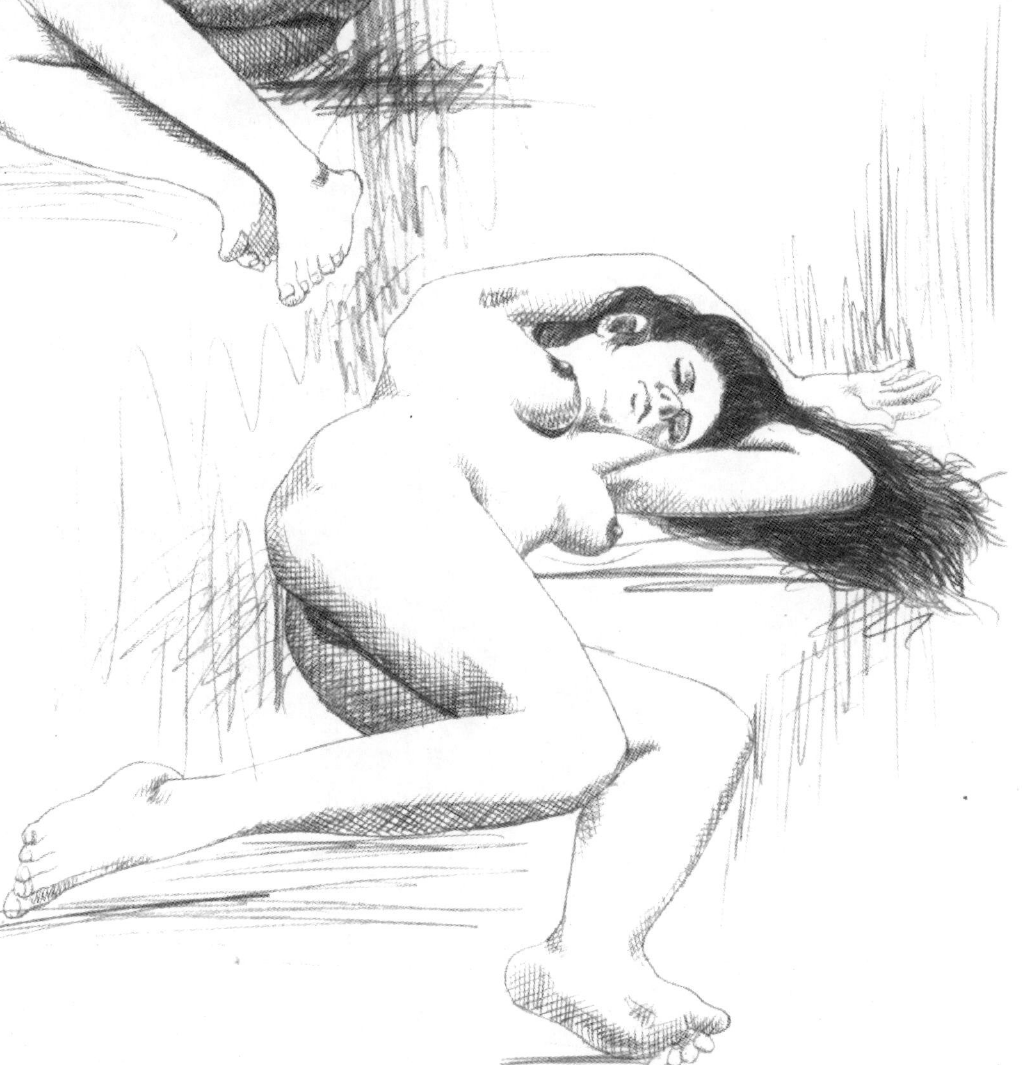

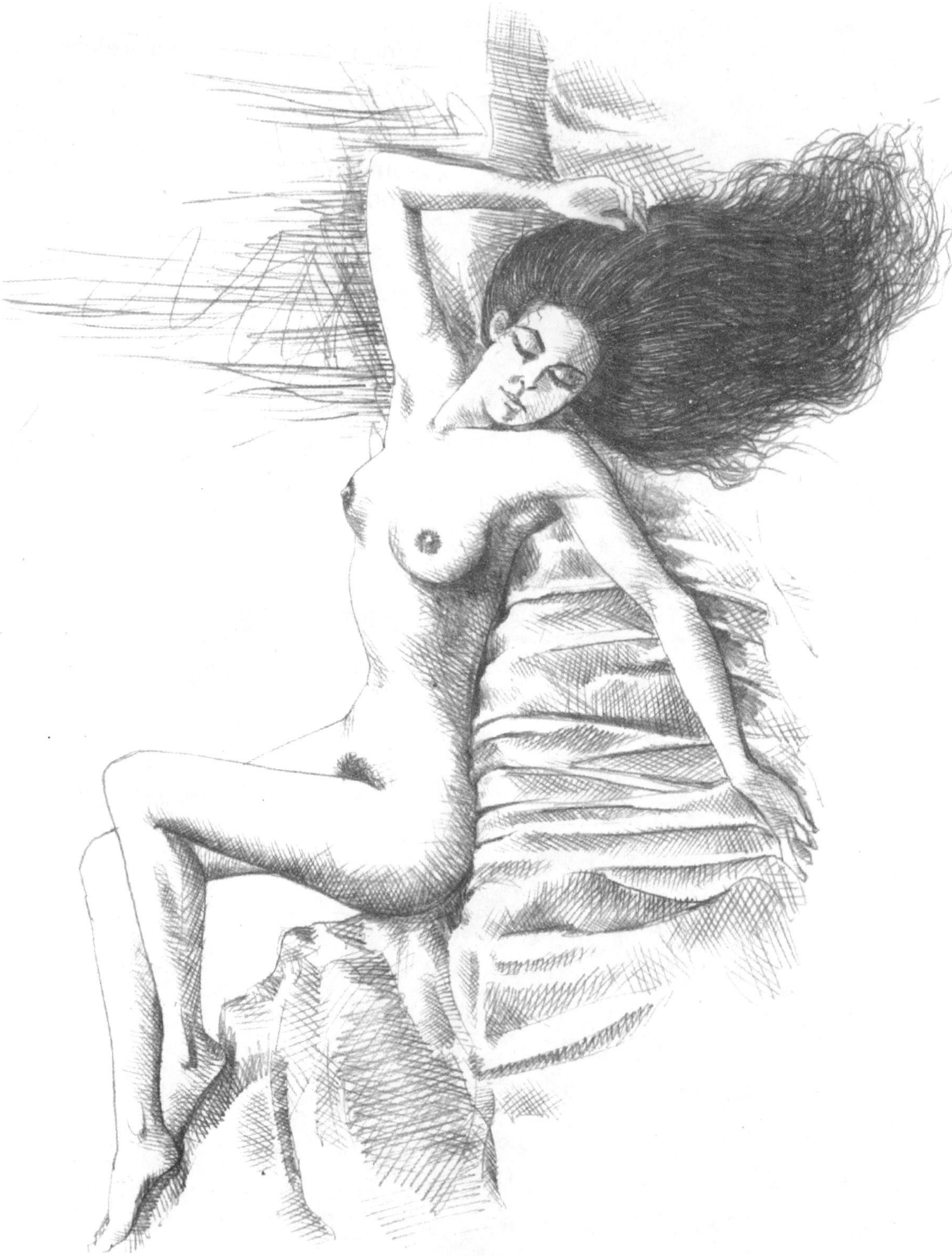

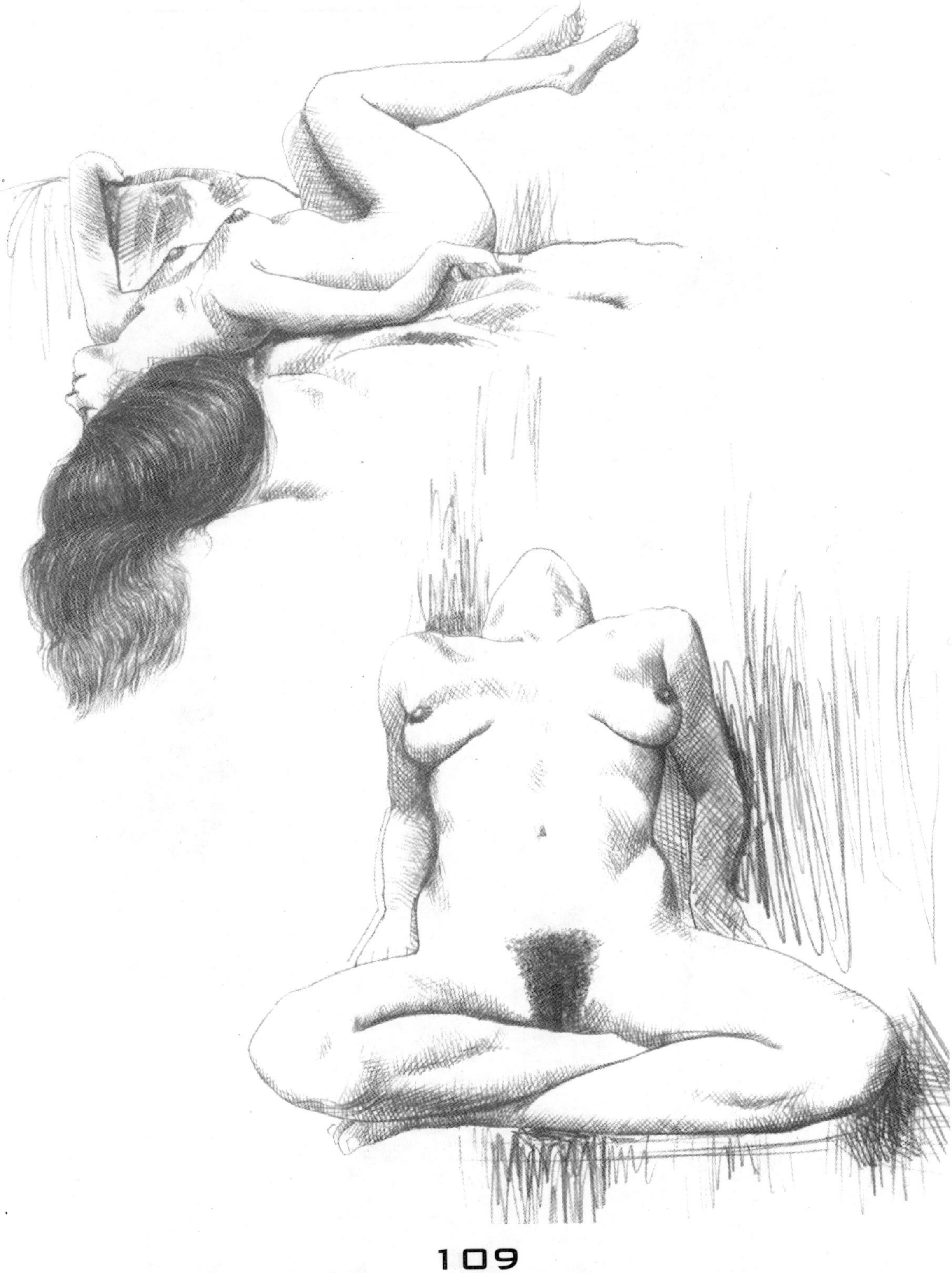

The Reclining Figures

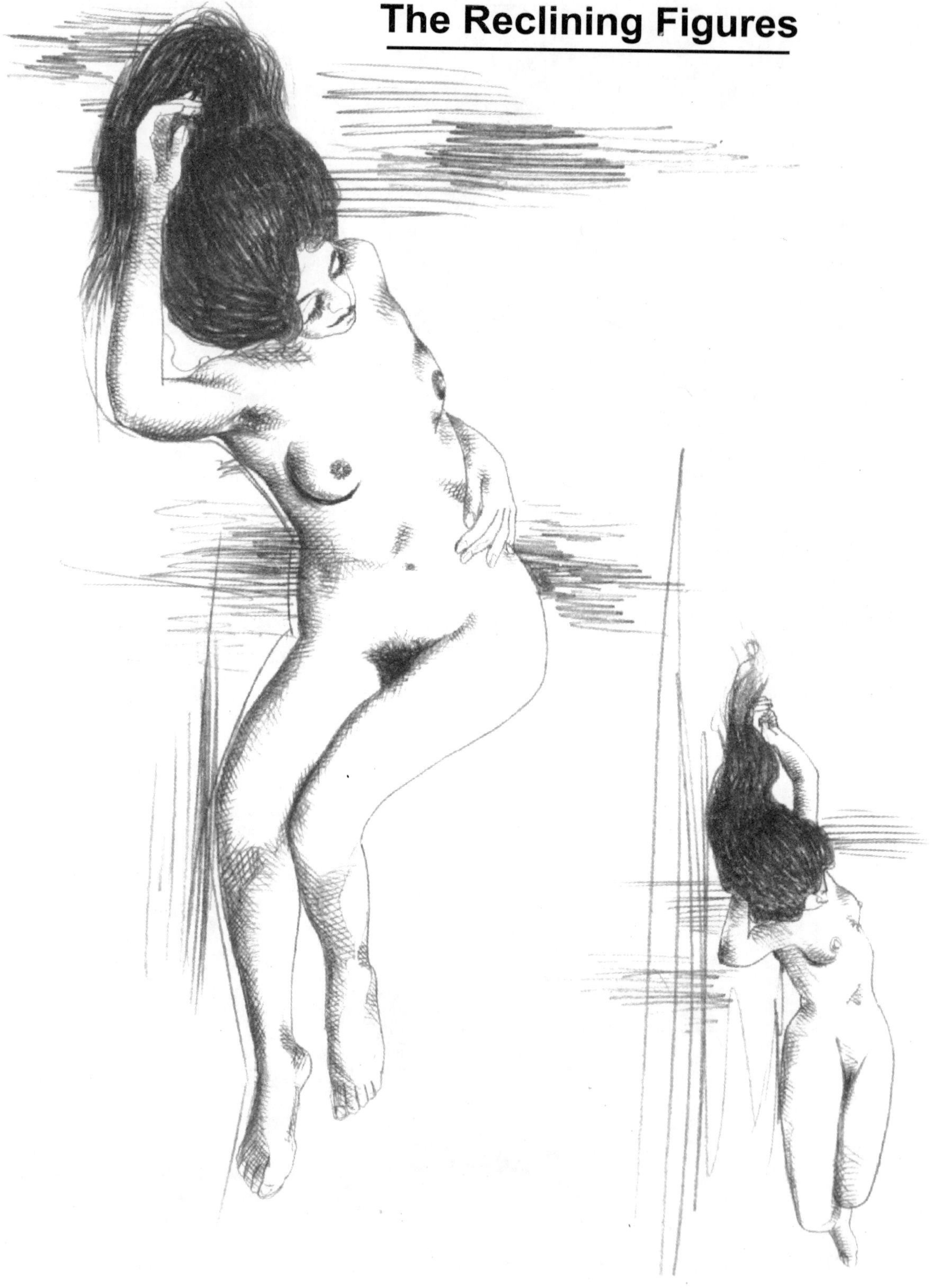

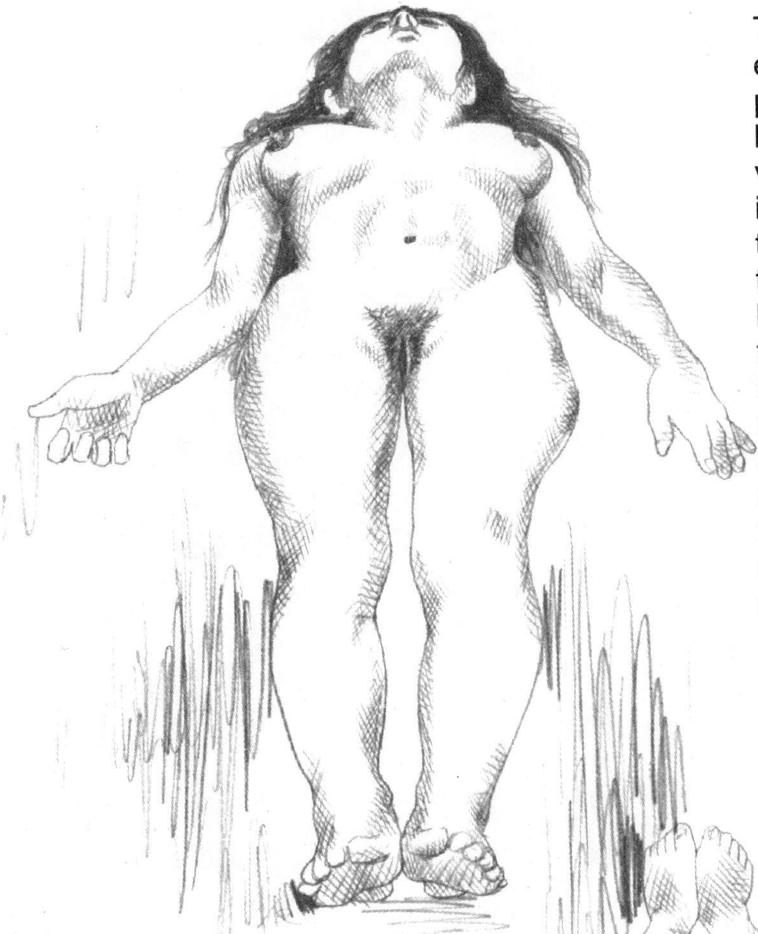

These types of figures in exaggerated perspective present a few difficulties, because of their unusual view in unnatural and indelicate position. However these figures are interesting to study the anatomy of the human figure, and to draw the nude in these positions, it is more necessary than usual to have recourse to measurements or comparisons based on bony protuberances and other relatively stable bodily structures.

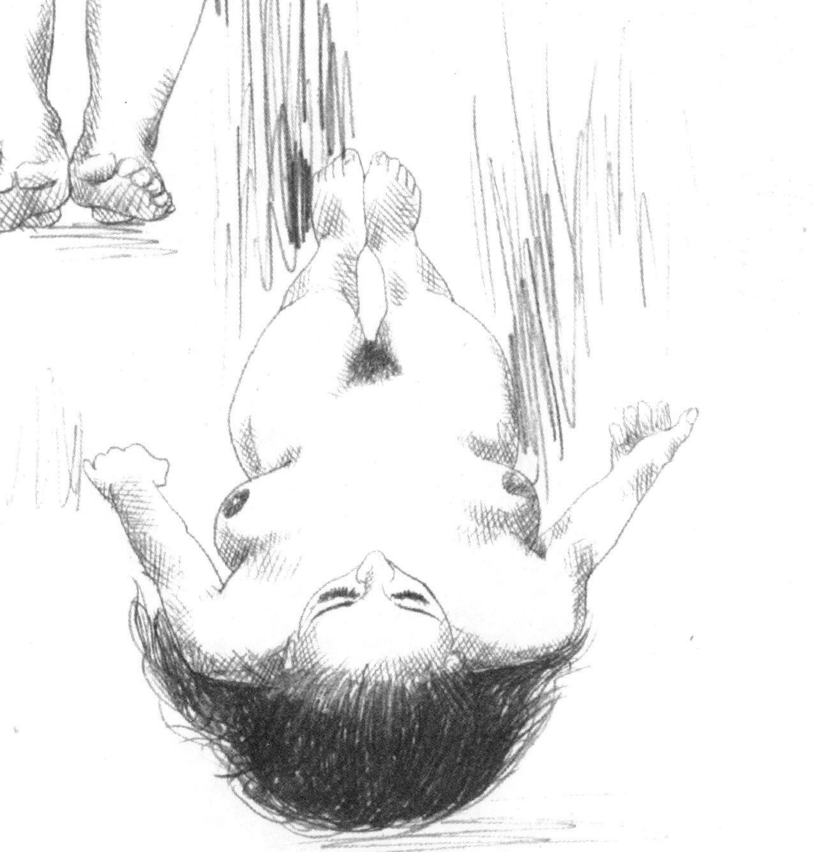

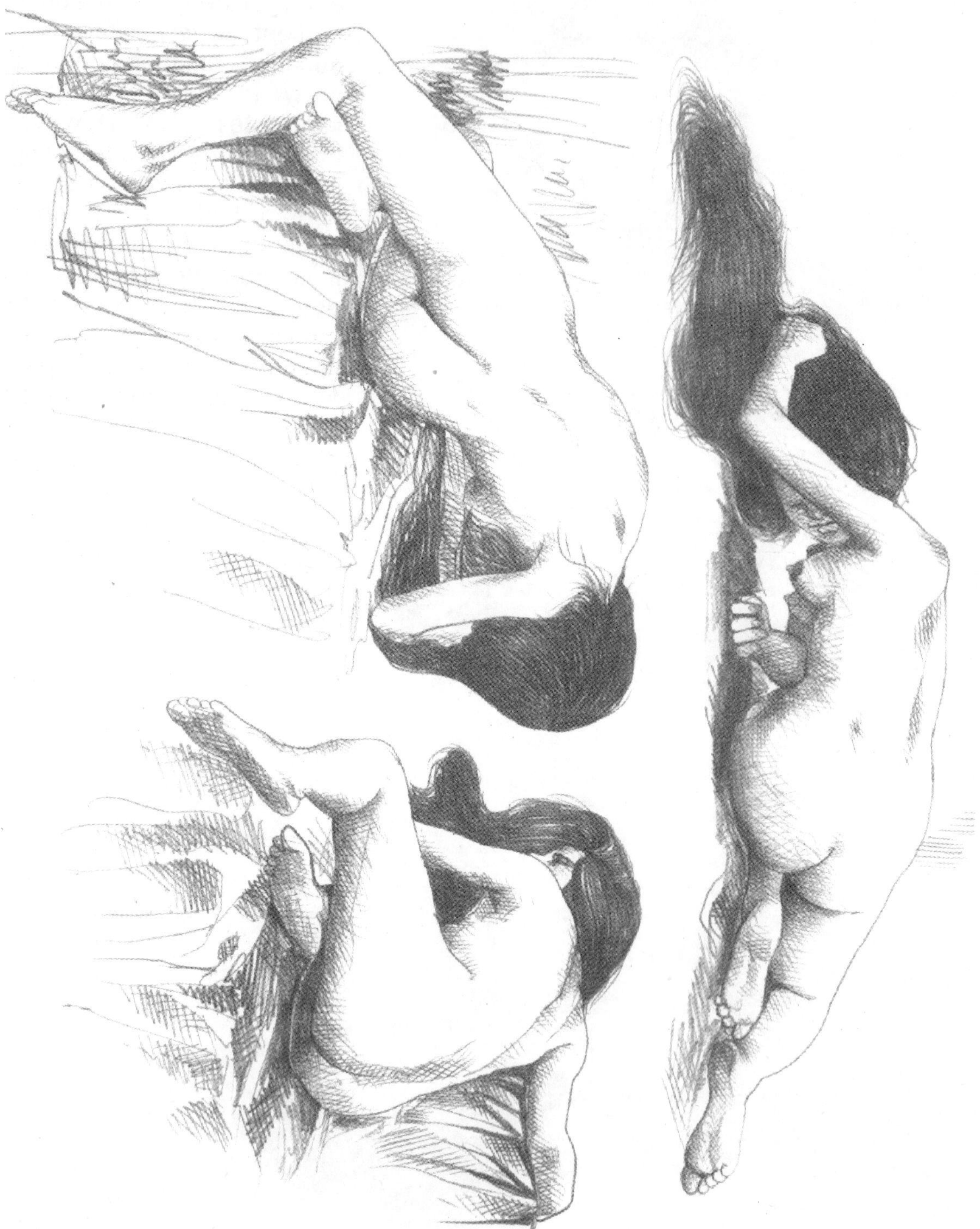

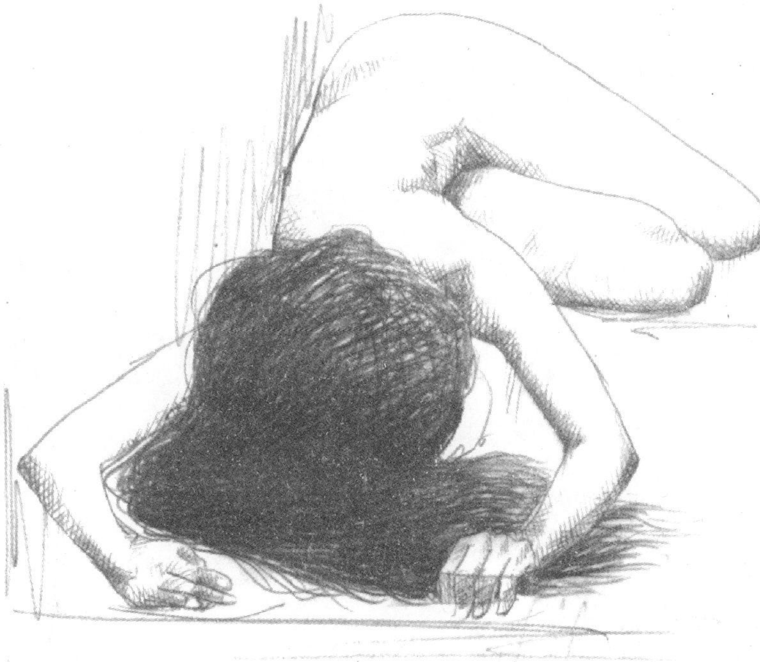

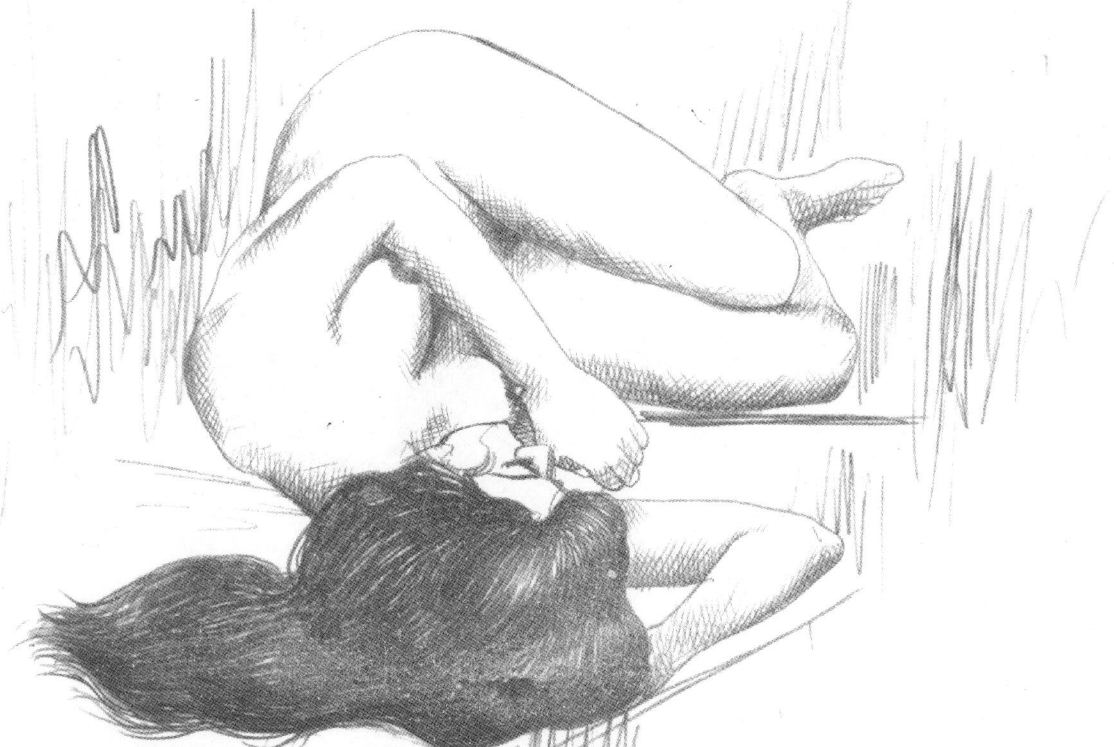

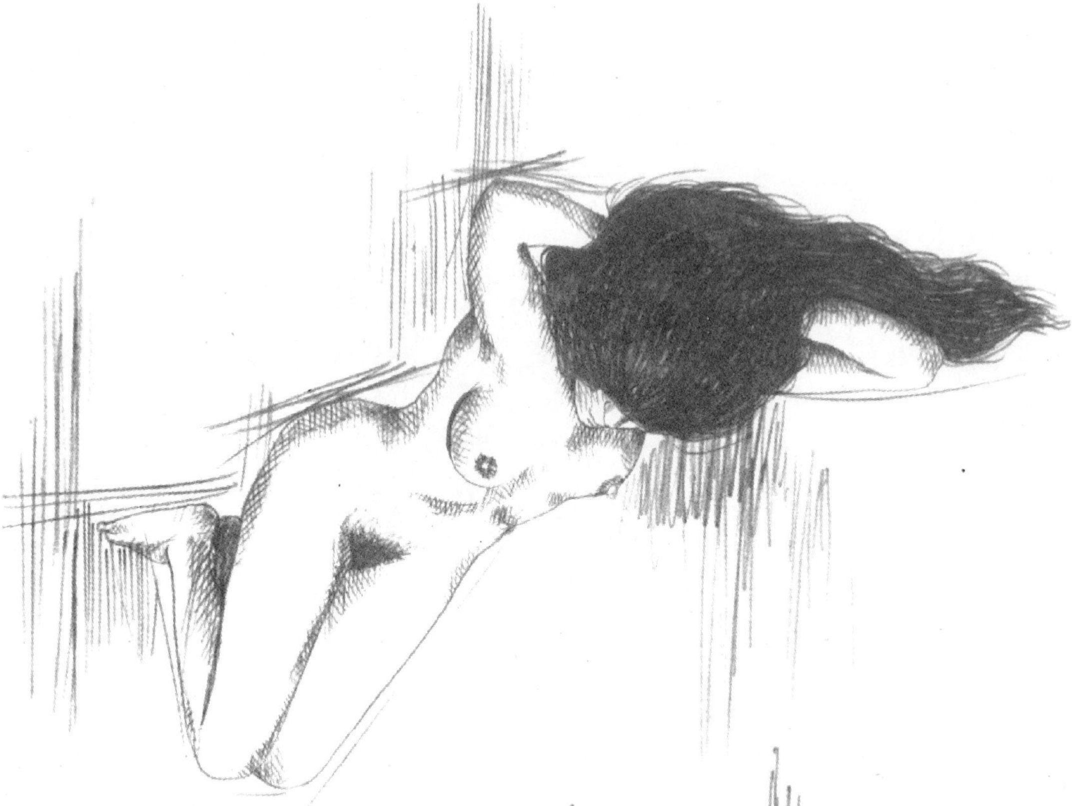

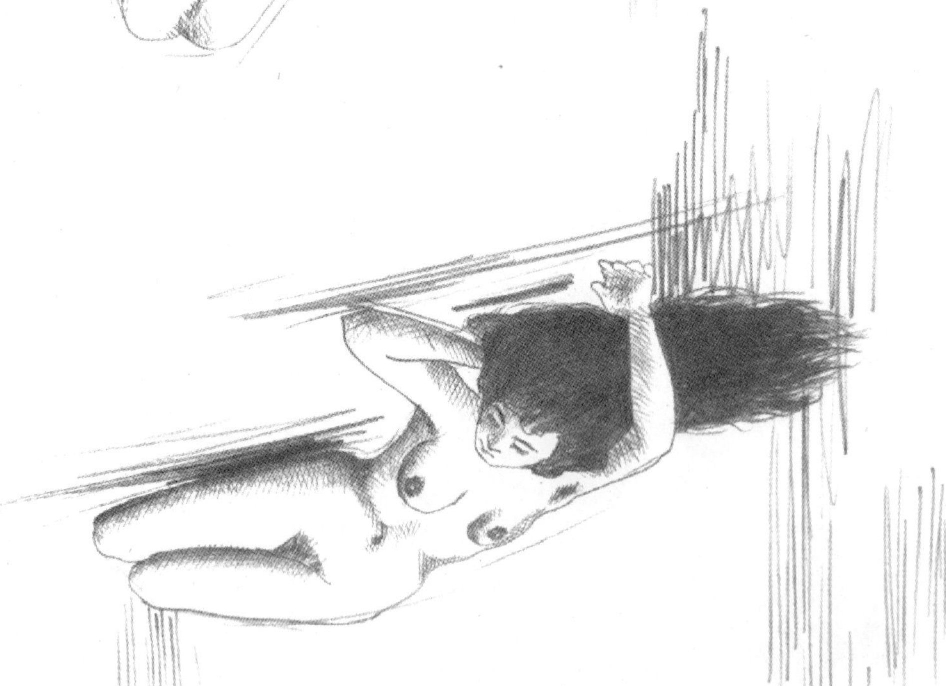

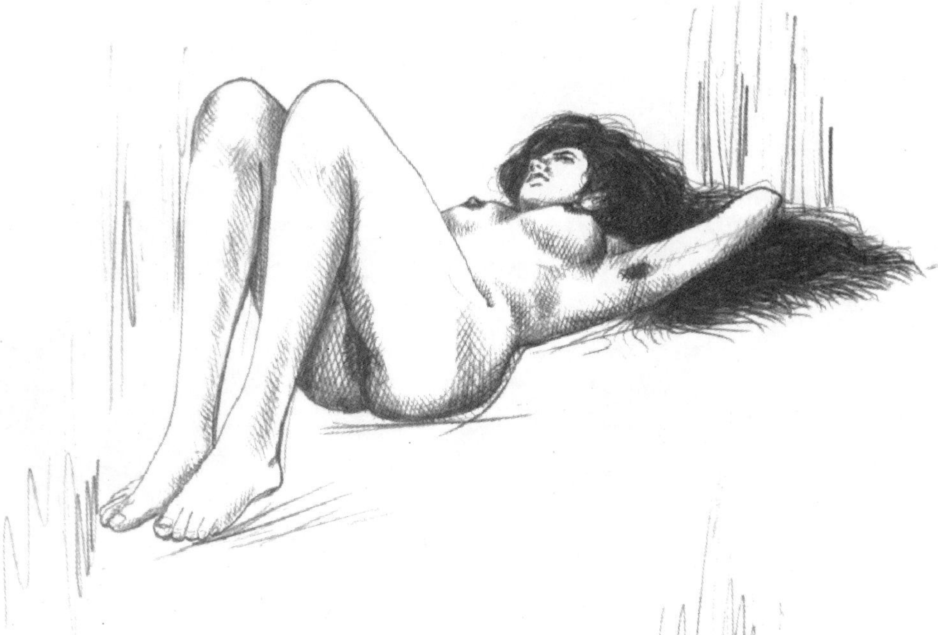

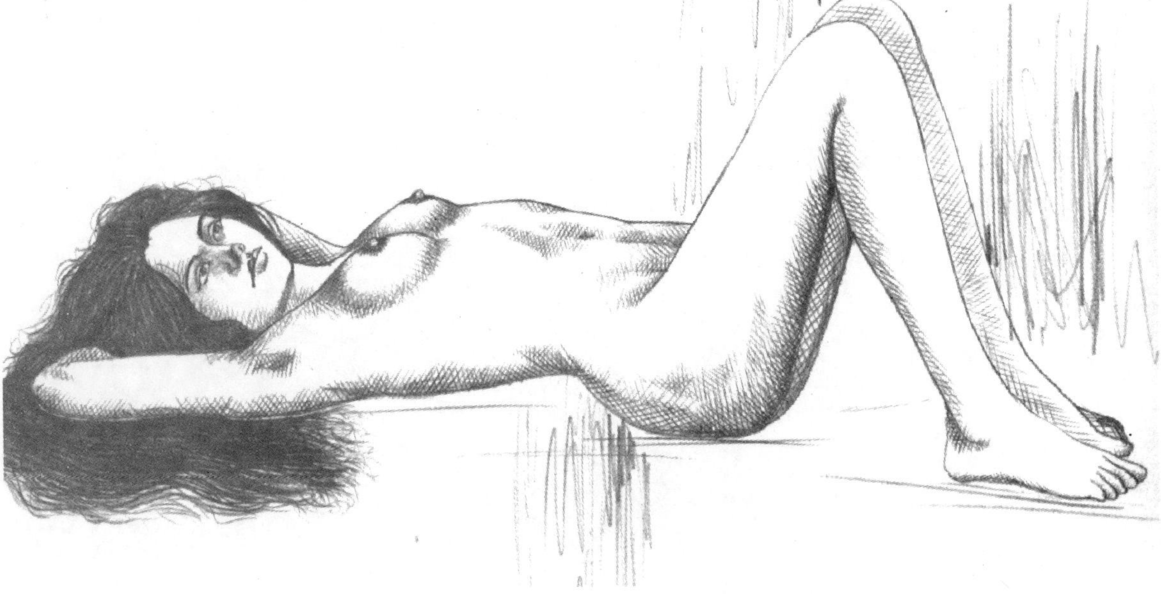

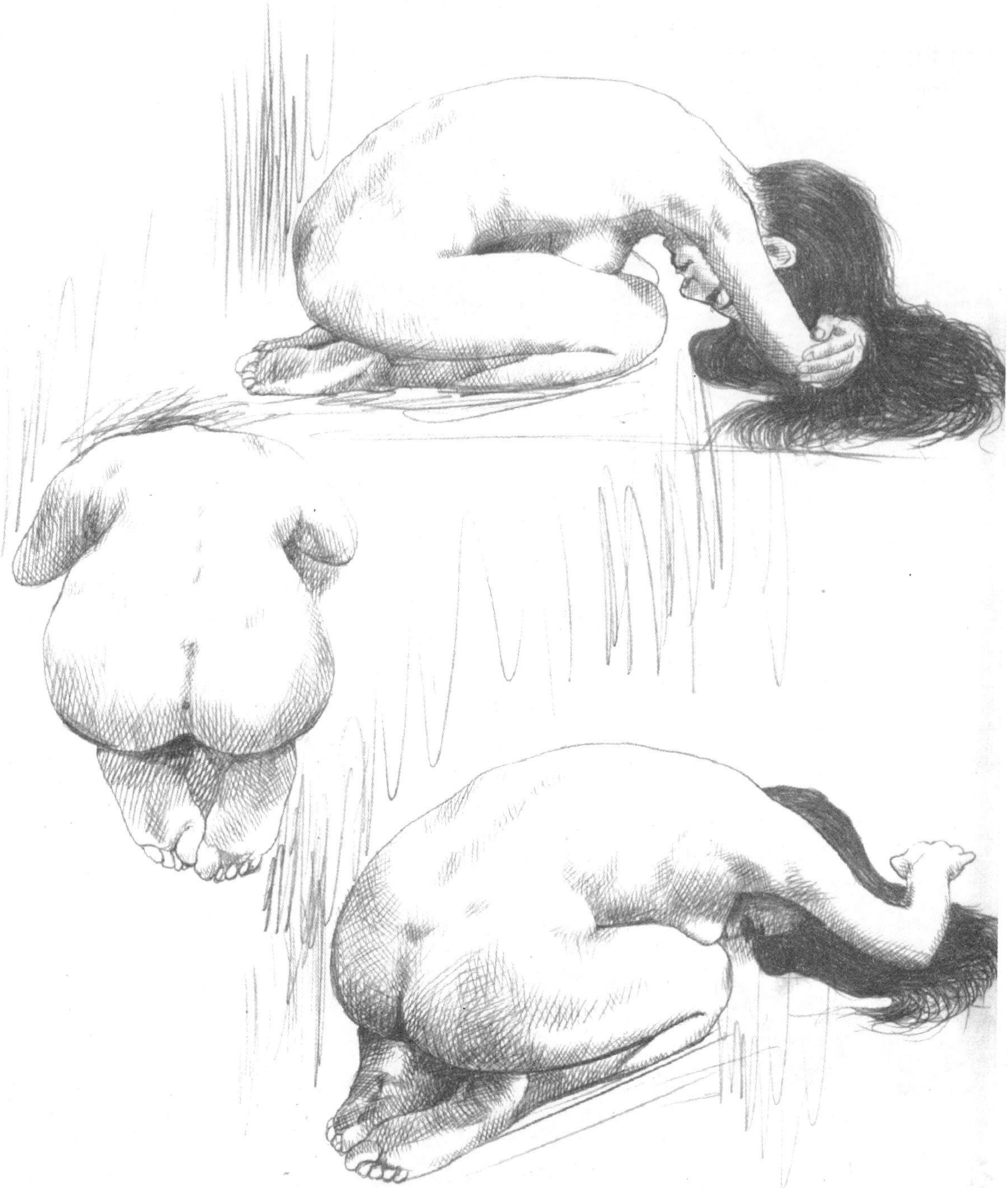

The positions suggested in these illustrations are of great value in studying the flexion of the vertebral column and the consequent lengthening of the trunk in relation to the thigh. From behind the model shows clearly the oval shape of the thoracic cage.

When the model's thighs are spread apart, the adductor muscles which draw the thigh towards the medial plane, are much in evidence. Here the thigh is sharply flexed against the body.

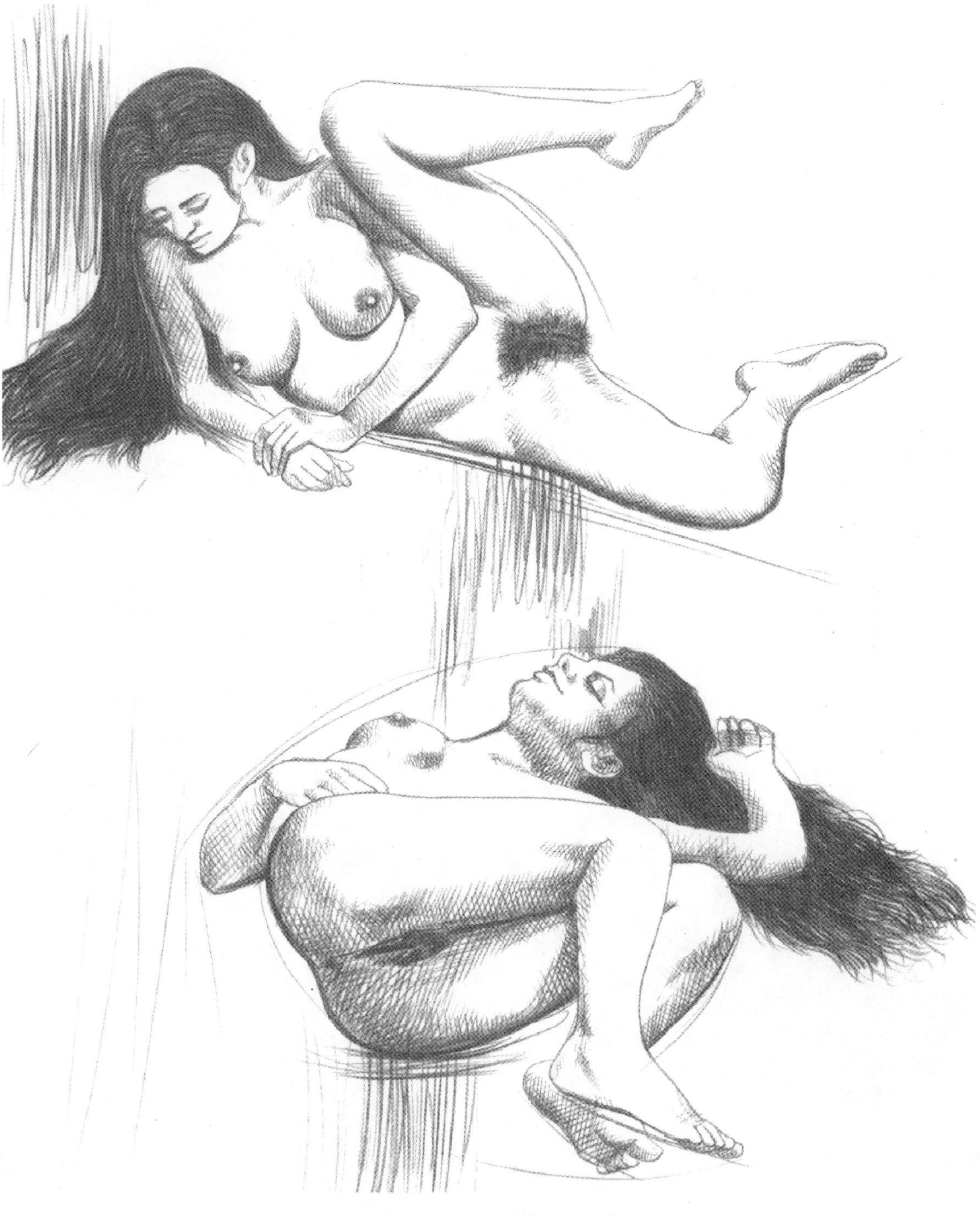

The model is curled up hugging her knees to her body, shows a centripetal tension and allows the various proportional relationships of the different parts of the skeleton to be studied in close and unusual proximity to one another.

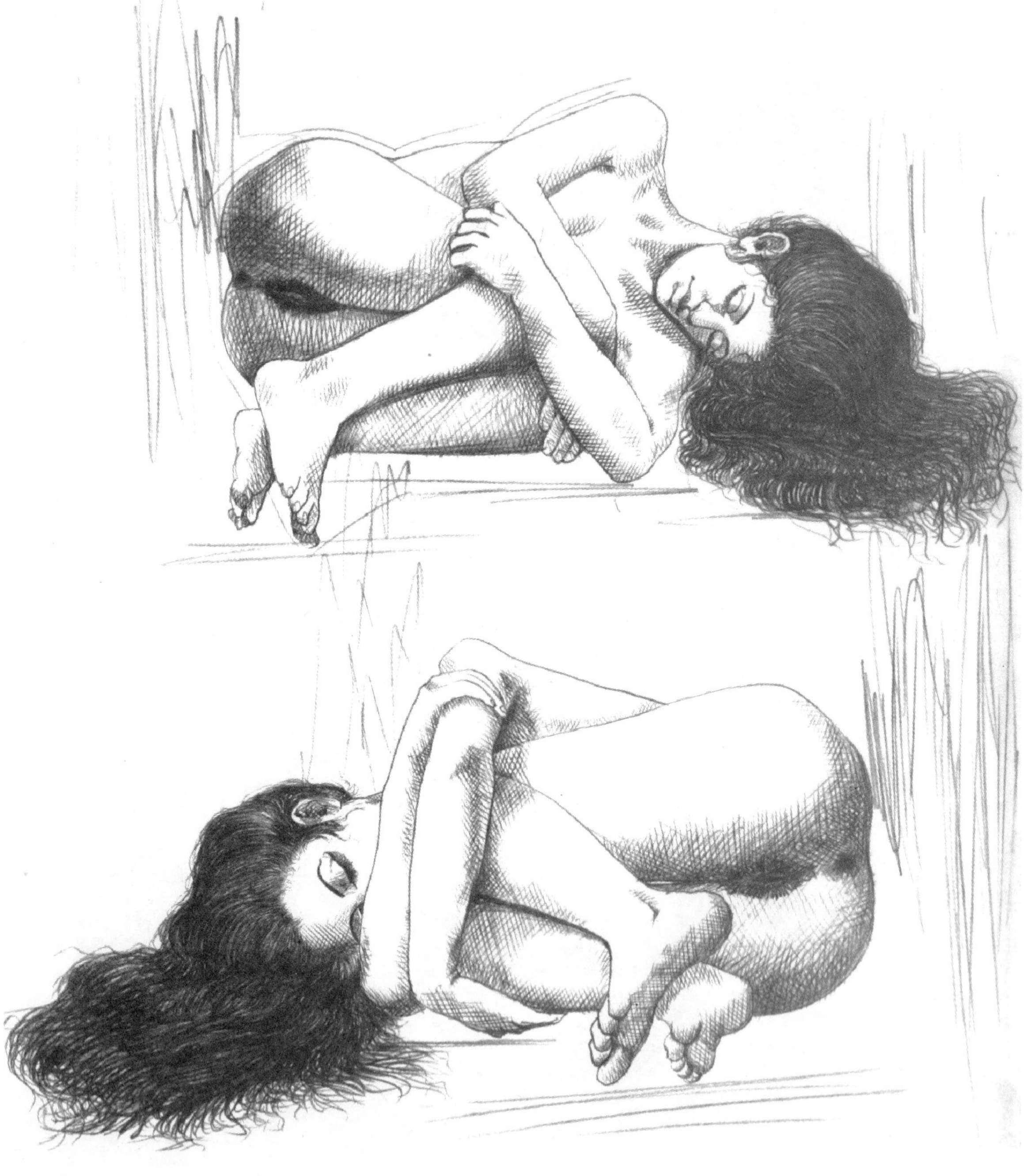

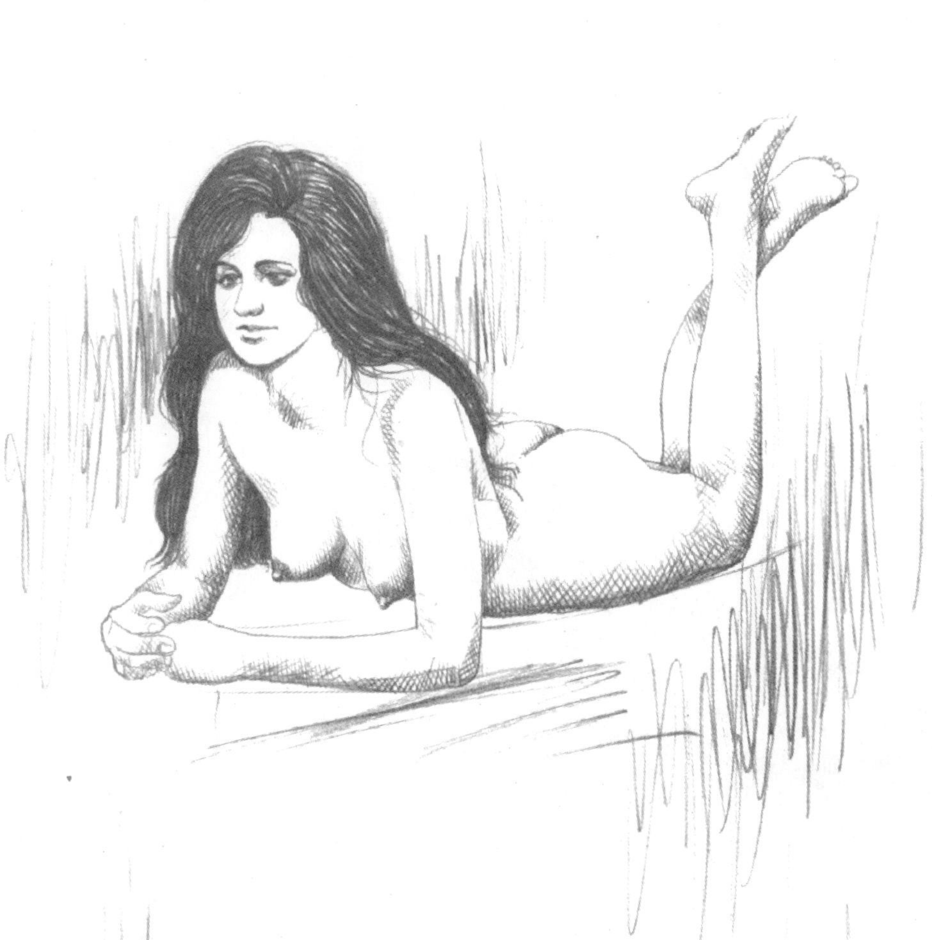

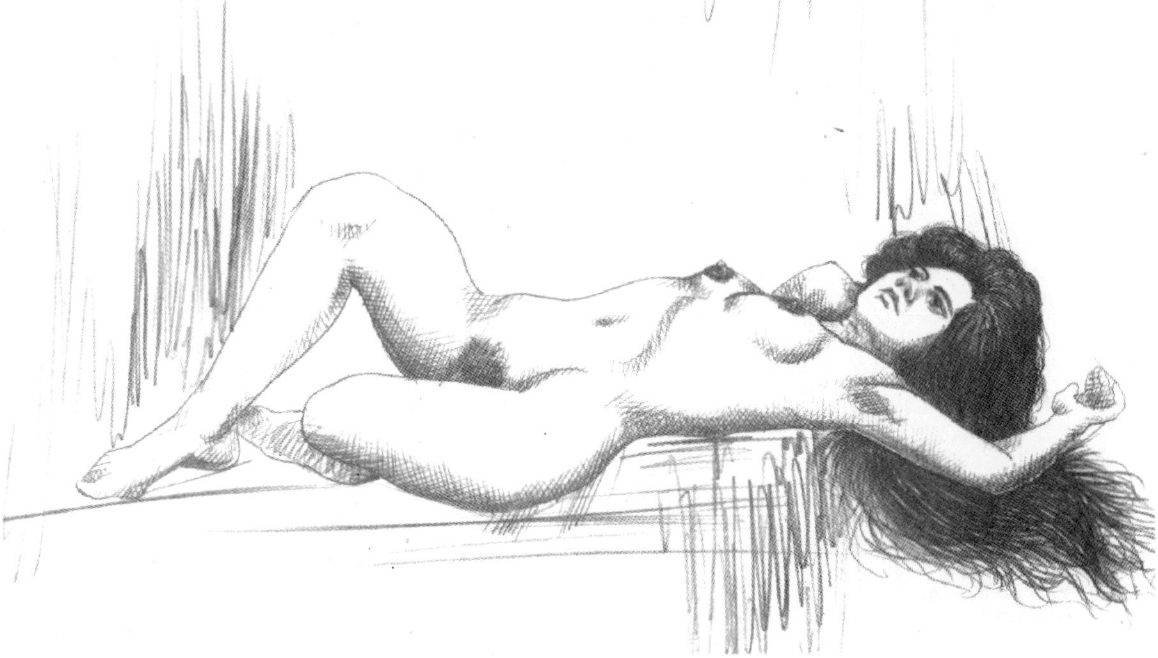

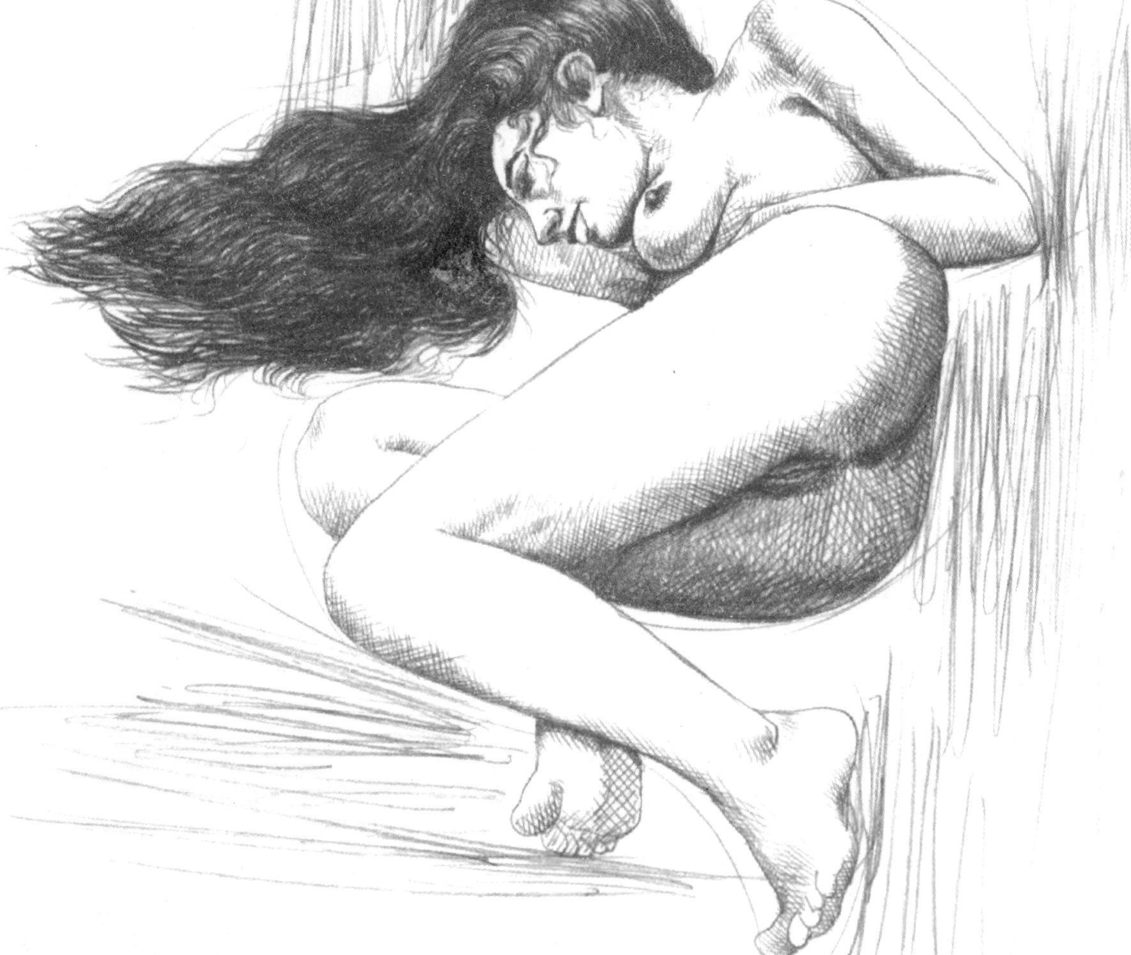

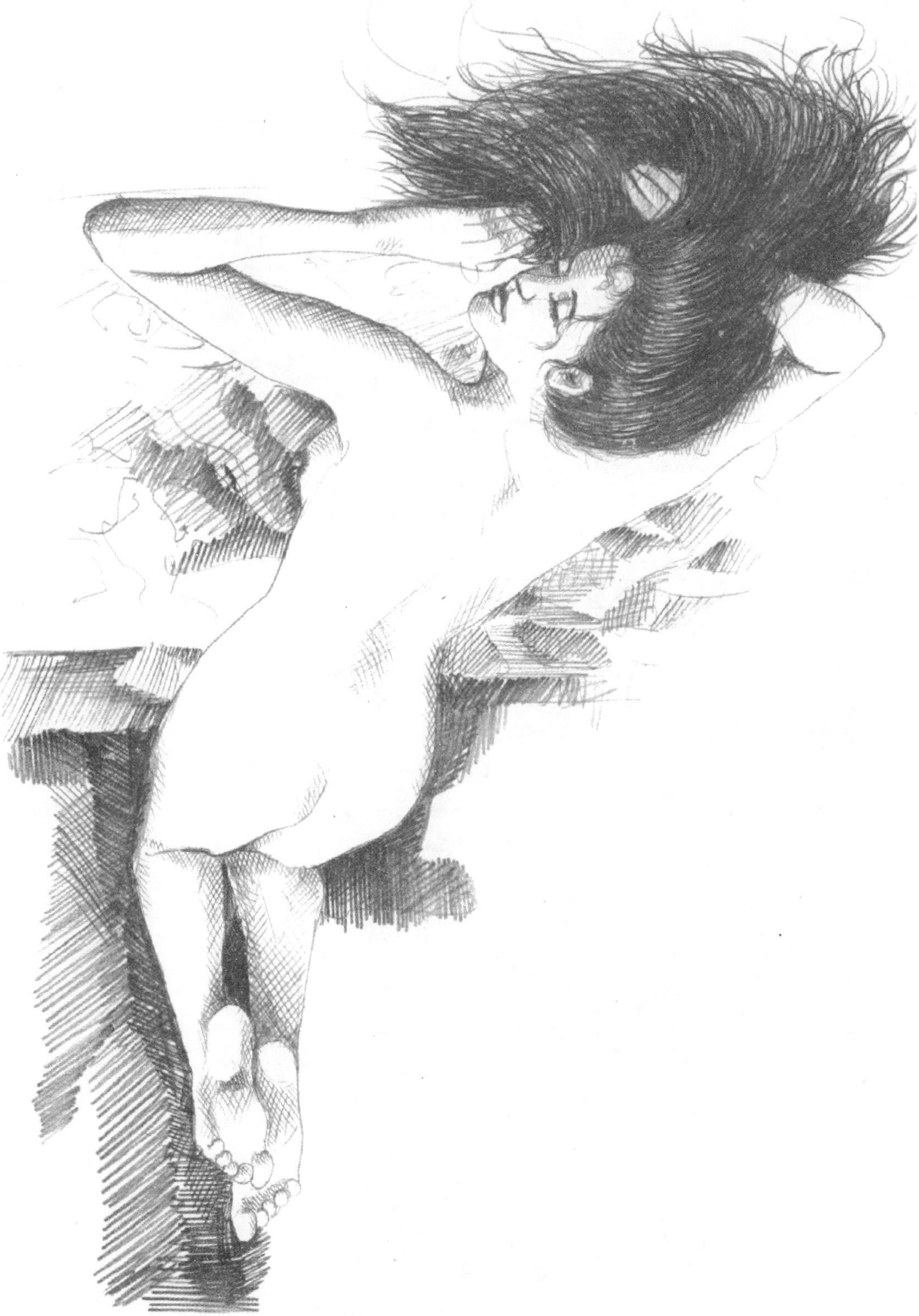

The Seated Figures

Seated positions lend themselves to careful study of the figures. These poses in sequence show the changes that occur in the trunk. In the position which shows the trunk extended and the arms raised, the backbone is bent in the lumbar tract.

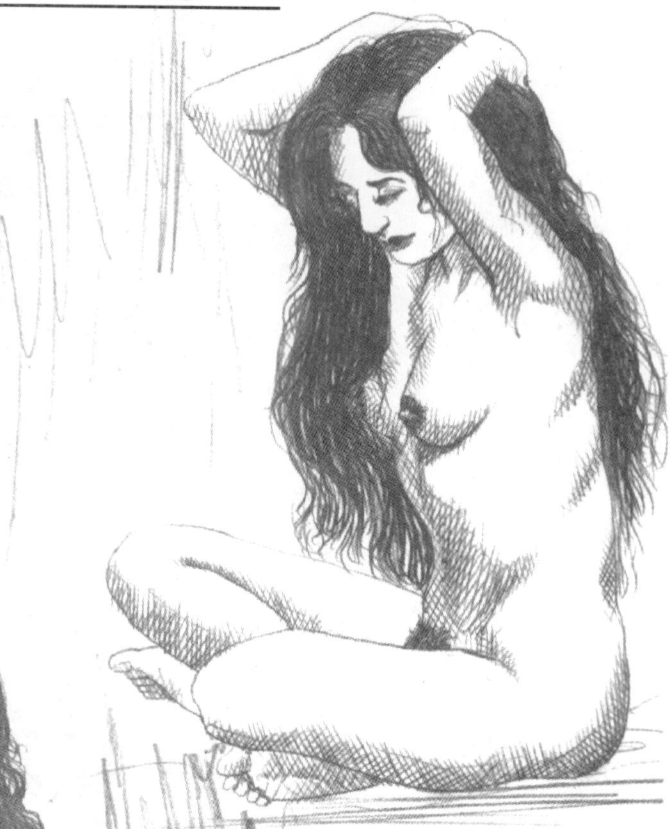

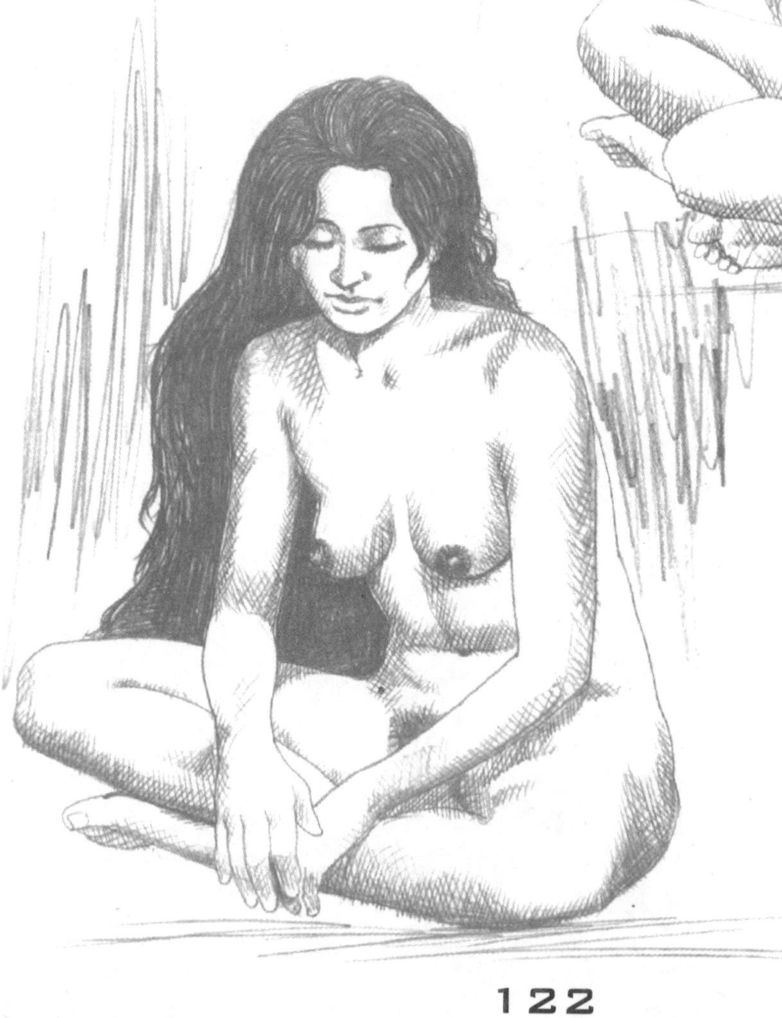

Look at the dimensions of the part of body in foreground, even if the figure in this position is not seen in perspective from the front. Here the feet and left arm are slightly enlarged. There is a fold at the top of the thigh where the flexion is greater.

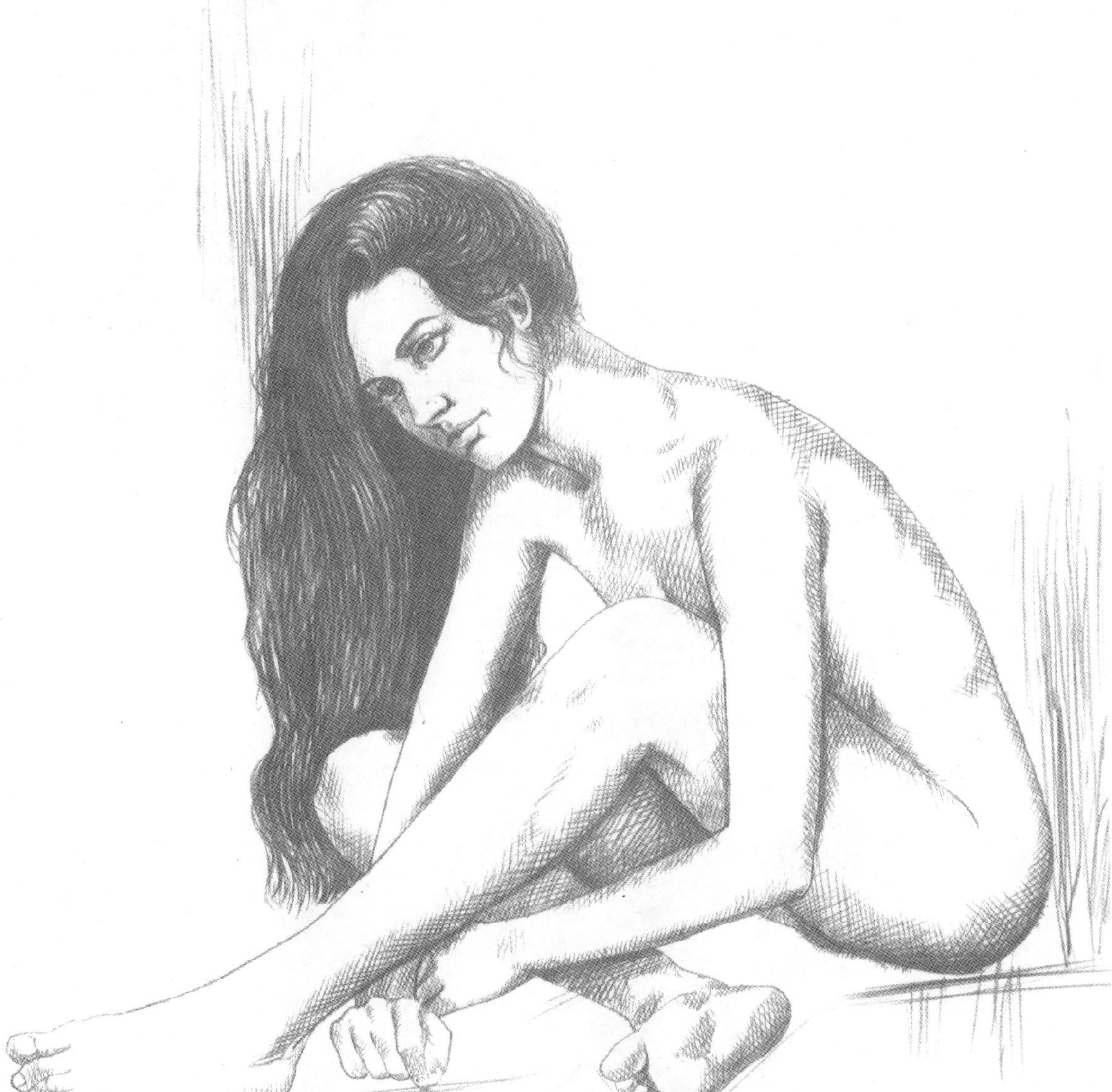

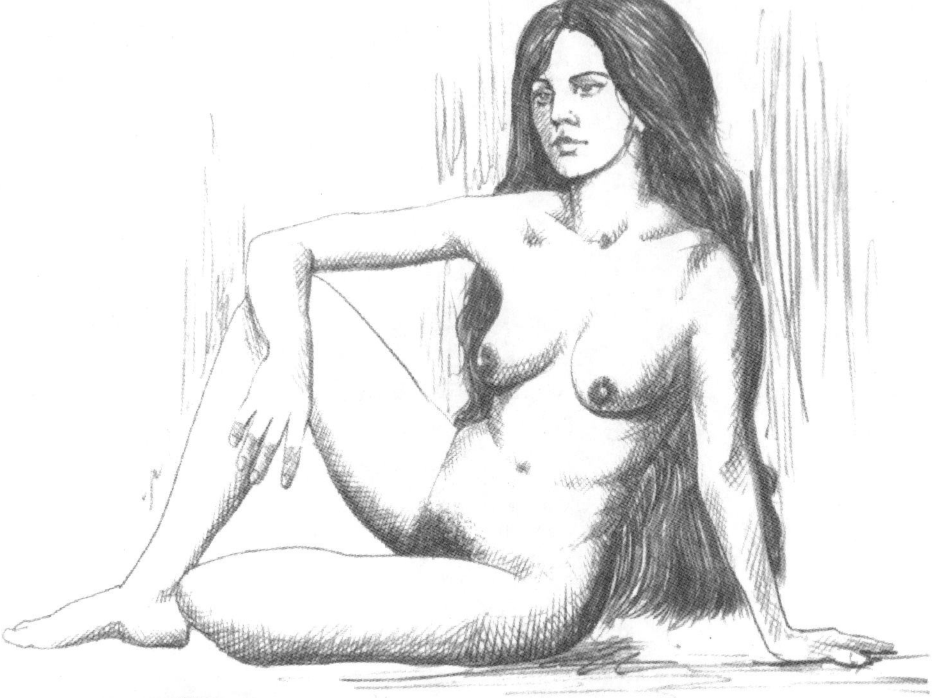

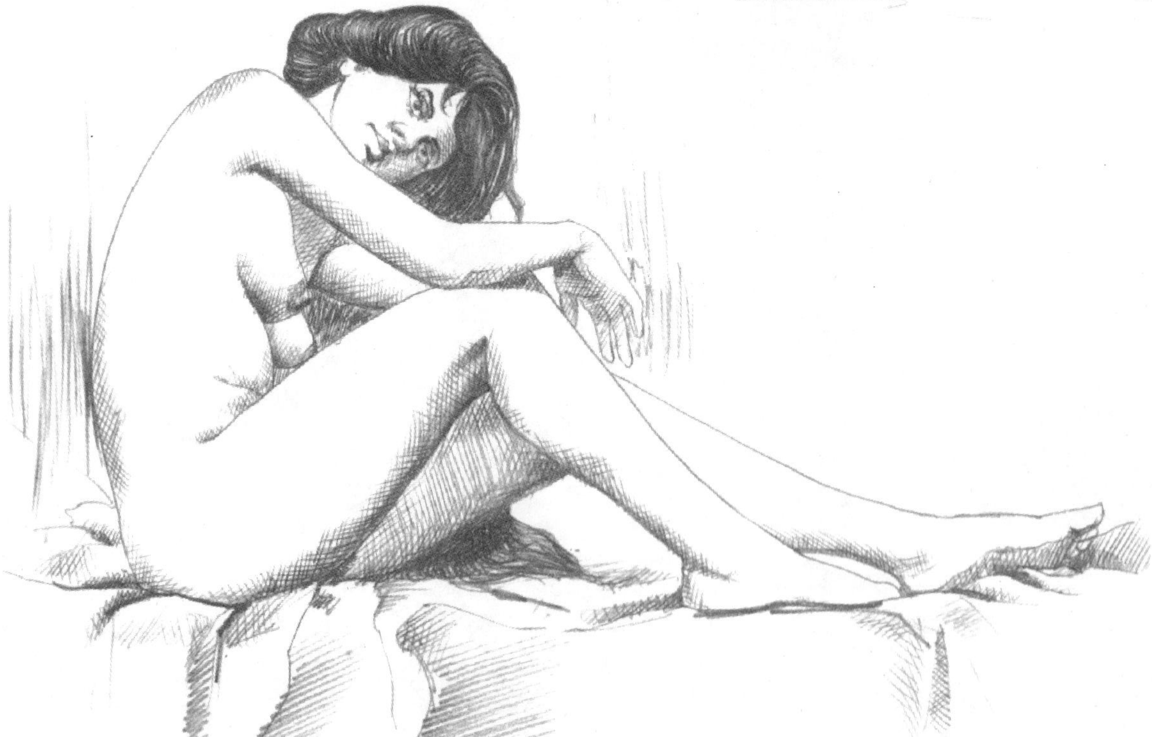

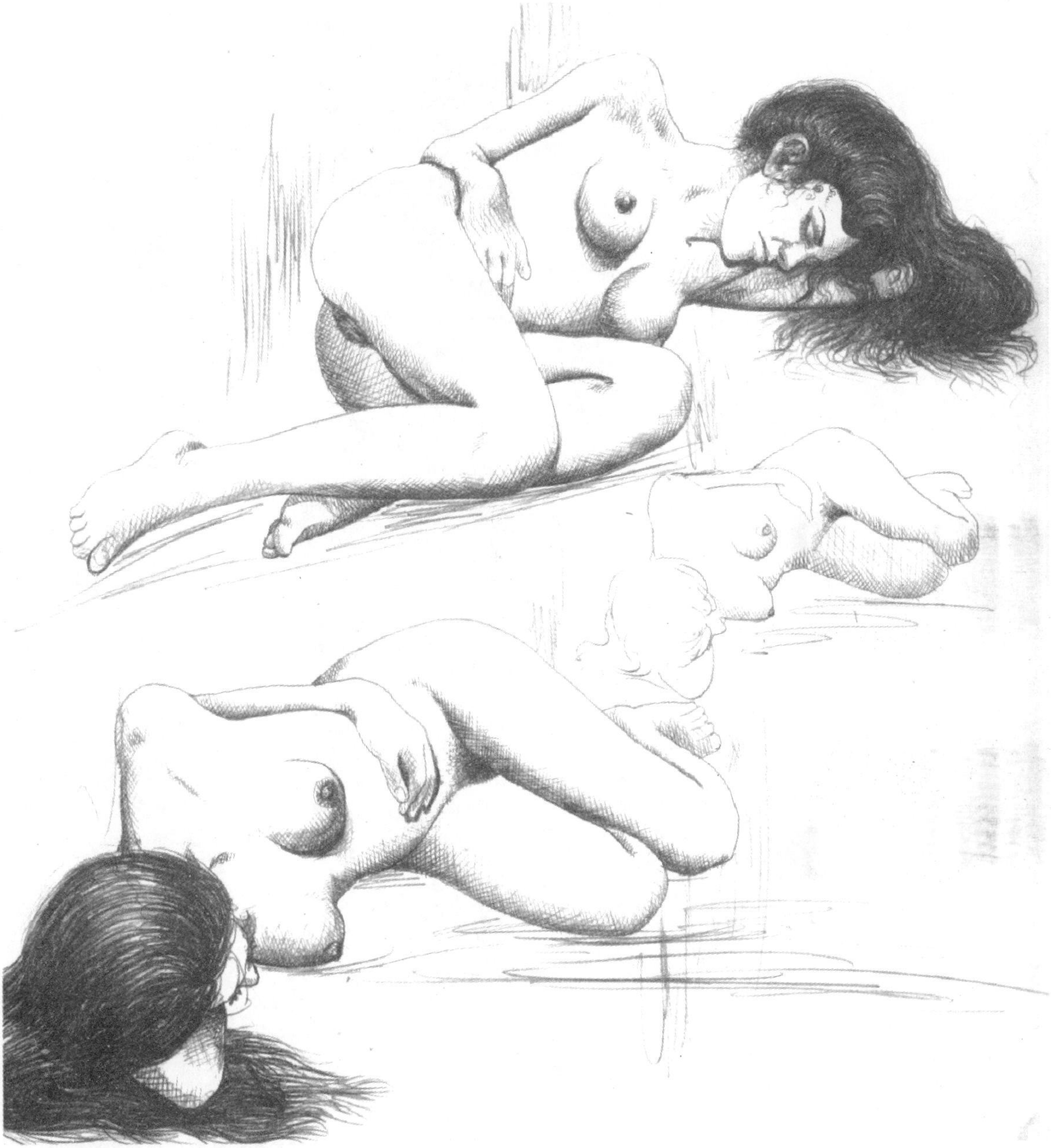

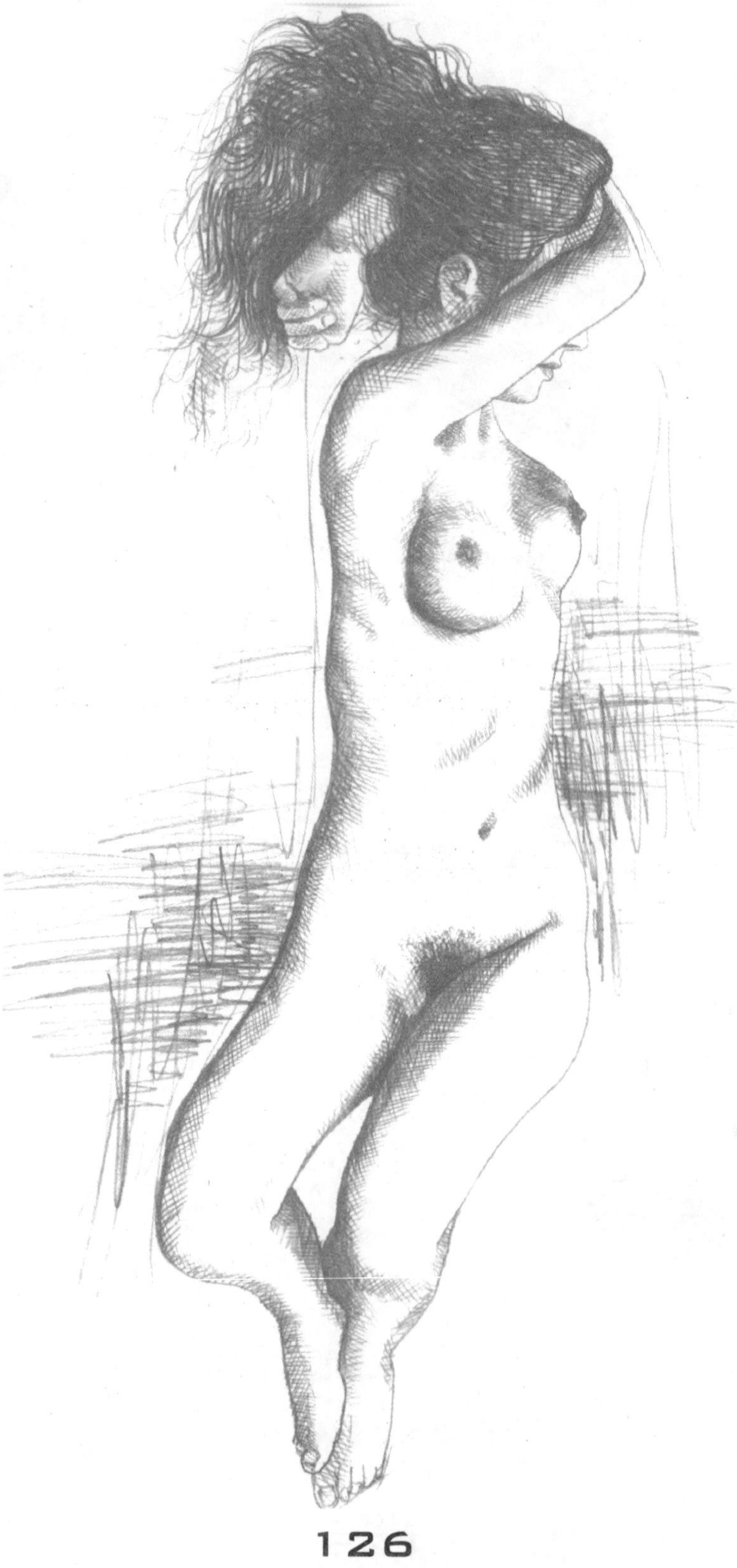

In these difficult positions, try to observe the model from above, in order to appraise the true dimensions of the body, and to convey them even in the distortion produced by foreshortening.

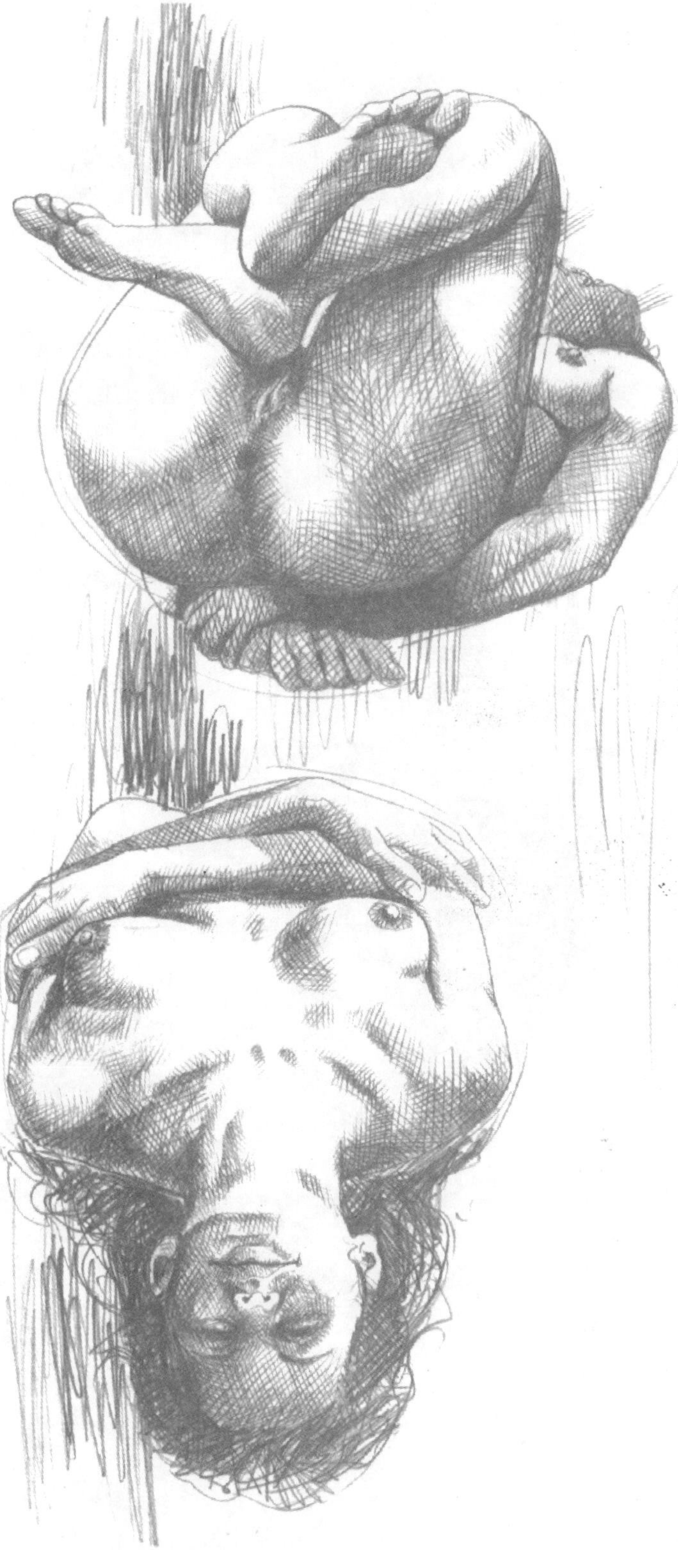

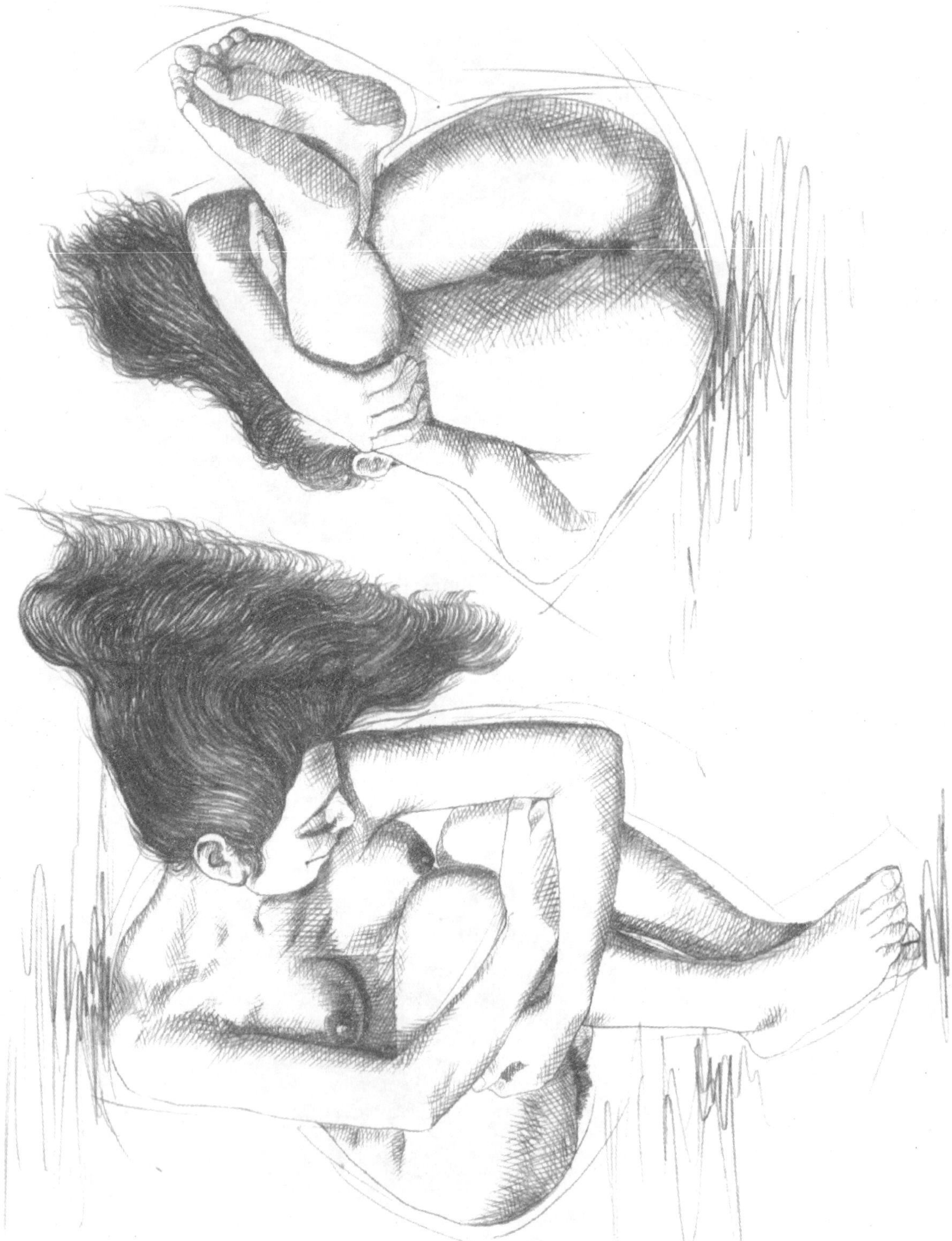